$\mathscr{S}$ILENCE

OF THE $\mathscr{H}$EART

$\mathscr{D}$ialogues
with
$\mathscr{R}$obert $\mathscr{A}$dams

Edited By
The Infinity Institute
Acropolis Books, Inc.

Acropolis Books, Publisher
Santa Barbara, California

Silence of the Heart
Dialogues with Robert Adams

First Acropolis Books Edition, 1999
Second Printing, 2007
©1997 by Robert Adams

For information contact:

The Infinity Institute
2370 W. Highway 89A
Box 11- 182
Sedona, Arizona 86336

Acropolis Books, Inc.
www.acropolisbooks.com

Library of Congress Cataloging-in-Publication Data

Adams, Robert, 1928-1997.
  Silence of the heart: dialogues with Robert Adams; edited by The Infinity Institute, Acropolis Books, Inc. - - 1" Acropolis Books ed.
      p. cm.
  Originally published : Sedona, AZ. : Infinity Institute, 1997.
  ISBN 1-889051- 53-5 (pbk. alk. paper) ISBN13: 978-188905-153-6
  1. Spiritual life-Hinduism. I. Title
BL1237.36 A33 1999
294.5'44-dc21   99-056019
                                                                        CIP

In Loving Memory
of
Our Beloved Robert

Who Transmitted the Entire Teaching in His Smile.

January 21,1928–March 2,1997

They say that I am dying, but I am not going away.
Where could I go?
I am Here.

Sri Ramana Maharshi

Robert's Presence on this Earth was the greatest gift of the Universe. He was silence. He was love. He was being. His simplicity and sweetness were his teaching. His vast understanding which was all inclusive, gave him wonderful humor, sincerity, compassion. Robert was everyone's best friend. In his presence one became like a child, like the child they could never be even in childhood. Innocent, openhearted, natural and simple. Nothing could remain in front of him. There was no room, no space. The fullness of his presence left no room for anything else, no mind, no past, no attachment. One was relieved of all but here and now. This was his grace.

Looking into the endless vastness of his eyes, I said, "Robert, you don't mind, do you?" He said, "Just put nickels in my ears to keep my eyes open." What an ordinary guy, but so extraordinary! The delight of his emptiness! Empty of judgement or opinion, he loved unconditionally. The utter joy of his unconditional love left one completely open. One could see that any thought of feeling was coming only from one's own mind, and therefore so easily dropped. We are free. We only think we're not. "Robert," I said, "am I not free just because I think I'm not?" He replied directly, his face in front of mine, his eyes looking fully at me. "Because you think."

There is nothing to hide, nothing to be, nothing to do. There is a free relationship. There is unconditional love. There is revelation, there is understanding which goes beyond understanding. He told the story of our suffering, and he told the way out. There was nothing he did not understand. If we remember his words, his life, his manner, his walk, his talk, his gentle hands, his humor, his vast eyes. If we remember this in our lives, we are free, and we are with him in freedom.

For that is what he was—freedom. No name, no form, no limitation. Know your Self, and know Robert for what he was and remains. Know your Self and be free! Free without separation.

We remember Robert in freedom. The freedom that he was and always remains. The freedom that we are. The freedom that I Am. Robert rarely had a preference. He flowed with life.

. . . Again, he leaves us only with ourselves, looking within.

Ananda Devi

~

The first thing you should realize is that there will never be a time when you disappear or die, because there never was a time when you were born. You have always existed as Consciousness, and you will always exist as Consciousness.

After you awaken, what happens to you when you die? Where do you go? When you wake up, you stay where you are. There is nowhere to go, nowhere to come back to. You just are. You are your Self, Omnipresence.

Robert Adams

Some people tell me:

"Robert, why don't you just speak
the highest truth all the time?"
And some people ask,
"Robert, speak so that I can understand
what you are talking about."
So that is the dilemma.
So I do whatever I have to do.
I plan nothing.
Everything is extemporaneous.
I have no rehearsals.
I don't write anything down.
I just say what comes out of me.

∽

This book is dedicated to the teaching of Robert Adams. Great effort has been taken to present the words exactly as he spoke them during Satsang, 1991-1993. The tapes were transcribed, then organized and categorized under subject titles.

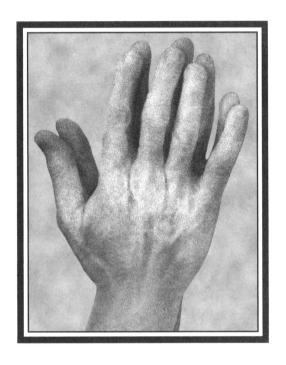

*"He sees the Infinite Self in all,
and all in the Infinite Self, which is his Being."*
— Robert Adams

Confession of the Jnani
by Robert Adams

For the Jnani who has realized the identity
of his inner being
with the infinite Brahman,
there is no rebirth, no migration and no liberation.
He is beyond all this.
He is firmly established in his own Absolute,
Existence-Knowledge-Bliss true nature.

The further existence of his body and the world
appears to the Jnani as an illusion,
which he cannot remove,
but which no longer deceives him.
After the death of this body, as in life,
he remains where and what he eternally is,
the first principle of all beings and things:
formless, nameless, unsoiled, timeless, dimensionless
and utterly free.
Death cannot touch him, cravings cannot torture him,
sins do not stain him; he is free from all
desire and suffering.
He sees the Infinite Self in all, and all in the Infinite Self,
which is his Being.

The Jnani confesses his experience thus:

I am infinite, imperishable, self-luminous, self-existent.
I am without beginning or end.
I am birthless, deathless, without change or decay.
I permeate and interpenetrate all things.
In the myriad universes of thought and creation,

I ALONE AM.

Table of Contents

Table of Contents

Table of Contents

Table of Contents

Table of Contents

Finding the Satguru

It began over ten years ago with a phone call to a fellow seeker whom I'd not heard from for a while. For months, then years, we'd run into each other in the Los Angeles area in our mutual search for answers to Life's spiritual questions. So I half jokingly opened the conversation by inquiring, "Well, have you found the Holy Grail yet?" To which he responded resolutely, "Yes!" He went on to explain that he had found an American guru in the nearby San Fernando Valley who was a direct disciple of Sri Ramana Maharshi (whom I'd never heard of); and I might add I was somewhat dubious of even the word guru, despite a certain attraction to Eastern mysticism.

Nonetheless, after repeated urging, I decided to go once to meet this somewhat unearthly-looking-and-behaving man whose teachings, other than a few brief sentences, were conducted mostly in silence. Although the first time I looked into Robert Adams' pale blue eyes, I felt as if I should hold onto something just to keep from falling in. My friend and I would still spend many hours over coffee, after weeks of satsang with Robert, debating with each other (and ourselves) whether he was ". . . completely nuts, or really onto something." Little did we know back then how blessed we were and always will be.

Beginning with that first Thursday afternoon, however, something about Robert in the ashram-like setting (a U-shaped apartment complex built around a central courtyard, with steps leading to a pillared streetside breezeway where he often stood waiting for less than a handful of students to arrive) was so compelling that I found myself returning to his presence from then on. The faces and places would, of course, change quite dramatically over time.

But for the purpose of this particular story, I suppose I could explain that I was quite ill at the time, didn't know my way around the Valley very well, etc., but suffice to say that it's been one of my lifelong samskaras (tendencies) to not only almost always be in a big hurry, but usually late arriving. Satsang was no exception. When my friend confronted me with how disruptive this was (although Robert never seemed to mind or even notice), I felt so humiliated that I vowed if I were ever late again, I'd simply sit outside the closed door to receive Robert's darshan (grace) there rather than in his apparent physical presence.

So . . . when on the following Thursday I realized that despite what seemed like my best efforts, I was running slightly behind schedule, it was with great relief when I arrived that I saw Robert standing, waiting as usual between the pillars. As I hurried from the car I watched him turn and walk toward the apartment where we met, losing sight of him only as I rushed, breathless, up the stairs just seconds behind him. When I entered the room, there sat Robert on the floor with the other satsangees, in the middle of an answer to a question someone had just asked him!

Was Robert a Jnani? To such questions, he would merely shrug and answer, "I have no idea what I am." Can a Jnani appear (as has often been recounted) in more than one place at a time? Had he come out to let me know it was all right if I was late, or was this an illusion? Is, in fact, everything we perceive with our senses (as Robert taught us) an illusion of the mind? Who is there to know the answers to these questions? I know less and less with every day that passes.

Jai, Robert, Maharshi
In His service forever, Dana

Robert Adams

Robert Adams is an American Self-realized master and a direct disciple of Ramana Maharshi.

He was born in New York City on January 21, 1928. His earliest memories were of a two-foot tall, white-bearded man standing at the end of his crib, who would talk "gibberish" to him. The little man stayed with Robert until he was seven.

Then Robert developed a siddhi. Whenever he wanted anything, a candy bar, a musical instrument or answers to test questions at school, he would repeat God's name three times, and whatever he wished for would come to him. One day, while preparing for a math test when he was fourteen, he repeated God's name as usual. Instead of the test answers, he had a complete enlightenment experience, a great satori, which left him stunned and changed. The world was no longer real to him. He could see only his Self, the Immutable, All-Penetrating, All-Prevailing Source of Existence. All things, the body, the world, the mind, were only images superimposed on the Unchangeable Self. In themselves, they had no real existence.

He began to change so much that his mother thought he was going mad. He was no longer interested in eating, in school, books, his friends or hobbies. He felt alone in the world among people that he had nothing in common with.

One day he happened on a book, *Who Am I*, by Ramana Maharshi. Seeing Ramana's photograph, the hair on his head stood straight up, as if he had been shocked. Ramana was the little man who had entertained him with gibberish for those seven years! But now Ramana's gibberish was completely understandable because Robert had realized his Self.

Two years after his enlightenment, he left New York to stay with Paramahansa Yogananda, who immediately made him a close disciple and friend. Robert Adams requested that he be allowed to become a monk at the new Self-Realization Fellowship monastery in Encinitas. Yogananda told him that was not his dharma, that he must go stay with Ramana Maharshi, who had a similar, spontaneous enlightenment experience when he was a youth.

Robert Adams then traveled to Ramana Ashram near Tiruvannamalai, India, where he remained for the last three years of Ramana's life. Robert has said, "It was with Ramana that my eyes were opened to the meaning of my experience."

After Ramana's mahasamadhi, in the ancient tradition of sadus and Buddhist monks, Robert Adams visited many great teachers over the next seventeen years, to verify his enlightenment, to make sure his understanding was complete. Wherever Robert traveled, where he stopped for a few months, he was discovered, and a group of disciples would grow up around him. Robert has always resisted being tied down in this way, to an ashram or community. He has preferred remaining alone, in Silence; fortunately, a few years ago he had a vision of many great teachers coming together, merging inside a mountain, not unlike Arunachala where Ramana Ashram is located. He understood it to mean that it was time to stop and to take on a small group of sincere devotees, to which he could pass on his understanding.

Many were blessed that Robert had chosen Sedona, Arizona, as his home. To have experienced a true master of

Jnana so close at hand is a great fortune indeed to those who sincerely seek the ultimate happiness, and the Ultimate Source of all things.

Satsang with Robert Adams is a special occasion where we can sit in silence, where we can chant the name of God, and where we can experience the grace and presence of a great being in darshan.

As Robert has often said, the three fastest ways to enlightenment are to attend satsang, to keep the company of great beings, to practice Self-inquiry.

If you are a sincere seeker, and if you find the all-important heart connection with Robert, your life will never again be the same. Doors will unlock, magic will happen.

I Welcome You with All My Heart

Om, shanti, shanti, shanti, Om. Peace!
It is good to be with you. I welcome you with all my heart.

If you came here to hear a lecture, you came for the wrong reason. I do not lecture. If you came here to hear a sermon, the church is down the hill. I do not sermonize. If you came here to hear a philosophical discourse, again you're here for the wrong reason. I do not philosophize. If you came here to hear nothing, you're here for the right reason. For there is only *One* nothing, and you are *That*. The most wonderful speeches are given in *silence*. *Silence* is eloquence. Words are just words. They fly away, they mean absolutely nothing sometimes. As we sit in the Silence, that's what the entire teaching is. Be still and know that I Am God.

If you don't react to conditioning, then you're always in the Silence. You can be in the marketplace, you can be anywhere. If you don't react, you're always in the Silence. You can also be in a cave, but if you have not learned to control your mind, your mind will drive you crazy, do all kinds of thoughts. Therefore, it makes no difference where you are. It's how you react where you are that counts.

I love every one of you unequivocally, unconditionally, just the way you are. Ask yourself this question. Why come to satsang? Ask yourself this question. You come to hear Robert mumble? You come to hear Robert give a lecture? Or did you come to sit with Robert? Of course the last is the right answer. You came to sit with me in the Silence. In the Silence is where all the power is. In the Silence is where all the answers are. Because when we talk, when we use words, words have their place, but what can the words really do? Think of the billions and billions of words that have been spoken since the beginning of time. Where does it end for us, for humanity, for the world? Think of how many words you spoke since you got out of bed. Think of all the words you spoke. What have these words done for you? They are worthless.

So sitting in the Silence is magic. This is when things begin to happen, wonderful things. Peace comes to you. Happiness comes to you all by itself. Joy comes to you. When you sit in the Silence you remember who you are. We come to see we are all one Self. What does this mean? It means we are not separate, we are One Self. Think of that. We are all the One Self.

Abidance in Truth

You are not an ordinary person, or you wouldn't be here.
There is something special about you.
You're ready to be out of the show, the show of materialism,
the show of relativity, materialism and relativity.
You're ready to break out of the shell,
the shell of materialism, the shell of relativity.
You're ready to break out of that shell.

Let it happen.
The mind will create all kinds of situations
to stop it from happening.
It will show you all kinds of nonsense.
But you know now that you have the power
to change these things,
to turn from the nonsense to reality!
You can do it.
Work with it.

Peace.

Satsang

Let me ask you a question. What is the purpose for your coming to satsang? Why do you come here? If it's to listen to a lecture, you came for the wrong reason. If it's for entertainment purposes, you came for the wrong reason. If it's to compare the speaker with other speakers, you came for the wrong reason. There's really no reason to come to satsang at all, unless you have an open heart! If you came to satsang with an open heart, Reality will be yours. Not my reality or your reality, but Reality, the Reality, what people call the kingdom of heaven, the kingdom of God. You are already That, but you have so many concepts you cover it up. You have so many feelings and dogmas and attitudes that you cover up the Godliness. So you have to open your heart and let your reality shine through.

How do you do this? By keeping silent, by not being judgmental, by leaving the world alone. There will always be something in this world to correct, either in yourself or in your family or in the world or people. You have learned from experience that you cannot do this. The correction is always made within yourself. It is yourself with a small "s" that sees the problem. But if you try to resolve the problem outside of you, it will never be resolved. It's resolving yourself, knowing the Truth, understanding who you are, that brings you peace and realization.

Always remember that this is satsang. It is not a lecture or a sermon or a speech. It is not Robert speaking to a group of disciples or students, or whatever you want to call yourselves. It is Consciousness speaking to Consciousness. And since there is only one Consciousness, you are actually speaking what I am speaking. You are feeling what I am feeling. There is only Oneness, Absolute Reality, and you are That.

Try to remember this. There is Consciousness. What you think you are, male or female, whatever your name may be, forget about that for a while. Think of yourself as Omnipresence, All-Pervading.

Do not question it. Do not analyze it. Just allow it to take over. The Presence, the Power. It starts within your heart, and begins to spread all through your body, encompassing your body. Your body merges with it, and it continues to spread until all of us in this room have become it. We're no longer human. We have become it. It keeps on expanding and expanding until the entire world is it. It keeps on expanding, expanding until all the galaxies, planets, stars and solar systems are it. It keeps on expanding, expanding until the entire universe is it. There is no longer anything that is separate from it. Everything is it.

We may call it Consciousness, the Self, Absolute Reality. This is it. This is your real nature.

What are you feeling? Try to let go of all your emotions, your preconceived ideas. All of your dogmatic beliefs, all about your body, or about others. Allow your mind to remain empty.

Feel that I am It, Pure Awareness. I have always been It. There never was a time when I was not It. The appearance of the body cannot fool me any longer. The world and all its manifestations cannot fool me any longer. The universe with its planets and galaxies and solar systems cannot fool me any longer. I can see through these things to the Source. I can feel the Source because I am the Source. I have always been the Source. There never was a time when I was not.

As far as thoughts are concerned, they do not exist. They can no longer bother me or make my life miserable. As far as others are concerned, there are no others. There is only the Source. I can no longer be deceived.

There is no thing that has ever transpired in my life that can hurt me. I forgive everyone and everything, and especially myself.

I am the power and the presence and the glory. If I am That, so is everybody else. So is everything else. All is well.

Awakening

Daylight breaks
The mind is stilled
Silent, at peace
Movement nil.

No pebble drops into its pool
No ever widening ripple
A placid mirror lake
untouched by thought
Serenity stands on its shore to watch.

The sun appears.
Rays of pure light
Engulf the landscape mind
And in the vanished scene
Birds sing for all mankind.

"Awakening" hand written by Robert
November, 1994

Spiritual Awakening

Never forget the purpose of why you're here. It is true in the Absolute Reality there is no purpose. The universe has no purpose for existing. You have no purpose for existing, in the Absolute Reality. But as long as you believe you are a body or a mind, then your purpose is to become no purpose. You spend your energy becoming nothing. But do not believe you're nothing when you haven't become nothing yet.

Be honest with yourself. See where you're coming from by the way you react to life situations every day. This will tell you where you are at, by the way you see yourself reacting to life's predicaments. Life will present to you many predicaments, and it's up to you to see these things in the right perspective: never to be frightened, never to believe anything is wrong, always to know, even though you believe you are a body, you are not alone. There is the Pure Awareness that is with you all the time, just awaiting your recognition, awaiting your understanding that you are not the body, that you are a spirit, called the Atman, Brahman, Absolute Reality. This is who you really are. This is your real nature.

You've heard me talk on many occasions on the subject of love, compassion and humility. These three things are very important to understand. They have to be nurtured and developed. When you understand what love, compassion and humility really are, at that time you become a living embodiment of the truth, and the Self will pull your ego into the Heart center, and you will become liberated and free.

When I speak to you of all these things, I'm referring to my own experiences. Therefore, do not take these things I say lightly, even though I tell you many times to not believe a word I say. It sounds like a contradiction, but it isn't. You are not to believe anything I say, yet you are to reflect and ponder on the things I say at the same time. Try to become a living embodiment of the highest truth.

When I had my spiritual awakening, I was fourteen years old. This body was sitting in a classroom taking a math test. And all of a sudden I felt myself expanding. I never left my body, which proves that the body never existed to begin with. I felt the body expanding, and a brilliant light began to come out of my heart. I happened to see this light in all directions. I had peripheral vision, and this light was really my Self. It was not my body and the light. There were not two. There was this light that became brighter and brighter and brighter, the light of a thousand suns. I thought I would be burnt to a crisp, but alas, I wasn't.

But this brilliant light, of which I was the center and also the circumference, expanded throughout the universe, and I was able to feel the planets, the stars, the galaxies, as myself. And this light shone so bright, yet it was beautiful, it was bliss, it was ineffable, indescribable.

After a while the light began to fade away, and there was no darkness. There was just a place between light and darkness, the place beyond the light. You can call it the void, but it wasn't just a void. It was this Pure Awareness I always talk about. I was aware that I Am That I Am. I was aware of the whole universe at the same time. There was no time, there was no space, there was just the I Am.

Then everything began to return to normal, so to speak. I was able to feel and understand that all of the planets, the galaxies, the people, the trees, the flowers on this earth, everything, were myriads of energy, and I was in everything. I was the flower. I was the sky. I was the people. The I was everything. Everything was the I. The word "I" encompassed the whole universe.

Love, Compassion, and Humility

Now here's the point I'm trying to make: I felt a love, a compassion, a humility, all at the same time. That was truly indescribable. It wasn't a love that you're aware of. Think of something that you really love, or someone that you really love with all your heart. Multiply this by a jillion million trillion, and you'll understand what I'm talking about. This particular love is like no thing that ever existed on this earth, consciously. There is nothing you can compare it with. It is beyond duality, beyond concepts, beyond words and thoughts. And since the I which I was, was all pervading, there was no other place for anything else to be. There was no room for anything, because there was no space, and no time. There was just the I Am, ever present, Self existent. The love of everything was the love of the Self. This is why, in scripture, it tells you to love your brother, and your sister, to love everyone and everything under all circumstances.

This love couldn't differentiate. It couldn't say, "You're good, so I love you. You're bad, so I don't love you." Everything was going on as myself. I realized I am the murderer, I am the saint, I am the so-called evil on this earth, I am the so-called goodness of this earth. Everything was the Self. And it was all a game. All of the energy particles changed from one thing to another thing. But the love never changed.

Another word for this love was compassion. There was this fabulous, fantastic compassion. For everything! For everything was the Self, the I Am. There was no differentiation. There was not me, what you call "me," and those things. There was only one expression, and that was Consciousness.

Of course, I didn't understand all these words at that time. There were no words like I'm talking about now. I'm trying my best to speak intelligently and try to use words to explain what happened, but I can't. All the games that people are playing, on all the planets, throughout the universe, are really the Self. It was all the Self, and I realized that nothing else existed but the Self. Yet all of these things, the multiplicities of planets, of galaxies, of people, of animals, were really the Self. Again, there are no words to describe this. I felt and knew that these multiplicities do not exist. Things do not exist. Only the Self existed, only Consciousness, Pure Awareness.

Yet, at the same time, creation came into existence. And there's no creation. We cannot understand this in human form. As long as we're thinking with our brains, it's incomprehensible. For how can they both be simultaneously creating each other? There was creation going on, and yet there was no creation at all! There was no creation taking place, and creation was taking place. Sounds like the thoughts of a madman. And it seemed normal. There's absolutely nothing strange about this at all, being nothing and everything at the same time.

So this great compassion was there. Since I was everything, the compassion was for everything. No thing was excluded, for the things were really the Self. And then there was this fantastic humility. The love, compassion, and humility are all synonymous. I'm trying to break it down to make you understand, to an extent, what was going on. The humility was there not to change anything. Everything was right just the way it was. Planets were exploding, new planets were being born. Suns were evaporating, new suns were being born. From the suns the planets came, and then life began on the planets. All this was taking place instantaneously, at the same time. And yet nothing was taking place at all.

Therefore the humility is that everything was all right. There was nothing I had to change. There was nothing I had to correct. The people dying of cancer were in their right place, and nobody dies, and there is no cancer. Wars, man's inhumanity to man, was all part of it. There cannot be a creation if there is not an opposite to good. In order to have a creation there has to be opposites. There has to be the bad guy and the good guy. I was able to understand all these things.

The next thing I remember is my teacher was shaking me. I was the only one left in the class, everybody had gone, the bell rang, and I had not even started the mathematics test. Of course I got a great big zero. But those feelings and the understanding never left me. From that time on, my whole life changed. I was no longer interested in school. I was no longer interested in the friends I had. I won't go on any more than that for now, as far as that's concerned.

The point I'm trying to make is this: If the end result of realization is love, compassion, and humility, what if we were able to develop these qualities now? Do you see what I'm getting at? If we are able to develop this love, this beautiful joyous love for everything without exception, without being judgmental, and we have a great compassion for everything without being judgmental, you can't have a compassion for one thing and not for another thing. Then, of course, there's humility. Humility means we don't have to try to straighten things out, to get even, to stick up for our rights. For there is no one really left to do that. If some of us were to work on those aspects, it would lift us up and make us free.

This is something for you to think about. We have to learn to leave the world alone. We become so involved in politics, in family life, in work, and the rest of these things we're involved in, that we forget that we only have so many years left on this earth in the body. And what are we doing with all of the time we have? We're spending the time on things that do not really exist, things that make no sense.

Imagine you're at a play in the theater, and you're playing a role, and you're playing a part, all the time you're aware that you're playing a part. You're not really that person. It's only a part you're playing. In the same way, you are now playing a part, but you have forgotten you're playing a part. You think your body, the way it looks, the way it appears, what it does, what it acquires, is real, and you put all your energy into the game of playing the part. This is indeed a waste of energy. If you'd only put your energy in finding the Self that you really never lost. And you can do this by developing the quality of love, compassion and humility.

This is another method you have to work on. As you're working on Self-inquiry, work on the love, work on compassion, work on humility. Do not just practice Self-inquiry for a while, and then react negatively to the world, and have your feelings hurt. Be your Self. Awaken from the dream. Refuse to play any longer. Look at yourself all day long. See the things that you do, the thoughts that you have, the feelings that you have. It makes no difference what situation you're going through. It makes no difference what's going on in your life. The only thing that matters is what's going on inside of you.

Karmically, you are put on this earth as a body to go through karmic experiences. Therefore, the experience you're going through is part of the maya, the karma. Do not reflect on these things. This is important. You have to drop this. Leave it alone. If you only knew nothing can ever happen to you. There never was a time when you were born; there will never be a time when you die. You have always lived. You are Consciousness. You have always existed. Identify with your existence. Merge into the existence of nothingness.

I tell you this again and again. Leave the world alone. Remember what I mean when I say to leave the world alone. I'm not saying that you should voluntarily, consciously, make a plan of how you're going to leave the world alone. You'll not be able to live up to it. By leaving the world alone, I mean entertain in your mind higher thoughts. Always have in back of your mind, "I am not the body. I am not the doer. I am not the mind." Feel this. Feel it deeply. Do not feel good or bad about it. Do not try to prolong your life. It's a waste of energy. What you call your life will take care of itself. It knows what to do better than you do. We're very limited in our understanding about the body, or the affairs of the body, what's going on in the body. Do not try to do anything with your body. Your body will do whatever it came here to do. It knows what to do. Separate yourself from that. Of course, you may do this by inquiring, "To whom does the body come? Who has this body?" and remain in the Silence.

Many of us here this evening are making tremendous progress. I've been talking to many of you who are really getting there. Of course I use all these terms loosely. There's nowhere to get. But I have to talk to you this way, to remind you to leave yourself alone. I know some of you may be in pain sometimes, and say, "Well, I want to live a life free of pain, therefore I have to do things to myself so I don't feel that pain." This is really a mistake. If you could only realize who has the pain. To whom does the pain come? "I" have the pain. Then who am "I?" If "I" have the pain it means that the person who is thinking these things does not have the pain. For it is "I" that has the pain. You are free of pain, for you are not the "I" thought. Remember the "I" we're talking about now is the thought, the "I"-thought that has the pain, and the experience of being born, the experience of dying, the experience of having problems. This is the "I"-thought that has these things. Not you.

You have to vehemently make up your mind that the only thing that matters to you is to become free, liberated, and let go of all the other things that keep you bound. This is why you have to work with love, compassion and humility. For if this is the end result of awakening, if you do this first, the awakening will come faster.

Even while I'm talking to you, some of you are thinking about your body, you're thinking about the mind, you're thinking about your work. This is what keeps you back. Destroy the thoughts through Self-inquiry. Become free. Do not fight, do not fear. Observe, watch, look, but have no opinions for or against. Some people think if they act this way they will not be able to function in the world. You will function. Always remember, there's an appearance of the body, and it came here to do certain things, and it's going to do those things. It has absolutely nothing to do with you.

It's interesting, I'm really talking to myself because there's only the Self. So why am I talking to myself? I must be crazy. Many times when I talk to you I have to keep from laughing, explaining all these things, talking about all these things when you're already free and you already know these things. Sometimes we're pulled into the illusion. For there's really no thing. When we talk of God we're speaking of nothingness. God is nothing. And that nothing is you. We get deeply involved, when we study, when we read, we get deeply involved in maya.

Why can't you be yourself and wake up? Why do you have to go through all these things, and make me sit here talking to you like this? Just think what I could be doing if I didn't have to talk to you. (laughter) I could be watching *Tales from the Crypt!* All is well.

Robert, I don't mean this irreverently, quite the contrary, but you tell us to try to develop these qualities of love, compassion and humility that you've described as beyond our comprehension. How do we try to develop something we can't comprehend?

Simple. Be your Self. When you are your Self the thoughts come slowly to you until they cease. When the thoughts become slower and slower into your mind, and the thoughts begin to disappear, you automatically become loving, compassionate, and you develop humility. In other words, the faster you get rid of your thoughts, the faster these other things, these other qualities come. So it's a matter of stopping your thoughts. It is the thoughts that see everything in this world as good and bad, right and wrong. As the thoughts begin to subside, love comes by itself, compassion, humility come by themselves. So again, we have to stop thinking.

Consciousness

Consciousness is not a thing.
You cannot describe it.
It is not the opposite of the world.
And it's not an object,
and there is no seer to see it.

Consciousness is another word for being.
Being what?
Being no thing.

Everything Is Consciousness

Everything is Consciousness—everything. When you ask what is Consciousness, there is no valid answer. When someone asks me to write a book or give a lecture, then I have to explain Consciousness in about fifty different words, and each word has another fifty words to explain that, then those words have another fifty words. So your volume of the book is written. What does it say? "Everything is Consciousness." I could have written one page. And in the middle of that page I would say: "Everything is Consciousness," and the rest would be blank. This is the reason why I do not write books, because there is nothing to say. See how confusing it is? You read so many books during the week. Usually you do not remember what you read, and if you do, it's intellectual. You are using somebody else's words and not having your own experience.

I don't know what Consciousness is, but I am That. If I knew what Consciousness was, it wouldn't be That, because I would be voicing a word and the word would be limited by the very voicing of the word. So Consciousness is a no-thing. It's nothing you can pin down. It's nothing you can describe. It's nothing you can write a book about. Consciousness is Silence. Sometimes I'm saying Consciousness is Absolute Reality, which is more words, and I have to explain Absolute Reality.

Consciousness is Ultimate Oneness, Pure Intelligence. Consciousness is all of those things. But what are those things? Again they are just words. Sometimes I say Consciousness is Love, Bliss, Sat-Chit-Ananda, Knowledge, Being, Existence. Those are just words. And you get a good feeling from the words, but the feeling doesn't last too long, for you have not digested the words. You have not become a living embodiment of Consciousness.

You are an asset to the human race, an asset to your Self, an asset to God. You are a wonderful person just the way you are. Just the way you are! Do not judge by appearances. Do not even judge yourself. You are a beautiful person *just the way you are*. When I say just the way you are, I am referring to your real Self, Consciousness. You are beautiful just the way you are. Not what you think you are. Not what you appear to be. Not what the world shows you, but just the way you are right now.

Stand up tall. Do not be afraid any longer. There is nothing that can hurt you. There is nothing in this world that can actually do anything to you. *You are free!* You are the substratum of all existence. Everything is an image on *Consciousness.* The whole universe, all the planets, all the galaxies, are all images on *Consciousness.* And *you are Consciousness.* Know yourself and be free!

There's only one way to bring peace to the world. There's only one way to bring peace to yourself. There's only one way to overcome problems. There's only one way to find yourself. And that way is to realize that everything is Consciousness.

What do I mean by that? Take everything in this room: the glass, the lamps, the chairs, the couch, the rug, the light, and your body. They are not real. They are Consciousness. I am not saying that Consciousness has produced these things. I am not saying that first there is Consciousness, and these things came out of Consciousness. On the contrary. I am saying that everything that appears to arise, that you hear with your ears, that you taste with your mouth, that you feel with your hands, is Consciousness.

There is a substratum of existence called Consciousness. Another name for this Consciousness is Bliss. It is all-pervading. As you begin to merge with it, it becomes you. It is your real nature. It is self-contained. The world, the universe, did not come out of it. I'll repeat that. There are teachings that tell you that the world is a modification of Consciousness, and we have to return to Consciousness. There is nothing to return to. Consciousness is Pure Awareness. It is aware of Itself as Absolute Reality. The world is like a reflection in the mirror. Where did the reflection come from? From nowhere because it doesn't really exist. You cannot try to grab the image in the mirror, for you grab the mirror. When you awaken, you understand that you are the mirror. And the reflection of the world is like the water in the mirage, like the snake in the rope, like the sky is blue. Why does this happen? It doesn't. It appears to happen. Why does it appear to happen? It doesn't. The appearance appears to happen. Why does the appearance appear to happen? It doesn't. It appears to appear to appear to happen. And we can go on like this all night. It is difficult for the human mind to grasp that you are not what you appear to be. This is exactly what we have to do. It is not what it appears to be. It is not duality. Remember what I'm trying to convey. There is not Consciousness and the world. There is only Consciousness, and you are That.

A paradox. A contradiction. You are the paradox. You are the contradiction. You are not what you appear to be. You are not what you see. No thing in this world, in this Universe, is as it appears to be.

Consciousness—the Screen of Reality

Now what is Consciousness? We can say that Consciousness is a power that knows itself. It is self-contained Absolute Reality. In other words, there is nothing but Consciousness. There is not Consciousness and you, or Consciousness and the world. There is only Consciousness. Consciousness, you may say, is the screen of reality and all of the images of the whole universe are superimpositions on the screen of reality. When you go to a movie and you begin to watch the picture show, the screen is covered by images. You forget all about the screen. You do not think of the screen any longer. You're looking at the images. You identify with the images. You're enjoying the movie. The screen is far away from you. Yet if you try to grab the images, what do you grab? You grab the screen, not the images. The images never existed, you will grab the screen. And so it is with us. We forget that we are superimpositions on the screen of life. And we are really the screen, which is Consciousness. We believe through many incarnations that we are the image, we are a person, and there are others, and there are external things to contend with in this world. But I say to you these things are false. The images are like water in the mirage. Like the snake in the rope. Like the sky is blue. Yet there is no sky, and there is no blue. And when you find out that the snake was really a rope, it will never frighten you again. When you try to chase the water in the mirage, you become disappointed, you grab sand. In other words, they are optical illusions. This universe, my friends, is an optical illusion.

It is a dream just as when you're dreaming. No one can ever tell you that the dream is a dream as long as you're dreaming. You'll always stick up for your rights and say this is not a dream. Look, there are riots going on in Los Angeles, fires are burning, people are being killed. How can you tell me this is a dream? Yet you awaken from your dream, and the dream never existed. It came out of you and it returned to you. Ponder this. The dream emanated from you, it externalized itself from you. The dream was not limited at all, was it? You didn't dream that you were just in one space. You dreamt about the whole universe, all kinds of things taking place. You took airplane rides to Africa, you went to the Belgian Congo. You were a little boy and you grew up, a little girl and you grew up. All this is in your dream. And again you will fight for your dream. You will stick up for your rights in the dream. You will even kill in the dream. Yet, when you awaken, the dream is gone. The dream never existed. I can assure you, my friends, that there will be a day in your life when you awaken to the truth.

This world in which we live is the same thing. There's absolutely no difference. You are living the mortal dream. Consequently, great sages have told us we have to identify with Consciousness, with the Absolute Reality, not with what's going on. The only freedom we've got is not to react to anything, but to turn within and know the truth.

But how can this be? We look at each other. We see the things of this world. We feel the pain. We feel sorrow. We feel happiness. We feel joy. And yet I'm saying to you, that these things do not exist. There is only Consciousness.

You can only know this when you experience it. So you're saying, this is good for you, Robert, but what about me? I feel the world. I get hurt easily. I'm sensitive. Things bother me. I see man's inhumanity in the world, and I cry. I perceive all these dastardly things going on in the world, they make me sad. How can you say these things don't exist? How can you say there is only Consciousness, when all these things face me every day?

That's just it. You have to be ready to turn away from the worldly things. You have to be prepared to jump within yourself. To dive deep within yourself. And to sort of ignore the world for a while.

This doesn't mean that you have to give up anything. It means that while you're going through your daily chores, while you are doing your work in this world, you simply have to become aware every once in a while that everything is Consciousness. Just by being aware of these things that I'm talking about, you awaken. You become free. Just by being aware. By thinking to yourself when you get up in the morning, "Everything may appear real to me, but all is Consciousness. Everything is Consciousness. Consciousness is space, pure choiceless Awareness."

Consciousness—the Substratum of All Existence

Again, what is Consciousness? Consciousness we can say is the substratum of all existence. On the scale of evolution, if you take an object and you dissolve it into its most minute particles, you will get molecules. This is true of any object on this earth, whether it's a human being, a chair, a tree, a cat, everything will return to molecules. You dissolve the molecules and you'll get atoms. When I speak of atoms you can't imagine how small they are. Seven million atoms can fit on one pin head. It's incredible when you think of atoms. We know they exist because we can look at them through an electronic microscope. Now when you dissolve the atom, you get sub-atomic particles which are even smaller than atoms. And we cannot even discuss these things or talk about these things because they're just amazing. The whole universe is made out of these things. You go further, you dissolve the subatomic particles, and you get energy waves. Scientists tell us the whole universe is composed of millions of energy waves. We can't see them, yet great sages in meditation have gone to that stage. And here is the important part. You dissolve the energy waves and you get nothing, the void, that Buddhists talk about. No-mind, Nirvikalpa Samadhi, it's the same as the void. We go beyond the void, and we have Consciousness.

How can you prove this scientifically? If you got a giant electronic microscope, and you put your body under the microscope, you would see atoms separated by a vast amount of space. And if you obtain an ultra electronic microscope which hasn't been invented yet, you would see your body as pure space. There would be no atoms, for the ultra electronic microscope would see through the atom, and you would see space, total space.

That space is Consciousness. This is not only true of your body—it is true of the chair, the building, a tree, a flower, an animal. Everything is space.

That's why I say so often, we are all nothing. All of us are nothing. So we are no thing. We are no thing conceivable. We are no thing that you can ever imagine. Your imagination only goes down to atoms. You know about molecules. You go down to atoms, pure energy, but go beyond that. Go beyond the pure energy. There's absolute nothing. That nothing is you. That nothing is Consciousness.

There was once a class being conducted like this. And a particular student said, "Master, I don't know what you're talking about. How can everything be Consciousness? How can everything come from nothing? This doesn't make sense."

And the Master pointed to a fig tree, said to his student, "Go bring me a fig." The student went and pulled a fig from the tree and brought it to the Master. The Master said, "Break open the fig." He did. "What do you see?" "Seeds." "Bring me one of those seeds." He obeyed. He gave him a razor blade and he said, "Cut open the seed." It was a pretty hard job, because the seed was so small. And he cut his finger a couple of times, blood all over the place. He finally managed to cut open the seed. And the Master said, "What do you see now?" "Nothing. In the seed there's a hollow, absolute nothingness." And the Master said, "From this nothing, the entire universe is produced."

And this is true of everything on this earth, and in this world and this Universe. Everything is nothing. There is absolutely nothing that exists. Remember I am saying that things do not come from Consciousness. I am saying that everything is Consciousness. Things do not exist.

Human beings appear to be made so that they see things, hear things, smell things, touch things, and feel things. Therefore they think they are living in a material world. In a relative world. Yet the ultimate truth is, everything is an optical illusion. Like the snake in the rope. Like the sky is blue. Like the water in the mirage. These things do not exist. You, as you appear, do not exist.

Just thinking about this will free you. You really do not have to do anything else but to consider this. To ponder this. To try to realize everything is really space. Everything is Consciousness. To think about this and rest, something begins to happen to your mind. You begin to lose your mind. (laughter)

So you see what Consciousness is on the scale of evolution. Consciousness is the substratum of everything, of all existence. And your true nature is Consciousness. This is what *you* really *are*. But you see what you have to do to get there? You have to go beyond these levels. You have to become a molecule, an atom, a sub-atom, an energy wave, and then you return to your real Self, Absolute Reality, Pure Consciousness, the screen of life.

Why Transcend Duality?

Now why would you want to do this? Why would you not say, leave me alone and let me have a drink? Who wants to go back to atoms and sub-atoms and become Consciousness? Well, this is why the highest spiritual teaching is not for everyone. Most people are satisfied with life the way it is. But they are going to die. They're going to go through experiences. As long as you live in this world or any other world, you go through the law of cause and effect, which is like a pendulum. It swings to one side, which means things are looking up for you, you're doing well, everything is great in the physical world. Then the pendulum swings the other way and things begin to reverse themselves. Your world starts falling apart. You may get sick, develop cancer, AIDS. You may lose everything in the stock market. Your family can be wiped out in an accident, you can become crippled, and if you have nothing to hold on to, what do you do? You curse life, you become suicidal. Then the pendulum swings to the right again, and things get better and better. You become like a yo-yo. You go up and down, up and down, up and down. This is the way of the world. This is the way of the universe.

We live in a world of duality. Therefore this is the reason to become free. For if you go through life the way you are now, and you've not worked on yourself in order to transcend good and bad, up and down, right and wrong, forward and backward, you keep appearing again and again and again on these various planets throughout the universe, taking on various bodies, and going through various experiences. It never ends. You may leave your body tomorrow and come back when the planet is again in the dark ages, and they are having another Spanish Inquisition. And you become a prisoner and you're tortured. Your fingers are cut off one by one. You are reduced to nothing. Then you come back again in another life, you become the Vice-President of the United States. You become Dan Quayle. This is the way of the world. This is life. It will never change.

Many people have good intentions. They want to make this a better world in which to live. By a better world they mean they want to make the world go their way, what they think is better, what they think is right. All of these things show you that you are identified with images. Think of the energy put into this world. Your projects that you do. The work that you are involved in. The things that you believe in. The energy that you expend. All the clubs you belong to, the societies you belong to. These are the things that pull you back to the earth. They pull you back into bodies, one after the other.

Turn Within–Awaken to the Truth

Consciousness is not a thing. You cannot describe it. It is not the opposite of the world and it's not an object, and there is no seer to see it. Consciousness is another word for Being. Being what? Being no thing. Now we go beyond the realm of creation, where it becomes ineffable and indescribable. That's why we can only explain to you what Consciousness is not. Consciousness is not the world. Consciousness is self-contained, Absolute Reality. It is yourself, when you do not identify with the world. And that only happens to the average person just as they are falling asleep and just as they wake up. At that time you are Consciousness. But the feeling leaves you almost immediately. You begin to identify with the world. You forget about reality. The method to remember is to catch yourself all during the day. "Who believes this? To whom does this come? Who feels this?" over and over again. When you say, "Who am I?" for some people it is better to say, "Who is I?" The same thing. What you are really doing is, you're finding the source of the "I." You're looking for the source of "I," the personal "I." "Who am I?" You're always talking about the personal "I." "Who is this I? Where did it come from? Who gave it birth?" Never answer those questions. Pose those questions, but never answer them. Keep it up. Don't give up.

It's fine for me to sit here and say the world doesn't exist, nothing exists. But when you walk out of this door, the world hits you right in the face. Some of you become depressed because you have to go home by yourself, perhaps. You wish you had a relationship. Some of you feel depressed because you have a relationship, and you wish you were alone. Nobody is happy. Everybody thinks something is wrong with their life. Some of you are depressed because you can't get enlightened.

Think about what you're doing. Think about what you're feeling. So we begin a program. And from my own personal experience, I found that Self-inquiry is the fastest way to awaken, for some people.

Therefore, you passionately get yourself involved in Self-inquiry. As I said before, it is true that listening to these words, and realizing that everything is Consciousness, can awaken you. But this is only if you are prepared. By prepared I mean you've already transcended all the things we were talking about. All of the emotions and all of the fears. All of the hurts and all of the frustrations. If you have already transcended these things, then that's all you've got to do. All you have to do is hear the word, and you're awake. But for most people it doesn't work this way. Therefore you have to practice some form of sadhana.

Self-inquiry becomes very useful. You simply allow thoughts to come to you, and you inquire in a gentle way, "To whom do these thoughts come? Who is thinking these thoughts? I am." You wait, and you inquire sincerely, "Who am I? What is the source of this I?" When I say you have to dive within yourself, that's how you dive within yourself. People often ask me how do you dive within yourself? That's how you do it. You inquire, "Where does the I come from?" The I is deep, deep, within yourself. "What is the source of the I?"

Then thoughts will come to you again. And you repeat the same thing over again. "To whom do these thoughts come? They come to me. Who is this me? What is the source of me?" Me and I are synonymous. "Where does the me come from?" You do it over and over and over again.

You do not look for a time. Forget about time. Do not worry about anything. Spend time by yourself. Most people cannot spend time by themselves. Many people tell me they stay by themselves a lot. But if you're going to their house, the TV is on, the radio is on. That is just like having people in your house. When I say spend time by yourself, I mean in the Silence.

Take the time. Sit down in a chair and watch your thoughts, and begin to inquire, "To whom do these thoughts come? They come to me. I am thinking these thoughts. Who is this I? What is the source of the I? Where did it come from?"

It makes no difference how many times you've practiced this before. Whenever you do it, it's like the first time. This may be the time for you to awaken. That's why you should never give up. You simply sit still. Do not try not to think. For if you try not to think, you will have thoughts that you can't get rid of. You will be full of thoughts if you try not to think.

You do nothing, absolutely nothing. You're watching the thoughts come. As soon as the thoughts come, in a gentle way you inquire, "To whom do these thoughts come? They come to me. I think them. Who is this I? Where did it come from? How did it arise? From where did it arise? Who is the I? Who am I?" You remain still.

The thoughts come again. You do the same thing again and again and again, in a gentle, peaceful way.

Who Am I?

Feel your reality,
in the stillness,
in the quietness,
when there is no mind,
no thoughts, no words.

Who are you then?
You just are.

I AM. I AM.
I am not this.
I am not that.
I AM.
I am That which has always been.
I am That which will always be.
I AM THAT I AM.

"I" Is God

When you take a true picture of yourself, when you look at yourself, when you get up in the morning and you sort of become the witness to all of your actions, you will notice that you revolve around three words: "I," "me," and "mine."

There is usually never a moment in your material life when you do not use these words. If every time you said "I" you were aware of what I really means, that would be a different story. But, unfortunately, we do not use I that way. When we refer to I, we're talking about the body. We say, "I feel wonderful, I feel sick, I feel happy, I feel sad, I feel this, I feel that." We also say, "This is mine, this belongs to me, no one else can have it. It's mine alone." Me, me, mine, mine, I, I. We're always involved with those three words, aren't we?

And this is what keeps us human. This is what keeps us back from realization. Those three words. It would be difficult to speak without those words. For instead of saying, "I feel good," you'd have to say, "Feel good." Instead of saying "I feel sick," you'd have to say, "Feel sick." Instead of saying, "I feel depressed," you'd have to say, "Feel depressed." Instead of saying, "This is mine," you would say, "This is." Instead of saying, "I am angry," you would say, "Angry."

It would make you sound ridiculous. But, at the same time, it would make you understand that you are not that "I." You are not the "mine." You are not the "me."

You will immediately catch yourself and realize when you say "I" you have to be very careful what you say after that. For "I" can never be sick. "I" can never know anything unhappy or happy, good or bad, rich or poor. "I" is beyond all those things.

I is Consciousness. I is God. I is pure Awareness. Imagine if you will, whenever you said "I" you realized truly what this I means to you. You're no longer speaking of the small I, the body I, the I that does not exist. You're speaking of God. Whenever you say "I," you're speaking of God.

Therefore, if you said, "I am sick," that's blasphemy. How can God be sick? If you say, "I am unhappy," same thing. How can this thing called God be unhappy? Even if you say, "I am happy," how can God be happy according to human standards?

As you begin to realize what this I really means, you'll automatically be lifted up to a higher state of Consciousness.

Just by realizing continuously what I really means. Yet you have to do this every day. You have to catch yourself every moment.

Think how many times today you used the term "I." And what you said after that. Think how many times today you said the word "me" and "mine," as if you were an individual. As if anything can belong to "you" personally. As if you really own anything, and you have to protect it and take care of it as if it is yours.

Am "I" My Possessions?

Everything belongs to God. Everything is God. It is true that you appear to be using it. But never for a second believe that it belongs to you.

This is why when people realize this truth, it's so easy for them to share. But when one believes they are the body, then they have to hoard, and hold onto something and fight for their existence and stick up for their rights.

Is it any wonder that you don't wake up? How can you wake up when you're fighting for your rights as a human body? When you're trying to protect the things that you think you own? This is maya, total maya. The belief that you own something. That you are something. It's all an illusion. There is only God, there is only Consciousness. Everything else is an appearance.

Enjoy the world if you can. But do not allow the world to be your master. Do not allow the world to tell you how things are. Do not allow the news or the newspaper or the way of the world to confound you and confuse you. Or to make you sad or angry, or upset you. After all, it's the same as seeing a movie. You look at the movie and you see all kinds of dastardly things going on. But then you catch yourself and you say, "It's only a movie! It's not the truth." And so it is with life. You observe everything that's going on in life, you watch, you look, you see. Yet you never react. You're never for or against. You understand, and this makes you free.

Where Did the "I" Come From?

What do you think is the difference between this teaching, jnana marga, and the rest of the yogas, prayer, religions or whatever? What is the basic difference? In every teaching besides advaita vedanta, there is a personal I. Think about that. Let's take hatha yoga. The "I" learns postures and the ego becomes expanded because you can say, "I can stand on my head and twist my feet," and you give it a Sanskrit name. But you still say, "I can do this." So the I has become inflated. Take raja yoga, the eight-fold path. Now these things are good. There is nothing wrong with these things. I'm not putting them down. But there has to be "someone" to learn the yamas and niyamas, the virtues. There is someone who is learning all these things. The I has learned to become virtuous. Take kundalini yoga. I am focusing on the chakras, on each chakra. There is always I and I and I. Take prayer. I am praying to God. Again there is nothing wrong with these things. But the reason we call this the direct path is because this is the only teaching that investigates the I. We're not interested in the effects. Whatever the effect may be, we realize that the I is behind it. We realize that if we find the I, then follow it to its source, everything else will be wiped out and we'll become free. This is why it is called the direct path.

Also, what is the difference between meditation and jnana marga? Because most of you realize that on this path it is not really necessary to meditate. So what's the main difference between meditation and this path? In meditation there's always an object of your meditation. And again the I is concentrating on something else, where you exclude everything except the mantra or the words of your meditation, whether it's God, or whatever. In this teaching you simply inquire for the source of the I. "Who am I? Where did the I come from?" Even when I say to you, where did I come from, some of you are relating to your body, aren't you? You're thinking where did I come from, as a body? But that's not what we mean. You want to know where the I came from, not where you came from. If you find out where the I came from, you will realize that you do not exist. You never did and you never will. That's the point—where did "I" come from?

And after you get used to this kind of thinking, whenever you use the word "I," you will never refer to your body again. For instance if you have a cold, you usually say, "I have a cold." Only now you will catch yourself and you will laugh, because you will say, "I has the cold." Sounds like bad English. I has the cold and it has nothing to do with me. So where did the I come from that has the cold? And as you follow the I, it will lead you to the source where there is no I, there is no cold. You can use this method for everything. "I am hungry." Well, catch yourself and realize that "I" is hungry. I is not my real Self. I is hungry. Yet my real Self can never be hungry. I'm tired, I'm depressed, I'm happy, I feel beautiful, I feel wonderful. It's all the same thing. As long as you are referring to your body you are making a big mistake. Separate yourself from I.

Silence Is Understanding
There Is No Mind to Quiet

There is only one I actually. That I is Consciousness. When you follow the personal I to the source, it turns into the universal I, which is Consciousness. Begin to catch yourself. Begin to realize your divine nature. You do this by keeping quiet. The fastest way to realization is to keep silent. Yet you have to know why you are keeping silent. This is why you can't tell this to the average person. If a person has no inkling of advaita vedanta, you can't say, "Keep silent." For then it means just to be quiet. They don't realize it means to go deep, deep, deep within to that place where Absolute Reality lives, and that's the Silence.

Actually, the human body cannot keep silent. There is something else that enters the Silence. It has nothing to do with your humanity. Then suddenly after years, perhaps, of meditation and previous lives, you can be mature enough to really know what this path is all about. When I give this practice it's not for you as a human being. You appear to be able to go through it as a human being, but I can assure you that your humanity has nothing to do with it. When you enter the Silence, you have gone through a profound peace, bliss, Pure Awareness. That's what the Silence is. It's not being quiet. It's beyond that. It's not just quieting your mind. Like I say all the time, it's understanding that there is no mind to quiet. When you realize there is no mind, you automatically become silent. When you still think you've got a mind, you make every effort to quiet the mind and you can't. How many of you believe that you can quiet the mind through effort? You can't do that. It's not the effort that makes you quiet your mind. It's the intelligent understanding that you have no mind to begin with, then you just keep still and everything takes care of itself.

If you have to meditate, by all means, meditate. This path is never against any other method, due to the fact that they all eventually lead to awakening. You have to do whatever you have to do. But for those who can understand what I'm talking about, and realize that you're dealing with no mind, no body, no world, no universe, no God, the awakening comes immediately because there is no one who is sleeping. Do you follow this? If you think you've got something to overcome, if you believe that you've got to work on yourself, you've got to make some kind of effort, it will be hard. After all, who makes the effort? The ego. Who is telling you all these things you have to overcome? The mind. You think you have to overcome your bad habits, you have to overcome past karma, you have to overcome samskaras. That's all a lie.

I realize that I talk about these things sometimes. It sounds like a contradiction, but I am sharing with you the highest truth. There are no samskaras to overcome, because they never existed. There is no karma to overcome because it doesn't exist. But it does for the immature students. They have to work on something. So I explain to them there's karma, there are samskaras, there are latent tendencies that have got hold of you, and you have to transcend them. Yet I'm telling them a lie. But they really need to hear that at this time of their evolution, otherwise they cannot work on anything else.

"*I*" *Has Nothing to Overcome*

But the truth is, you have nothing to overcome. Think about that. If you had something to overcome, you would never overcome it. For it is the nature of the mind to play games with you. As soon as you overcome one thing, another thing pops up, and you have to overcome that. When you overcome that, something else pops up. Say you have a drinking habit and you say, "I've got to overcome this." You may overcome it. It leads to bad temper. It leads to you telling lies. Then you have to overcome telling lies. It never ends until you begin to realize "I" has nothing to overcome. Then you start working on the I. It is then you finally realize it's this personal I that's been giving you this trouble. That's an advanced state, but that's also a lie, due to the fact that the personal I never existed. But you don't know that. Because you think the personal I exists, you have to use Self-inquiry to lead you to the place where you realize the personal I does not exist. It never has, and it never will. Yet wouldn't it be wonderful if you could just sit down and realize all this in a flash and become free?

We'll not allow ourselves to do that for some reason. We want to play the game of overcoming. So we say, "I've got to work on myself. I've got to practice. I've got to meditate. I've got to be alone. I've got to do this and I've got to do that." But I say to you, there is nothing I have to do. You just have to realize what I'm saying and awaken. And that's it. Again, who has to awaken? It's all a pack of lies, but I'm using words. How can the Self awaken? The Self never went to sleep. Do you not realize who you are now? You're not a mortal human. There are no words to express what you are. You have to find out. So you practice. But while you're practicing your sadhana, keep it back in your mind someplace, there is really no one who practices. After all, who does the practice? It's your body and your mind. If you can only remember there is no body or mind that exists, then there is no one to practice. So while you're practicing, remember that.

I know you're going to walk out tonight and you'll say, "Well, what do I do now?" Look at it this way. As long as you feel body consciousness, and as long as your mind, so-called, still has the power to make you feel this way and that way, then you have to do some practice. Otherwise your body/mind will control you. The highest practice is Atma vichara, Self-inquiry. The reason I'm talking to you like this is because I can feel that all of you who are here have been through many paths and you're not newcomers, so you're ready for this. You're ready to hear that there is no practice, there is no God, there is no enlightenment, there are no past lives, there is no you, and you're free.

The Finite Cannot Comprehend the Infinite

People still want to know, when everything is gone, what's left? What is the substratum? The cause? The underlying cause of all existence? There has to be something that holds it all together. Says who? There is nothing to hold together. Remember also, that the finite cannot comprehend the Infinite. So when I say there's nothing that holds anything together, I mean there's nothing that words can describe. When I use words like Bliss or Pure Awareness, Consciousness, Sat-Chit-Ananda, Parabrahman (and Parabrahman is very powerful because I mean it's beyond Brahman), what can be behind Brahman? Silence. There is no such thing as Parabrahman, due to the fact when you think of it, it signifies an object to you. For instance, a place to be in. A place to be in the Silence, that is Parabrahman. You're wrong. There's no place. There is no Silence. There is no Parabrahman. Then what is there? Find out. Only you can know, yourself. For there are no words to describe it.

You have to come to terms with your life. That takes total honesty to do that. You can't go on fooling yourself. Look how you run around from pillar to post. You go here, you go there. You're always searching. You're always looking. You're always striving. For what? Some of you think that you're going to find a teacher up in the sky someplace, and you're going to go searching for that teacher until you find him or her. No such teacher exists. When you finally settle down, and start going into the Silence more often, your teacher will appear to you and you will find he is none other than yourself. You may ask then, "What am I doing here with you people?" I am yourself. I can see that very clearly. There is no difference between you and me. When you feel depressed, when you feel angry, when you feel out of sorts, that's me you feel. When you feel happy, when you feel enlightened, when you feel beautiful, it's also me you feel. All this is the Self, and I am That. Some of you still think I'm talking about Robert. Robert has nothing to do with this. I'm speaking of Omnipresence. I'm speaking of nothing. And I think to continue speaking is a waste of time.

Am I the Body/Mind?

"I" is the first pronoun. The second pronoun is "am."
When you realize "I am," you become free.
This is called "Being."
Not being this or being that. Just plain Being.
I AM.

It's quite a different situation than identification
with the body.
The body will continue to have experiences, yet you will not.
You will be free from the whole ball of wax.
Yet to other people, to others, it will appear as if you're doing
whatever you're doing.

It appears as if what you're doing is a reality.
Yet when you discover the truth about
yourself and you awaken,
you will no longer be connected to your body.
At the same time you will appear to be a body to others,
and they will see the games you are playing.
But you will be free from that.
Yet your body will continue to play the games.

It's a paradox.
Your body appears as the water in the mirage,
as the snake in the rope.
But yet, when you awaken, you are no longer the body.
And there is nobody.
But the body appears to others as being real.

This is why when a Jnani dies, or appears to be suffering,
nothing is really happening to the Jnani.
But to the ajnani all kinds of things are happening.

They see suffering.
They identify with sorrow, or death, and
with everything else.

Therefore, I say to you, do not disturb yourself
by these things.
Inquire "to whom do they come?" and be free.

You Are Not What You Appear to Be

What would you do if you woke up in the morning and found that you have no body? There is no body there. You look under the cover. You're looking for it but you can't find it. And you also realize the thoughts that are thinking these things are not you. You are somewhere as the witness to the thought that you are no body, and there's no body there. Yet you feel your Essence in everything. In the furniture, in the bed, in the windows, the whole Universe. And when your wife or husband comes in, or children, they see you as a body. Yet you know one hundred percent that you're not a body. You never were a body. There is no body. This is an awakening. The paradox is that you are sure there is no body, yet the body appears. And when you become adjusted to yourself, you see a body which is supposed to be you, but yet it's not there. You know there is no body, and there are no thoughts. Yet something is thinking, and something appears to be a body. This is a great paradox. What we call maya, the grand illusion.

Right now you believe that you are a body. You are certain of this. But I can tell you truly you're not. You never were. And you will never be. Yet you identify with what you call a body, you go through experiences in life, you're happy, you're sad, you cry, you laugh, you're sick, you're healthy, you're poor, you're rich. And you go through all the vicissitudes of life, making a career out of yourself, putting yourself in various positions, sticking up for your rights, fighting for your survival, and going through all these things that do not exist. This is the way you are now. This is the truth about you right now. You do not exist. Yet you appear to exist. You appear to have two arms and two legs and you move around, and you do things, and you feel things, and you go through things. But do you?

I can tell you for sure you don't. You never have and you never will. When you realize this about yourself, you stop being hurtable. No thing can ever hurt you again. Your feelings can never be hurt, because you have no feelings. You just exist as Pure Consciousness, Pure Awareness. Try to follow me on this. This is our true nature right now, Pure Awareness, right now. There never was a body that you had to deal with. Yet the impression is so strong with many of you, that not for a moment does the thought leave you, that you're not a body. The thought is always with you, that I am the body, I am the mind, I am the experiencer. All spiritual teaching ends with this understanding. Even the priests and the rabbis and the ministers and the yogis and the rest of these people. What they are trying to teach and what they are trying to tell you is this ultimate truth, that you are not a body, but they don't realize this themselves yet. But all spiritual teaching is for that purpose.

All Is Well

On Tuesday I attended my mother-in-law's funeral. So somebody asked me, why am I not crying? I therefore started to cry, and I cried louder than anybody else. They had to go get me a towel. That's how much I cried. And it made everybody happy. I cried for about ten minutes, I don't know why. Somehow when people ask me to do something, I do it. Yet my feelings never change. What feelings are those? *All is well.* Those words never come to my mind. But there is something that knows, all is well. There is some mysterious power that is continuously felt. This power of course is the Self, Consciousness. It is beyond Consciousness, beyond the Self. What is called I is simply an image superimposed on this power. Therefore, I can be the body and the power at the same time. So the body can cry, can laugh. It can go through all sorts of experiences, but no body is affected. The experience is like a burned rope. It's of no value. You can't do anything with a burned rope. If you try to touch it, it falls apart. So the feelings and the emotions and everything else that this body expresses is like a burned rope. It's of no value.

There are no words to explain this, but I can assure you that everything is unfolding as it should. No matter what's going on in your life, or what appears to be going on in your life, believe me it's all for your ultimate good. There is nothing in this universe that can ever hurt you, no matter how things appear and how they look. First of all, you're not your body. There is nothing hurtable. You're not your mind. So there are no thoughts that can attract you or destroy you or repel you. You're beyond that. You're above that.

As long as you believe that you are the body/mind phenomena, you're going to have problems. That's that. I don't care what kind of problems you may think you have, it makes no difference how severe. As long as you believe you are the body/mind phenomena, you're going to have problems. You may feel justified in having problems. You may feel it's not your fault. You may feel it's karma. You may feel it's all kinds of things, but as long as you believe or you feel the body/mind, you will have problems, because this is the kind of world in which we live, the world that doesn't exist. Seems real to most of us. And if we believe we are the body/mind, then we believe the world is real and we believe we have to pray to God for solutions. We do all these things and we still suffer.

Suffering will only stop, not when God answers your prayers, but when you awaken to the truth of your own Being. Then you are born again, so to speak, in a new reality and all is well. But you say to me, "But Robert, sometimes you appear to have problems too. Your karma evolved as it does all the time, or your physical body doesn't feel too good, or something is going on." My question to you is this. Who sees this? There has to be a seer and an object. You're seeing yourself. When you catch on to your awakening, the world does not change. You just see it differently, that's all. You acquire a feeling of immortality. A feeling of divine bliss, so to speak, when things no longer have the power to affect you. In other words, in the state of enlightenment, cause and effect does not exist for you. But those who are living in the world are going through their karma, and they're beholding themselves everywhere they look. For the world, remember, is only a projection of your mind.

Now what kind of a projection is it? It depends on your state, where you are coming from. We're all looking at the world and we see something different. All we are seeing is ourselves. There are no problems. None exist. None will ever exist. The only problem that exists is what? Who can tell me?

Kuwait.

You're close. What do I always say, "Why does a problem exist?" It has to do with your nose. That's right. You're allowing your thoughts to go past your nose. That is the only reason you have a problem. If you catch yourself quickly before it gets past your nose, where is the problem? The problem is in your thought, only in your thought. When your mind slows down, when the thinking process slows down, where is the problem? It doesn't exist. But if you allow the thoughts to go past your nose, then there are all kinds of problems which you come up with. You believe this is wrong, and this is not right, and this is hurting me, and you become doubtful, suspicious and apprehensive and fearful and so forth. Because you're thinking. You may say how can you exist without thinking? Quite well, thank you. The trees do not have to think. The grass does not have to think. The world does not have to think of itself. Everything is taken care of.

There is a power that knows how to take care of everything, and will also take care of your body, so-called, if you stop thinking. But as long as you think I am the body, then you have to take care of your body, and watch it, and feed it aspirin and cold remedy and proper foods and do all kinds of strange things with your body. But your body and your mind are not your friends. They come under a law of their own. Did your body ask you today, this morning, when it's time to get up? It got up. Did it ask your permission? It does what it wants. You have nothing to do with the body or the mind. When you become depressed, does your mind ask you if it can become depressed? It does what it wants. When you become fearful, does your mind ask your permission? It does what it wants. When your body catches a cold, does it ask you if it can catch a cold? It does what it wants. But what have you got to do with those things?

Identify with the Source, I Am

A lady called me this morning from Santa Cruz. And she asked me, "How long do I have to come to satsang before I become Self-realized?" So I told her, "Before I answer let me ask you, 'What do you mean by "I"? And what do you mean by satsang?'" And she hung up. I wonder why she did that. But it's something we can talk about, or I can talk about since I have nothing else to do. How long do "I" have to come to satsang? How long does "I" have to come to satsang? Does "I" need to come to satsang? What is this elusive "I"? What does it mean? How long does I have to come to satsang? The reason you would call it I, is because you misinterpreted the I. You identify the I with the body. So you're saying, "How long do I have to come to satsang?" Then what is satsang? Sat means Being, being with the Self. Therefore I and satsang are the same thing. What this means is, satsang is your everyday experience. It's not a place you go to. It's how you live your life. I makes the separation, but there is no separation. There is one Whole, and you are That. But as long as you are separating I from your Self, then you always question. I feel sick. I feel happy. I feel depressed. I feel out of sorts. Who is this I? Where did it come from? How does it originate? What is its source? Find out. Dive deep within and find out where the I came from. A good way to do this is, before you go to sleep say to yourself, "I'm going to find my 'I' when I get up this morning."

Just before you wake up, before you start thinking, the I presents itself as I Am, as pure Consciousness. Catch it then. That's the best time to catch it. As soon as you awaken in the morning, in that split second before you wake up and start thinking. Before the thoughts come of the world, that is the time to catch the I Am, the Absolute Reality. For at that moment, this is exactly what you are, Pure Awareness, and then the thought comes, it covers it up. So remember this: If you tell yourself when you go to sleep, "Tomorrow morning as I open my eyes I am going to identify with my source, I Am," and you will. Even for a second, it will change your life.

As you keep on doing this every morning, every morning, every morning, the time between your awakening and the thought coming to you will become larger. And the space will expand and expand and expand, until you are able to stay in the Awareness. Of course at that time there will no longer be a you. There will only be the Awareness. Try it. You have to investigate. You have to intelligently dive deep within yourself and find the Source of your I.

Do not accept your feeling. Do not accept your thoughts. Watch yourself feeling miserable, and do nothing about it; you can become the witness to it. That will help too. But it's better to ask, "Why am I feeling miserable?" And realize that you said why am "I" feeling miserable. I. I'm identifying with my body as I. Again a mistake. The I in itself is pure harmony, joy, happiness. But when you identify the I with your body/mind, it becomes the personal I which doesn't even exist. But you're making it exist. You're identifying with it. Why do you want to identify with your personal I? Your personal I never existed. Why have you befriended it? Why do you keep giving it power? Why do you make it grow?

Take your power back. Expose yourself, the real you, and forget all this nonsense about a mind and a body and thoughts and the world and God and everything else that appears to be real. Compare yourself with no one. Be true to your Self. Never mind how much progress somebody else is making. Forget about saints and sages and other people. You are the only one that ever existed and there is no one but you. You are all the saints and the sages and the seers. You are everything. Everything is the Self, and you are That. Why not awaken to this? Why do you want to play games with yourself so long? By believing in reincarnation you just come back again and again and again, and hoping to have a better life next time. There is no better life.

As long as you are born of the flesh you have to suffer. This is the way of the flesh. Do not try to improve your life. You're making a big mistake. For there is no question about it, if you use positive thinking and use your mind, you may appear to improve your life. But remember, this world in which you live is a world of duality. For every up there is a down. For every forward there is a backward. For every good there is a bad. Therefore, whatever improvement comes in your life, it will last for a while, then will subside, then you become miserable again. Then you will be happy again when you get what you want, and then that will not last, and you will be miserable again. You'll start sticking up for your rights and fighting for your survival. Then as you get what you want, you'll be happy again. You're like a yo-yo. You go up and down, up and down. And no matter how much I talk to you about this, you're going to keep on doing this. So why am I talking? I don't know. I have no choice.

You know, I never asked to do this. Strange how things turn out.

Too late now.

All I know is that all is well, and everything is unfolding as it should. All I know is, that happiness is your true nature. That you are not what you appear to be, and things are not what they appear to be. Nothing can ever happen to you. Why do you worry so much? What are you afraid of? Your life? You have no life. What you call your life is nothing. It doesn't exist. It's no thing. You worry about your hair falling out. Worried about needing a new pair of shoes. You're getting fat. What a waste of energy. Like feeding a dead horse. We're all going to wind up in the cemetery, so what difference does it make what you do.

Last week I was talking to a body builder. He was telling me about his muscles. And what he does for this muscle, and what he does for that muscle, and how well he eats. So I told him, that's great, you'll be the healthiest man in the cemetery. And that's about the gist of it. Why not use your energy for constructive purposes? Now this does not have to mean that you ignore your body. Your body will always take care of itself. As a matter of fact, the more you practice your sadhana, or realize your true identity, your body will be able to take better care of itself than you were ever able to take care of it, because it comes under a different law. It knows what to do. It will do whatever it came to this world to do, but it has absolutely nothing to do with you. Wake up to that fact.

Stop thinking about yourself so much. About getting a new job, losing a job, about working or not working. No one is ever happy. Those people who work are miserable because they have to work. Those people who don't work are miserable because they can't find a job. And when they find a job they join the miserable ones who can't stand the job. Where is peace? Peace is your real nature. It's within you. It is you. Look for it and you'll find it. Seek and ye shall find.

When the Mind Is Destroyed, Consciousness Appears by Itself

Even in religion, they try to focus on the God of their religion in meditation, focus on an item. This does not awaken you. It may improve your concentration, make you a little more one pointed, yet it will not awaken you. The only time you will awaken, is when your mind is destroyed. There has to be no mind left. When the mind is destroyed, Consciousness appears by itself.

When I talk about losing your mind, I am referring to emptying the mind. Actually destroying the mind. Annihilating the mind. Totally, totally transmuting the mind. Not to change it to something else.

For in truth, you are already That. You have always been That. But as long as you go on crying over spilled milk, when you look at your life you see the things that upset you. You see the things that make you angry, the things that make you worried. The things that make you fret and become excited. What a waste of energy. What a waste of time.

There is no thing in this world that is that important. As long as you believe it is important, you will never awaken. You can't. For you are caught up in maya. You are playing the game. You are still involved in the leela. You're feeling things. You're reacting to things. You're arguing about things. You're debating things. You're still not sure.

As long as you keep acting this way, you cannot awaken. Just think of the things you thought about today. Just for today. Since you woke up. The things that went through your mind. The actions you took. The emotions you had. The worries you had. The feelings of sadness or joy, or any kind of feelings. All this is a waste of your precious energy.

This is what keeps you back. This is what makes you a human being. This is what makes you worldly. It's up to you to understand what I'm saying and to begin to get a program of non-action in your mind in not reacting.

When something takes place in your mind or in your world, you become the observer. You become the witness. You do not react. You try to keep your mind centered in the now, in the moment. You do not think about ten minutes ago, or about yesterday, or about last week, or about last month, or last year, or five years ago. You do not consider what some-body did to you ten years ago, or how you were wronged. Those are the things that keep you back.

Do not consider where you are going to go next week. Or what you have to do to become enlightened next month. Or the teacher you have to go to see next year. Or the book you have to read next week. You do not think about these things. All of these things are part of maya. They are part of the grand illusion. They pull you back into materiality.

How can I do all the practical things I need to do in the state of mind of "I am not my body?"

If you really knew you were not the body, that question would never come to you. The body will always take care of itself. Who grows oranges on the orange tree? Who makes the grass grow? That same power will take care of your body. You don't have to worry about it. Everything will be okay. Your body will not walk into the street in front of a truck, unless you are day dreaming. You will be awake! Being awake is not being in a stupor.

Because you believe yourself to be a body, you believe you are the doer, in charge of everything, making meals, walking, shopping. But you have nothing to do with that. Being awake is being aware of all of this that is happening spontaneously, which has nothing to do with you. Grass grows spontaneously, but we can imagine we are making it grow with our willpower. The same with the activities of our bodies. Actually, they function better when you don't think about them. Therefore, be yourself and watch what transpires.

Why do we have to go through such trials and tribulations in the world? What is that part of it about? If we are Consciousness, then why do we have to bother with the material world?

You don't. Ask yourself who has to bother. There is no one to bother. It is like a dream. You are dreaming the mortal dream. Pinch yourself. Wake up. Be free. There is no one who has to do this. See, we're caught in mesmerism. We're hypnotized into believing we have to go through experiences, so it's natural to ask why. But the truth is, no one is going through any experience. It just appears like that. Just like the water in the mirage, or the sky is blue, or the snake in the rope. It appears that way, it appears real. But once you know the truth you're free. There will be no one going through anything. Only when you hold on to the "I am the body" idea, do you appear to go through experiences. But as soon as you give up the body idea by realizing I is the body, not you but I, then you become free. You never were the body. There is no body. But I do admit that in some people the mesmerism is so strong that it is most difficult to believe you're not the body. Because you see it, you observe it, it feels and acts. This is the reason you have to do Self-inquiry.

What is the difference between the no-mind state and enlightenment?

The no-mind state is where you come from practicing to the place in the Silence where there are no thoughts to bother you any longer. You get there through Self-inquiry. That's the fastest way. But that's not Self-realization. Self-realization is when the mind is pulled into the spiritual Heart. Liberation, moksha, Self-realization, is when the mind that's left over in the Silence is pulled completely into the spiritual Heart. At that time the whole mind, the I, dissolves completely, and you are free. So the no-mind state is a very high state. It's a state of bliss, but there's still somebody left to experience the bliss. When the bliss is pulled into the Heart, there is no one left to experience anything. Therefore, you no longer say, "I'm in the no-mind state." At that time there is nothing to say. Can you understand that?

Seems clear to me.

As clear as mud. Again, the important point to remember is that you should keep asking yourself questions. Do not make statements. Ask questions to yourself. The mind hates that.

Robert, it seems that it comes down to the mind or the ego trying to dis-identify with itself, and trying to identify with the mystery. Is that enough to produce the shift?

That's enough to produce the shift. When the mind begins to wonder about itself, it becomes weak. So the more you ask the question, the weaker the mind becomes. If you make statements, you keep saying to yourself, "I am God, or I am Consciousness, or I am Absolute Reality," the mind likes that, because it wants to become God. It wants to be God, so then the ego thinks it's God. And you walk around with a chip on your shoulder. But when you go the other way, wher "Who am I, where did the mind come from?" t becomes weak, it doesn't like that. As you said, it begins to see the mystery and becomes weaker and weaker. It devours itself, so to speak. But of course the ultimate truth is, there is no mind, so do not concentrate on the mind doing anything. But ask, "To whom does the mind come?"

But Robert you said to ask questions, but earlier you said to say that "this is not me." That's not asking a question.
It's like asking a question. This is not me!? Who am I?

Robert, can this all come about if you just surrender?
Oh yes, definitely. If this appears to be complicated, all you've got to do is give it all up. Say, "Take it God. It's all yours." And let go so completely, there's no room for a question. You say, "Take this, God. Take the whole burden. I no longer care." But it is difficult also because it means you have to give everything to God and not worry about a thing. Do not concern yourself with anything in this world; realize God is taking care if it. That's true surrender.

Maya

Everything that you feel, hear, touch, smell and taste is maya.
Everything is maya, the grand illusion.
Most of us really do not understand what maya really is.
My trying to explain maya is maya.
Everything that your eyes behold,
that you believe is so important, is maya.
Everything that you hear,
Everything that you read,
Everything that you try to do to better yourself,
It's all maya.

The water in the mirage, that is maya;
Something that appears to be real,
but upon investigation you find it's not.
The whole world is like that.
The whole universe is like that.
Do not be fooled again.
Do not take anything seriously.
Turn within, do not react.

The turmoil, the chaos that appears to be in this world,
is not the truth. It is not Reality.
It is something that comes and goes.
This too shall pass.
But your center is God,
Consciousness, Absolute Reality, Brahman.
Those are all synonymous.
That is the Peace that exists.

Maya–the Grand Illusion

What we call maya is very powerful, and so it appears. It grabs you in its clutches and makes you believe that things are happening in this world, and makes you believe that things are moving, changing. That's the picture it shows you. There are very few people who can go through a day without being affected by maya. Think about yourself. Just today, how have you been affected by maya? Believing something about your body, or about somebody else. Or about a situation in your life, or about the world. Or about the universe, and feeling it. That's maya.

Here's an example; I've told this story before. One day Buddha and his chief disciple, Narada, were walking along a country road. Buddha was discussing maya. He explained that the tree, the river, the mountains, the beauty, all of the bugs and the mosquitoes, animals, it's all maya.

And Narada said, "But Master, how can this be? It sounds virtually impossible. I can grab the tree. I can grab your arm. I'm stung by a mosquito. I feel this thing, there's a bump on my arm. How can this all be illusion? I don't understand."

And Buddha said, "I'm thirsty. Go get me a glass of water." There was a town nearby, so Narada went to the town and knocked at the door of the first house he saw. An old lady opened the door. She said, "What do you want?" Narada said, "My master would like a glass of water." She looked him over and saw that he was handsome, well built, healthy, and she said, "Come in."

He went into her house and there was a beautiful lady sitting on a chair. The woman said, "This is my daughter. Isn't she beautiful?" Narada was astounded at her beauty. He said,

"She is the most beautiful girl I've ever seen." The old lady said, "How would you like to marry her?" And Narada said, "Why not?"

So, he married the girl. They had a big wedding, and all the people in the village came. The next day, he got a job. He was a potter by trade, and he made beautiful pots out of clay. He did this for a living. After the first year, they had a child, and he was able to afford a beautiful house. He had a mortgage payment, had to pay taxes. So he had to work harder and hire people to help him. He had employees. He had to pay them salaries, take out taxes, workers' compensation, everything else. Then, after two years passed, another child. He was completely enmeshed in family life. Some days were good. Some days were bad. A couple more years went by, three years, four years, five years.

One day there was a big hurricane, very powerful hurricane that came into the town. The place was getting flooded. Narada said, "What are we going to do?" All his furniture was being ruined. Everything he believed he owned was getting wet, totally ruined. He took his family up onto the roof. There was a clothesline on the roof. All hung onto the clothesline. The hurricane became stronger and stronger and stronger. His mother-in-law was washed away by the flood. Narada said, "I guess we didn't need her anyway, she was old." But the hurricane was still very strong, and his wife and two children were holding on. One of the children was washed away, and Narada became very distraught. But he was holding on with his wife. Then the other child was washed away. He became very upset, but he said to himself, "At least I have my wife. We can have more children." Then his wife was washed away, and he said, "What happened to my family? They're all gone!

Everything I worked for is all gone! Everything I strived for is all gone! I'm going to end it all, commit suicide." So he let go of the rope.

The next moment, he found himself sitting next to Buddha, with a glass of water. He looked at Buddha and Buddha said, "It's about time you brought me my water!" (laughter) So Narada looked at him and said, "Now I understand what maya is!"

This is just like us. We become so enmeshed in the world. We think things are real. Everything bothers us. We become angry. We become upset. But the truth is, you are not maya. You are Absolute Reality. You are Total Awareness. You are the Self. Know who you are and wake up. Awaken and be free!

It's so simple. Words make it so complicated. The fact is you were never born, you can never die. There is no power that sustains you, maintains you. You do not exist the way you appear. The same is true for the whole universe. It's only a reflection. It's an optical illusion. Like the mirage in the water, or the water in the mirage. They're both the same. The water is the mirage and the mirage is the water. So the appearance is of water. But when you try to grab it, you grab sand. Everything you grab in this world is like sand. It seems so real. And then your emotions grab a hold of it and give it more power so that the maya becomes stronger and stronger and stronger. Until you're in such a state that it takes you many incarnations to get rid of all your fears, all the frustrations, thoughts about the past, samskaras. You have made these things real for you, but they do not exist. None of these things are real, but you have made them real. You have done it to yourself. Therefore when you leave your body, you appear to go through an astral plane, and you take a rest. You meet your long lost relatives that you couldn't stand. And then you go onwards and you go back into a body again. And you continue and continue and continue. But it's a lie. You are making it the truth. It is your truth because you believe in this. And you refuse to let go.

Of course you've got a choice. And this is your choice. Whom shall I follow this day, God or mammon? Which simply means, following mammon is following the world. The world of illusion, which keeps tricking you, making you believe you should do this and do that and to go here and to go there. When you follow God, you're following yourself. You're following the dharma, swarupa. You no longer feel sorry for yourself. You no longer feel guilty about the sins of commission/omission of the past. Your mind becomes clear, peaceful. Your mind becomes like a mirror. And since the mirror is unable to see itself, it sees its reflection in the world as peace, love, harmony, joy. As you continue to work on yourself this way, the day comes when all this is gone, and you are gone. You become nothing. A good for nothing. You go beyond nothingness, which is ineffable. Something that can't be explained. For there are no words or thoughts to understand this. Yet, you've got it all within you. Everything you need is within you. You are the One.

Have Dispassion for the World

One of the things you have to work on yourself is passion. You must give up all passion for this world and the things in it. You must develop dispassion. Now to some of you this sounds terrible, not to have passion for the things of this world. Never to be passionately in love. What I'm referring to is having dispassion for the world of maya, and having total passion for the Self. As an example, if you're intimate with a boy friend or a girl friend or a husband or a wife or a camel or a yak, whatever turns you on, you no longer think you're with that kind of a being, whatever it may be. Rather you start to understand that you're loving your Self. The camel becomes your Self. Your partner, your lover, becomes your Self. It is your Self that you are in love with. Not the self called Robert or Mary or Jane or Joe, but the Self as Consciousness. You have total passion for your Self. As you love the trees, the sky, the world, you no longer think it's a world of maya, a world of illusion, but an extension of your Self, the Absolute Reality, the Effortless, Choiceless Pure Awareness. It is your Self you're making love to. When you think it's another human being, this spoils it. When you think it's a person, place or thing, this spoils it. It is always the Self.

When you begin to understand this, you begin to move in the right direction. Otherwise, if you're looking at people as a person, place or thing, you're making a terrible mistake. That brings sorrow. It brings unhappiness, brings jealousy, fear, frustration. The way you know you're with the Self, there is freedom. No restrictions. No laws. No rules. No regulations. You're always with the Self. You've always been the Self.

Self Is the Reality of the World

So there are two ways of seeing this world. One is maya, the grand illusion. You want nothing to do with this. This is what creates problems. This appears to create animosity, sorrow. But then there is the real world. The world of the Self. The world of Bliss. The world of total joy, unalloyed peace and happiness. This is what you really are. This is your real nature, your swarupa. You have always been this and you will always be this. Forget about the past. Do not worry about the future. Have total faith, total joy, in yourself. Only when you can understand yourself as All Pervading Consciousness can you possibly understand that all the universe is an emanation of your mind. Everything that you see comes out of you.

You are the Creator. You are the God. You are the Avatar, the Atman. All the Gods that you've heard of, the Buddha, Krishna, Jehovah, Allah, they're all *you*. You are That. You are nothing else but That. You've always been That. Tat Twam Asi. This is you.

Do not concern yourself about this world. For mortal man can never understand this world at all. This world appears very confusing, very chaotic. There seem to be so many wonderful things in this world, and yet there seems to be so much destruction, man's inhumanity to man. Dastardly things going on everywhere, intermingled with the beauty and joy of this world. It becomes very confusing to the mortal man. Then you see yourself getting older and older. All of your material plans have gone by the wayside. And even if you have accomplished great things, you have to leave them when it's time to go. You start to think to yourself, "What is life all about? Who am I? What am I really? What is the Source of everything?"

And no one has ever explained these things to you. So you believe life is a chance. A chance that you've been born, you've gone through prevailing conditions. You get old and you die. You have no idea what's going on. Therefore I say to you, leave the world alone. Do not believe you have to bring peace to this world. There is a greater power that knows the way, that takes care of this world, this universe. And it needs no help from you. The only way you can help this world is by awakening, becoming Self-realized. How do you help this world by becoming Self-realized? When you become Self-realized, you are no longer a body. You are All Pervading Consciousness, the Absolute Reality. You are Boundless Space. You become the trees, the mountains, the rivers, the animals, the insects, the birds. You have become everything. You are the Self. The imperishable, immutable Self.

But when you can't see this, you act as an independent agent. Thinking you're going to make this a better world in which to live. Sticking up for your rights. Trying to change people's opinions. Protesting about this and about that. I admit all these things are necessary in this world, but this is what maya is all about. Maya is a wonderful illusion. It makes you believe you've got to do something to change things in this world. But I can assure you, nothing will ever change. It will appear to change for a while. Things will appear slightly better at times, and they'll be slightly worse at times. There will be cataclysms, destructions. All sorts of things happening to this world. This is the nature of this world. It has absolutely nothing to do with you. Yet at the same time you are the world. I always contradict myself, this is the teaching. It's a total contradiction. But the ultimate reality is, let go of everything. Know yourself as Omnipresence, and you'll be total happiness and total freedom.

Everything begins to take on a projection of yourself. And since you are beginning to discover that you are Pure Consciousness, the world starts becoming Pure Consciousness also. It's like going to a movie, and the screen is pure Consciousness, the images are the world. Prior to your awakening, you've been identifying with the images and you have no idea there's a screen. Oh, you know it somewhere in your mind. You have a slight image of the screen, but you don't think of that, because the images are very entertaining. You watch a love movie or a war movie, or this kind of movie or that kind of movie, and you get all wrapped up in the objects. But of course if you try to go up to the screen to grab any objects, you're going to grab the screen. This is what happens when you awaken. You realize that you are the screen, which is Consciousness. And you realize that everything in the world, everything, the whole universe including God, is superimposed on you. It's not Reality. It's a superimposition. But you identify with the screen which is Consciousness, and you tolerate the superimposition. Yet you realize it's not you. You have nothing to do with it and you do not identify with it.

So in the same instance your body goes through all kinds of experiences, good and bad and in between, but you are always aware that you are not the body and no body exists for you. You know in reality, there is no superimposition at all. It does not exist. It appears to exist, but it does not. It's like hypnosis. You're hypnotized to believe a white poodle is following you. And sure enough, when you wake up out of the hypnosis you keep looking back; you actually see a white poodle. Your mind will actually picture the white poodle, and you will believe it's real. Nobody else will see it, but you will, until the hypnosis wears off.

In the same way we see people, places, and things, and they appear so real to us. We identify with them, and we suffer accordingly. But as you practice every morning, catching yourself between waking up and thoughts coming, little by little, slowly but surely, you will begin to realize yourself more and more. And the day will come when you awaken. Never mind how long it takes. Do not look at time. Think of how long it took you to be what you are now. Be yourself. Identify with your reality. Try to be yourself at all times.

What Is the Cause of the World?

Why do you appear to have a body, if you don't have one? Why do you appear to be playing these games, if they're not real? The answer is, you're not playing any games. There is nobody doing anything. This is something difficult for most people to comprehend. Nothing at all is happening. But I move, I swim, I play golf, I go to work, I watch television, I'm doing all these things. These things appear to be happening. You have to remember the question. To whom is it happening? Who is experiencing this? And of course we remember it's the ego that is experiencing this. Then you remember again you have no ego. There is no ego. An ego never existed. If it did, where did it come from? Who is its creator? Whatever you believe in, there has to be a creator to have created it. If you believe you're human, something created you. You say your parents created you, and you go back in time to who created them, and who created them. You go back to the very beginning. Everything you believe in, there has to be a cause. Even when I tell you there is no cause. Therefore there cannot be an effect. You think I'm crazy, and I am. Who wants to be sane? To be sane means you conform to society and to the happenings of the world. You think alike. I can assure you, nothing exists. And I can assure you when you think about nothing, the nothing that you are thinking about does also not exist. Once you think about nothing, you spoil it. Because it becomes something.

Be aware that the world is egoless. The world has no cause, so where is the effect? If there is no effect, there is no cause. How could the world have a cause? Where would it come from? When you dream, you can say that your dream has a cause. You are the cause, because you are dreaming. But can you say that while you're dreaming? While you're dreaming and you're in the dream, you believe that the world has a cause, like everyone else does. And you get involved in everyday activities in the dream. You have good experiences and you have bad experiences. And then I come along and I tell you you're dreaming, but you don't believe me. You say, "I'll show you if I'm dreaming, Robert." And you pinch me. I say, "Ow." And you say, "See, is that a dream?" And I try to explain to you it's a dream pinch, but you don't believe it. You think it's real. Then you go across the street. And then you're walking down the street and a car hits you, and you're bleeding all over the street. I run over and I tell you, "You're dreaming, don't be too upset. It's okay." You start cursing at me and shaking your fist at me. "How can you say that? Look, I'm bleeding all over the place." Then something funny happens. You wake up. Where does the dream go? Where did the blood go? Where did the car that hit you go?

Think of your personal experiences that are upsetting you right now. Think of the problems that you think you have even while I'm talking to you. Some of your minds are thinking of something else, problems, and you believe it's real. You're thinking of who you like or don't like. What you're going to eat for dinner tonight. All these thoughts come to you because you have not trained yourself how to deal with your thoughts. And you've got preconceived ideas. You have got concepts.

As an example you come and you look at me. You don't see me fresh and new like you see yourself. But you compare me with Krishnamurti or with this guy or the Bhagavan Ramana Maharshi or Nisargadatta or the garbage cleaner or with the janitor or whoever you wish to compare me with. This is exactly what I'm talking about. Your mind becomes filled with preconceived ideas. I am really nobody. I am nothing special. So what you see in me is not real. You're seeing your own projections. You're seeing yourself, in other words. And if you have not developed yourself and have awakened to Pure Consciousness, then you're seeing something worldly. And you make comparisons. You say I like, I don't like, it's good, it's bad and so forth. You've got to take control of your mind. You've got to realize your mind and your body are not your friends. They feed you the wrong information. It appears right for a while, but then it becomes wrong again. Do not listen to your mind. Stop the thoughts before they get to the edge of your nose. That's all I've got to say.

Self-Inquiry
(Atma Vichara)

Think how many years you'll be going through life,
believing you're a body, a mind, an ego.
The situations you've been through.
The agonies, the ecstasies,
the dualities.
You're beginning to see now that all of those things belong
to the I -thought, to the personal self,
which is not really you.
You are total freedom, having absolutely nothing to do
with the personal self.
You simply have to ask yourself, "Who is this personal self?
Where did it come from? How did it arise?
How did it get a hold of me, and make me believe
I'm human?
That makes me feel I was born? And I have to die?
What is this personal self? Where did it come from?"

And as you follow the personal self, the I -thought,
You'll begin to see it never existed.
It was never born.
It is absolutely nothingness.
And you'll become radiantly happy,
Full of Love,
Full of Peace.

Trace the I to the Source

As you try to understand these things, as you begin to
ponder what I'm talking about, you look for a way to remove

everything from your mind, to empty the mind. You begin to inquire. To whom do all these thoughts come? To whom does the feeling of humanity come? To whom does this universe come? To whom does the ego come? And you smile to yourself. You keep still.

You will soon realize that everything comes to you. It comes to you. I think these things. I believe this and I believe that. I feel hurt. I feel this way, I feel that way. A new revelation comes to you. "I." You begin to see that the I-thought is the culprit. From the moment you get out of bed in the morning, you begin with the I, and it never ends till you fall asleep. Therefore the only peace you ever get is when you are in deep sleep. When you are in deep sleep, the I returns to the Heart, to the Source. There is nothing going on. Nothing happening. At that time you are unconsciously Self-realized.

This is why when you get up in the morning and you say to yourself, "I slept well," you're talking about the I. I slept well. What you really mean to say is, the I wasn't interfering with your life. But as soon as you begin to think, you say, "I am late for work. I have to catch the bus. I have a headache. I have to eat breakfast." And you go on and on with this I, and it never stops. All day long it's I, I, I, I. Think about this. Am I not telling you the truth? You're always thinking about, "I this," and "I that." Till the night time comes again, you go to sleep. And again the I goes back into the Source, into the Heart, and you're at peace once more. Until you wake up and it starts all over again. After doing this for a million years, you get to the stage when you'll ask yourself, "Who am I? What is this I? How did it arise? From whence does it come?" And this is the beginning of wisdom, when you inquire for the Source of the I. You ultimately begin to trace the I to the Source. When you do this finally, when the I is in the Source, it is just like when you're in deep sleep, except that you're conscious. Think about this for a moment.

In deep sleep you have no I, for it has returned to the Source. You're totally happy, but you're unconscious of it. When you attain what we call Self-realization, it means the I has returned to the Source while you're awake. There's nobody left to think. There's no one left to worry, or to fret, or to be unhappy. You have merged with the Infinite, with the All-Pervading Brahman. If you understand this, and you practice this, you will become the happiest person in the world. For on the way to finding the I-Source you begin to feel happier and happier every day. The old thoughts melt away. The old you dissolves. You become free.

Whatever you identify with, that's what you become. Therefore, stop identifying with worldly things. Identify with yourself. Now, how do you do this? It begins in the morning, as I told you before. That's the time when your mind has been free. Because you slept, you've had a semblance of peace. Being in deep sleep is an unconscious method of Self-realiza-tion. You're realized when you are asleep, but you are uncon-scious. So you're not aware of it. You want to be consciously asleep. When you're consciously asleep, you're awake. You're awake to your Self, to Reality to what Is, to I Am.

When you get up in the morning, immediately before the thoughts come, identify with the Self. Now how do you do this? Simply say to yourself, "I . . . I." That's all you have to do. "I . . . I." You're doing this before your thoughts come. Maybe in the beginning you can only do this for a couple of seconds, but that's good. Even those couple of seconds will make your day fulfilled, and you'll feel happy during the day. As time passes, as I explained before, the space will widen and you'll be able to remain longer periods in I . . . I . . . I . . . I.

Now when thoughts come, simply ask yourself, "To whom do these thoughts come? They come to me." And you hold on to the "me." You do not let go. But do not concentrate on the me. Just hold on to the me. You concentrate on the Source of me. It's like you're holding on to a rope, and you're going to its source and you let go. Letting go is the Source. Total Awareness, Absolute Reality, I Am That I Am. Do not try to analyze this. Just allow it to be.

Remember, the finite mind cannot comprehend the Infinite. This is why it is important to always see where you are coming from. What were you involved in today, as an example? In retrospect go back to this morning. What was the first thing you did when you opened your eyes? You should have been aware that the I-thought has traveled from the Heart center to the brain. And now you are awake and you feel your body and you feel the world. You should not go any further. You should now attempt to work on yourself, where you send the I-thought back from the brain, back to the spiritual center, the spiritual Heart. You should immediately attempt to do this. In other words, you should not continue the game of the I-thought telling you things about your body, about the world. And you should not flick on the TV and watch the world news, for that pulls you further into illusion.

But you should immediately begin to inquire, "What happened to the I? Where is the I? Apparently it must be in my head, for I am aware of my body and the world, and I am identifying with it." This is the way you should talk to yourself, and you ask yourself the question, "But how did that I-thought get to my brain?" and you stop. As you begin to think about this, you are abiding in the I, and if you're really abiding in the I, the I-thought begins to travel backwards. It begins to leave your head and begins to travel backward to the Heart. But you have to catch yourself. This is the first thing you should do when you awaken.

I know most of you forget. Yet you should have some clue that tells you, "It is time for me to abide in the I. I'm not going to allow the I to bring all of these thoughts into my head." You forget about your work for the moment. You forget about getting dressed. You forget about the time, and you realize the reason you're thinking about your body or about anything else is because the I-thought has gone into your brain, and it now forms the body and the mind. You begin to see that the mind is nothing more than a conglomeration of thoughts. If there were no thoughts, there would be no mind. Can't you see what you're doing? As you begin to think this way, the I-thought begins to return to its source by itself. In other words, you don't really have to send the I-thought back to the Self or to the Heart center. You simply have to inquire what the I-thought really is. You'll come to the conclusion it is, after all, only your thought. If the I-thought really does not exist, then my body and the world does not exist. Just thinking about these things, you begin to feel peaceful, happy.

I know you're saying, "Well, I don't have the time to do this every morning. I'm late for work. I've got to get dressed. I've got to eat breakfast." But again I say to you, this is not yoga or meditation, where you have to take time out to meditate and then go about your business. This is the superior method of Self-inquiry. And if you just begin to practice this Self-inquiry, you will notice that when it's time to get dressed, eat your breakfast and go to work, your body will do this in record time.

You will not even be thinking about these things. But yet your body will shower, do what it has to do, and you'll be out of the house and you'll feel great. This is the difference between Self-inquiry and meditation. You are not meditating on anything. You're simply inquiring about your I-thought. And each step will come by itself. You will not have to think about what I'm going to say next. For instance, as you are working on yourself this way and thoughts come to you, something within you will immediately say, "To whom do these thoughts come?" You're not planning this. You have not rehearsed. And by the way, never rehearse. Never plan what you are going to do in the morning. Unless it's spontaneous it will not work. Remember this: Self-inquiry should be spontaneous. It should not be a drudgery. It should not be something you planned.

What Is the I-Thought?

You simply begin to look at yourself. You open your eyes when you wake up. You begin to realize that just before you woke up, you were in a total state of peace, in a no-thought state. You were in an effortless no-thought state. But now you have allowed the I-thought to go to the brain, and you're thinking about your body and the world. So the thought comes to you, how do I get back to the effortless no-thought state? By abiding in the I. Where did the I come from? Who am I? Surely the I must have a source. That source must be quite a powerful thing in itself, whatever it is. In other words, I'm assuming that you don't realize that the source is the Self. But just by thinking that the I-thought came out of it, it must be some-thing powerful. Then why did the I-thought come out of it? What is the I-thought? I keep calling it the I-thought. It's a thought. There is no I. This gives you a clue. It makes you happy. For you realize you've got nothing to fight. As a matter of fact, some people just become still and they say nothing else. In other words, when you realize the I is a thought you become still, and the I will immediately disappear. There will be no thoughts. You will feel wonderful. Then you can get dressed and go to work, but the momentum of what you did this morning will follow you through the day. It is true that you will get involved in the world, yet you will find that you have time to think of your Self. You will abide in the I. It will happen all by itself and you will find in your work that whatever you do, you're making the right decisions without thinking. Things do not disturb you. You are at peace with the world. You feel blissful. You have no desire to tell people about this. People have to be ready. They have to lift themselves up by their own bootstraps. People have to be prepared to be able to practice Self-inquiry. And the preparation was usually made in a previous life.

Therefore, something tells you it is a waste of time to write books, to go on public television, to try to expand the teaching, to do anything. You simply live your life in a wonderful way. Everything takes care of itself, and you notice that your consciousness is expanding. It began by thinking of yourself, and now it is expanding to take in the world, to take in the universe. And then you begin to see everything in this universe as an image on the screen, and you are the screen. You never worry again. You never fear anything again. You understand the wholeness of everything, and there are no mistakes. All is well. Nothing is wrong.

But you have to do these things every day, especially in the morning when you first open your eyes. That is the time to really work on yourself. If you wait until later, then maya becomes too strong and grabs a hold of you, causing you to get really involved in the leela and the game of life. But as you work on yourself every morning, the body takes care of itself, the mind becomes extinguished, the ego turns into humility, you become happy. There is nothing you have to do, and again your body will do whatever it came here to do. But you have nothing to do with that. You are at peace.

The mature aspirant of Jnani will always work with their I. That's where it begins. Trace the source of I. Where did my I come from? Watch it, observe it. Watch when you get up in the morning. You feel so peaceful in the beginning, but as soon as you start to think about I, all your problems, your troubles, the world, gang up on you. But if you begin to catch yourself, grab hold of the I, "Where did it come from? Where did it just come from? A moment ago I was at peace. A moment ago everything was all right, but now I'm worried, I'm upset, I'm thinking about my job, my future, my finances, my health. Where did the I come from that thinks about these things?" And trace the I back, back into the Heart, which is the Source.

People have asked me what they are supposed to look for in the Heart. Well remember, the Heart we're talking about is on the right side of your chest. Two digits from the center. That's your spiritual Heart. That's the Source. The I comes out of there. So don't follow the I externally, follow the I internally. You see the difference? Don't go catching the I as it thinks about the world. We reverse the procedure. You want to follow the I back to its Source.

So you can see the Source as a brilliant Light a thousand times more brilliant than the sun. You can imagine the I going back into that Light, merging with the Light. Or, if you're bhakti inclined, devotional, you can think of your favorite saint or sage, and feel the Heart center as that sage. And the I goes back into the sage or into the Light. The sage absorbs your I. I can assure you that if you practice this only a little bit, you'll have some amazing results. But for some reason, most people have to be on a spiritual path for years practicing some form of yoga before they can come to that stage where they can follow the I back into the Source. Yet there are those people who have had no previous experience. They were just able to see that the Source of their I is the Self. And they became liberated that instant.

The World Is Attached to the I

The secret is not to allow the I to take you over. How does the I take you over? You begin to allow it to identify with worldly things. And you do that by thinking about them. Now as an example, you get up in the morning and you start to think you've got to conserve water. You've got to pay your rent. You've got to buy new clothes. And a million other things about I, I, I. But if you keep remembering that all worldly things are attached to the I, you become introverted. And the I goes back into the Source.

As you keep doing this every morning, either watching the I, or asking to whom do the thoughts come, you'll notice a subtle change is taking place in your life. The first change you will see is, you develop a semblance of peace that you never had before. You'll just not be disturbed by anything, and you'll be surprised at yourself. You'll notice the things that used to make you angry no longer have the power to do that. You'll notice that the things you feared, for instance: depression, recession, loss of memory, whatever, your wife ran away with the milkman—maybe that's a good sign—but these things will no longer disturb you. You'll just feel good. You'll feel good all over. And that will turn into pure happiness. You're just happy for no reason. Can you imagine what it feels like just to be happy without interruption for no reason? It has absolutely nothing to do with the world. It doesn't mean you'll go round laughing hysterically all the time. It means you just feel happy.

You hear about the war in Iraq and you're happy. There's no war in Iraq, you're still happy. You work, you're happy. You don't work, you're happy. You have possessions, you're happy. You don't have possessions, you're happy. In other words it makes no difference what the world may seem to bring to you. You are no longer identifying with the world and its objects. You're seeing the world as yourself, or you're beginning to, slowly but surely.

Once the I goes back into the Source, even for a few moments at first, you become joyously happy. You have much peace and harmony. You feel it immediately. In the beginning it might not last. But at least you've had it for a few moments, and you were able to prove the truth of what I'm saying. Some of you have told me you've been able to do this for a few moments, and you felt a joy, a peace, and a bliss, that you never felt before. You're beginning to feel your Self, your real Self. As you continue to do this every day, especially when you wake up in the morning, those periods will last longer and longer. They will expand. And you will be able to rest in that space which is called the fourth state of consciousness, the gap between sleeping and waking. You will be able to stay there for longer periods of time, and you will feel what I'm talking about. Yet, there are some of you who do no practice whatsoever. If you are a bhakti, you really don't have to. All you've got to do is surrender, totally surrender, which leads to the same thing. But if you are an aspiring Jnani, and you want to get it over with, grab hold of your I, follow it to the Source, and become free totally and completely.

Abide in the I

It's not necessarily done with effort and intention. It's more a matter of letting go than a matter of effort, which can only take you so far.
Yes, true.

Sometimes it's that intense effort before you let go to realize how simple it is.
You wonder why you use effort to begin with.

I think it has a valid place. It builds up such intensity that one can awaken, and then when you awaken, you realize how simple it is.
But remember for whom the effort is. It is the ego that uses effort. It's much better to observe the ego than to resist it. You observe the ego effortlessly. You simply watch yourself the way you react to conditions. And see how much you react to given conditions that affect you. Are you still reacting as you always did? You notice how quiet your mind is. That your mind doesn't move so far any more. It doesn't go out so far. It stays still. And everything is happening around you, but not to you. Again, you become the observer of all of the things of life going on. You watch but you don't react.

Is that what you mean by abiding in the I?
Not really. Abiding in the I is holding on to the I by inquiring, "To whom does this come? It comes to me. I feel it. Then who am I?" That's abiding in the I.

When you ask "Who am I?" then the Silence comes?
The Silence doesn't come, because the Silence already is.

Your awareness of Silence appears.
You simply become still when you ask, "Who am I?"

Abiding in the I, is that the Silence you abide in?
You abide in the I by asking, "Who am I?" Holding on to the I is abidance in the I.

I still don't know what you mean by holding on to the I.
You become aware of the I by asking, "Who am I?" over and over again. "Who is this I? Where does it come from? Who am I? Who am I?"

That sounds more like questioning the I rather than living in the I.
It's the same thing. That's the way you abide in the I, it's the only way.

I'd follow the I and it would go somewhere and it would seem like it would go into the Heart. And once it went there, it dissolved whatever it was attached to. As I was working with it, it dissolved, everything dissolved in that place, and that's when I thought I was abiding in the I. At that point I followed it, and it took time. But it seemed like it went into the Heart and then everything dissolved in that place and that's when I thought I was abiding in the I. And would that seem like abiding in the Self? Is there a difference?

How did you abide in the I? How did you follow it?

I asked, let's see, what did I do? "To whom does this come?" To me. To I. And I grabbed hold of that I and I followed it, and there was something to follow. If I do it now, there's nothing to follow, but when I was doing it . . . .

What was the thing you followed?

Where is the source of the I? And it was nothing that . . . it was a sense of following it . . . it had nothing to do with anything.

That's right. You don't actually follow the I. You pose the question, "To whom does this come? To I."

And you quicken to a sense of following it into a space where everything dissolves in the end.

It happens by itself.

Yes, but for me it was a sense of following, even though there was no traceable means of following it at all.

There Is Only One I

What is the difference between abiding in the I and abiding in the Self?

When you abide in the I you're abiding in the ego. The I is really the ego, the small I. It turns into the Self eventually. So when you abide in the I, you abide in the Self, because there is only one I. This small I turns into the Self. Eventually only the Self exists, but in the beginning it appears like the I. And as you continue holding on by asking the question, "Who am I?" it turns into the Self, into I Am.

So it's pretty clear.
As clear as mud. (laughter)

So Robert, all the questions and all the answers are also part of maya. Maya can never be broken up intellectually.
No.

The only valid thing is to practice, to follow the teaching of the teacher. The method he advises, and that's it. Questions, answers—discussions out of questions.
You're right. Maya cannot be broken up intellectually, because it never existed. It doesn't exist. There is no maya. Once you realize that, you're awakened to your true Self.

So, all the instructions, the questioning, the answering, all of that is part of maya too.
It's all a waste of time. But you have to do something. (laughter)

Yes, that's what I mean. Follow the teaching of the teacher as a practice, follow the practice.
If you do that, you'll be okay. But the teaching is only to show you that there are no teachings. You simply awaken. And then you know you've always been awake. There never was a time when you were not. None of this exists. If you have a quiet mind, you're safe. But if your mind is always thinking,

thinking, thinking, looking for new methods, looking for new teachers, looking for new this, and new books, new this and new that, then you've got a problem. Be still and know that I Am God.

I would have said it another way, Robert. What I'm looking for, I'm looking with.
What you're looking for, you're looking with?

Yes.
Well, if you want to say it, that's good.

Robert, you said all you have to do is be still, be quiet. But it seems as though to find that stillness, that quietness, there's a battle with the mind.
To whom? To whom does it appear that way?

Well, if you do Self-inquiry, if you're quiet for a moment, then the mind comes back up. And then you do a Self-inquiry again, you're quiet again, and the mind comes back up.
Okay.

Well, that's the battle.
This is really no battle, if you ask, "To whom does it come?"

Well, that's your weapon. (laughter)
So use your weapon to win the battle.

Well, that's my point, that it is a battle. It's not so much "just be quiet." On the one hand it takes that effort, it takes the . . .
I understand what you mean. But as long as you talk yourself into a battle, you're going to have a battle on your hands.

Well, it seems as though if you ignore the battle, you'll have the battle. So the battle is inevitable, but you can choose the battlefield.
On the contrary, if you become indifferent and just watch, your mind will actually slow down by itself. Don't get involved. Watch. Be still. And there will be no battle.

Isn't it part of the illusion that there is some quiet or Silence that one's going to attain?
Quiet and Silence are your real nature.

Yes, but no it's not . . .
Silence and quiet . . .

I mean, I understand what you're saying and I agree, but it still has nothing to do with quiet and Silence.
That's because you're making noises right now. (laughter) You refuse to keep silent.

It's true; that's what I feel about you too, Robert.
I'm not really talking.

Well, if you were to witness and that becomes effortless and the mind becomes quiet, that's very understandable. But if you're doing vichara, that is like an effort.
Vichara is really done to quiet the mind, and if you look at it as an effort it becomes an effort. Try not to have any thoughts for or against. Just do it in a peaceful way, and watch what happens. But don't tell yourself it's a battle, it's an effort, or it's hard. Make it simple. Observe, watch, ask in a simple way, and everything will take care of itself.
It depends on your maturity. Everybody is different. I'm not saying you shouldn't involve yourself in the world; just do

not react in anything you do. Simply observe yourself and the things that you react to, and try to keep away from the things that you react to. Make your life simple and comfortable.

And do plenty of Silence.

If you don't react to conditioning, then you're always in the Silence. You can be in the market place, you can be anywhere, if you don't react, you're always in the Silence. You can also be in a cave, but if you have not learned to control your mind, your mind will drive you crazy, do all kinds of thoughts. Therefore it makes no difference where you are. It's how you react where you are that counts.

Spiritual Practice
(Sadhana)

Everyone here is Absolute Reality, Pure Awareness.
This is your real nature.
Right now, not some time in the future.
Not when you get enlightened.
Not when you search for the answers.
But right this minute. This is what you are.

Why will you not accept it?
When you think about yourself, do you think
you're a puny human
that has to struggle for existence and fight for survival?
As long as you believe this, that's the way it's going
to be for you.
But as soon as you accept the truth about yourself,
that you are a delight, Divine Sat-Chit-Ananda,
You will be free.
You simply have to accept this.

There are no rituals you have to go through.
There are no prayers you have to chant.
You simply have to awaken to your true nature,
Pure Awareness,
Nirvana,
Bliss,
Consciousness.
This is what you are right at this moment.

The Beginning of Wisdom

There is a story about a Jnani who was sitting on the edge of the road, with his eyes closed and his head on his knees, immersed in the Divine. A young boy walked up to him and said, "Master, can I be your disciple? Can you teach me? And the Jnani said, "I have no disciples and I give no teaching. But I will allow you to sit next to me for the day." The young man sat down and observed.

All day long people from various beliefs, religions, came to the Jnani, asked him questions, wanted boons, wanted healings, wanted different magical tricks to be performed. A lady came to have her daughter married. She wanted the Jnani's blessing so she could find a husband. Another came to be prosperous in his work. And this went on all day. The Jnani never opened his eyes, nor did he answer. He said absolutely nothing. At about four o'clock, a beggar came over with a bundle on his shoulders, he was disheveled, rags. He went over to both of them and asked, "Can you please show me the way to town?" And the Jnani opened his eyes, smiled, jumped up and said, "Certainly, follow me." He took him a quarter of the way, held his baggage for him, and pointed the road to town, and went back and sat down.

The young fellow was beside himself. He asked the Jnani, "I do not understand, Master, what you did. All these people came to you, lawyers, judges, various people from different religions, asking you profound questions, and you would not answer them. But the beggar made you smile and open your eyes, and you showed him the way. Can you please explain this?" The Jnani said, "The beggar is the only honest man we had come today. He knew what he wanted, and he had his way." What this means is, most people are hypocrites. They want teachings for their own benefit. They're not thinking of the Absolute. They're thinking of what the teaching can do for them materially. They want to remove a problem, change their lifestyle, gain material wealth, rid themselves of sickness, and so on.

Now these were all legitimate desires, but they have absolutely nothing to do with Self-realization. Self-realization is your true nature. It is what you are. It has absolutely nothing to do with your body. It has nothing to do with your mind. It has nothing to do with your affairs. So the one who is Self-realized is not the body. The body can never become Self-realized. The mind can never know enlightenment. People still believe, no matter how many times I say this, that it is the mind that becomes enlightened, the body rises in consciousness and becomes liberated. Nothing can be further from the truth. You are not the body. You have no body. You have no mind.

With all the religions and all of our spiritual practices, we say we want to become this, we want to become that. We want peace of mind. We want riches. We want all of these things. But what we really want is Absolute Freedom. The ultimate reality is Pure Awareness, Absolute Reality.

This is a goal that is someplace within us, and we don't know it. We're carrying it around. The ultimate reality is part of us already. But yet we go through all kinds of practices, meditations, sadhanas, trying to awaken the kundalini. Doing all kinds of tantric exercises, learning the Qabbalah, practicing Taoism, doing all these things that are completely unnecessary and ridiculous. They're all a waste of time. But then again, they're not a waste of time. They're not a waste of time because if you didn't do them, you wouldn't be here, and you wouldn't be in a class that teaches Advaita Vedanta. You wouldn't be seeking complete freedom.

Everything you've done has led you to this. Yet, it is all a bunch of nonsense. How can they both be correct? How can it be necessary and also be a bunch of nonsense? As long as you refuse to awaken, and you refuse to see yourself as no body, you're going to go through all these rituals and all these experiences. And practice all these teachings and memorize the Bible and the Sutras and everything else. You're to go through all kinds of teachings again and again and again and again, perhaps for many many lives. Until you awaken to the fact that it is not the teaching that's going to awaken me, really. It is no person, place, or thing that can ever awaken me and free me from bondage to myself, from bondage to maya, to the universe, to the world.

And this is the beginning of wisdom, when you realize this. Again, when you realize that all the teachings in the world, all the spiritual practices in the world, all the yoga practices, all the disciplines that you've been doing, are not going to awaken you one iota. You've been wasting your time. There is nothing that can awaken you.

You're waiting for me to tell you what will awaken you. There is no thing that can ever awaken you. If the thing awakens you, it would not be awakening. If you rely on something to wake you up, it would not be a real awakening. What happens is you simply begin to see. You become Pure Being. But nothing made it happen. Do not think that all the hard work you've been doing will make you awaken faster. I'm telling you these great truths for your own benefit, because most of you have been here for a long time. All of the things in this world will not awaken you. There is nothing that can awaken you, for you rely on some thing. And all the things simply pull you deeper and deeper into maya.

There Is No One to Awaken

You and I know many people who have been practicing spiritual disciplines for many years. They can recite the Bible backwards and forwards. They memorize beautiful stanzas and spiritual books. They're good debaters on points of Advaita Vedanta, or other teachings. They've been around the world to many teachers, many places. They're still the same as they always were. All they've done is add on to their ignorance. They keep adding and adding and adding all of the different teachings. They're filling themselves up with teachings. This will never awaken you. It's when you empty yourself out totally and completely, when there is nobody left to learn anything, that's when you simply see yourself as no body. You look at yourself and you realize what you are. But no thing can make this happen to you.

Therefore, what is the attitude to take? No attitude. What should you do? Nothing. What should you study? What should you learn? Nothing. Where should you go? Nowhere. With whom should you associate? No one. When you can get to this place, you are already awakened. For there was never anyone who had to be awakened. There was never anyone who had to practice spiritual teachings. There was never anyone who had a body. There was never anyone who existed. I know to some of you this sounds very strange, yet it is the truth. It is the whole truth and nothing but the truth. The only way you're ever going to learn this is by not learning anything. By keeping silent. Look how your mind is thinking right now. Some of you are saying to yourselves that guy is crazy. And you're right. Some of you are already thinking about lunch tomorrow, clothes you're going to wear, going to work, your mind immediately starts to think. The lesson you have to learn is how to stop thinking. And no one can teach you this, really. Because there are no teachings that can adequately stop you from thinking. You have to want it yourself.

In other words, instead of looking to me—I'm not a teacher, and a person who is going to give you a sacred mantra, or a person who is going to tell you a certain secret so you can awake—forget this. Turn within. See the truth. Become the truth. Do not look to others for advice, what to do, how to live. Be a lamp unto yourself as the Buddha said. All the answers are within you. Some of you are saying, "What about you Robert, can't we come to you for advice?" I am a guide, a mirror for you to see yourself. Look at me as a mirror for you, that's all. See me as a mirror for yourself. I can only see you as one way, perfection, Consciousness. I see you as myself. When you look at me, you're looking into the mirror. What do you see? You're seeing yourself. How are you seeing yourself? As depraved, homely, sickly, as an ego maniac? Drop it. Awaken. When you look at me you see Silence, if you're looking in the mirror correctly. There is no mind, there is no movement, there is no body, there is no one home. Then you see yourself. And you are just That.

Remember you haven't awakened to it, for there is no one to awaken. Always remember this. Many books, many teachings tell you, you have to awaken. Who has to awaken? There never was anyone asleep. There has to be someone asleep who is awakening. Yet, where you are coming from, you believe you are asleep. You believe you need a teaching. You believe someone has to touch you or give you a mantra, or do something to you. You always want something. You always think you have to get something from the outside. The outside is a total illusion, just as you are. Therefore the only thing you can get from the outside is total nonsense, foolishness, maya. That's all anybody is going to give you. You have to listen to these words and act accordingly. Just BE. Do not be this or that. Do not think of just being. Just BE.

Forget about your dreams, your goals, your ambitions, your future, your past. These are all illusions. If you want to look to your future, or to your goals, then the ultimate goal you're striving for is death. For that's where everybody appears to end. This is where your goals get you. This is where your future is, in the grave. This is where everybody appears to wind up.

Therefore the wise ones begin to know themselves as Absolute Reality before another day passes. They no longer keep thinking what am I going to do when I leave this meeting. I'm going to go and see a movie, I'm going to go out to dinner, I'm going home and watch a TV program, I'm going to go home and listen to records. Instead, the wise person thinks, I have nowhere to go, and I have nothing to do. Yet, you will do some things that you have to do. You will still go to a movie. You will still watch TV perhaps, if you want to. You will eat dinner. But you will realize you're doing nothing. Again this is a great paradox. How can you do something and yet at the same time be doing nothing? But this is exactly what is happening. Your body will appear to go through the motions and do all sorts of things, but you are doing nothing. When I speak of things like this, the finite mind cannot comprehend this. The finite mind wants to fight, argue, stick up for its rights. And many people forget about this kind of a teaching and go about their business. And they say, "Well, let whatever happens, happen." It is only very few people that can grasp what I'm talking about.

Everybody is ultimately going to come this way. Everybody is going to awaken one day. And yet as long as you are engrossed in the body the way you are, and in a world of persons, places, and things, you will appear to come back life after life after life after life after life. Until you come to the conclusion I've come to. We are all hell bound for heaven, so to speak. Everyone is going to get to this place, whether we like it or not.

You may ask if this is our true nature, nothing, no one, how did I get here in the first place? And this is a good question. Who asked the question? I did. So I'll answer it. Nothing is happening. You never got here. There is no here to get. It's like hypnosis. Many of you have seen people hypnotized. And in the hypnosis they seem to be seeing certain things that the hypnotist tells them. Yet these things do not exist. So it is with this world and your appearance in it. You appear to be here because you're hypnotized. You have certain thoughts, certain feelings, certain emotions, because you're hypnotized. You feel you want to become Self-realized, liberated, because you're hypnotized. Everything you feel or do or act is hypnosis. You are not the one who is acting or doing or being. You are beyond all this. You are boundless space, Nirvana. Sat-Chit-Ananda. You are not what you think you are. You are eternal happiness, unalloyed peace, joy. This is your real nature. You are the substratum of all existence, the underlying current out of which all things come. Yet you are not those things that appear to be coming from you.

There Is Nothing to Search for

You can tell if you're getting closer to this by the peace that overwhelms you—the happiness that takes you over. It is not a happiness because there is a thing happening in your life that you feel. It is not a happiness of something that you own that you did not own before. It is not a peace because you're in the right environment and you feel peaceful. It is a peace and happiness that is always with you. You are that peace. You are that happiness. It is always there. It never leaves you. As long as you believe you're a body, it is virtually impossible to have this peace and have this happiness. You cannot, for a body is part of the world conditioning. Therefore, you have to search for peace. You have to search for happiness. You believe that if you do this, you'll be happy. If you do this you will become peaceful. And when you do this and you do that, the happiness and peace, how long will it last? For a short while. Things change. Environments change. Conditions change. Your family changes. Everything changes. Therefore, again, it is virtually impossible to have real peace and real happiness as long as you believe you are a body. Consequently, we do not go searching for peace and happiness. This is a mistake. What we do, is become our real Self by not trying to become our real Self.

All this begins by quieting the mind. By not allowing the mind to react to conditions and situations. I'm not only speaking of negative conditions and situations, I'm speaking of everything that arises in the mind. When you wake up in the morning and you see the beautiful trees, sun up, the mountains, the flowers, birds, this also is a false image. It is not the truth about you. You're not trying to exchange bad for good. For the singing bird that you listen to will only last a fortnight. How long is a fortnight? Two weeks. That's enough. All the trees you see will die in the winter time, or change in the winter time. Everything you see changes. The beautiful flowers you pick for your morning breakfast table die within twenty-four hours, or less. They're no longer beautiful flowers. What I'm trying to show you is, you cannot depend on anything in this world for your happiness or your peace. It's a false premise. Things in this world only make you happy temporarily. When you come to the realization that you're not the body—and sometime you come to the realization that there is no world—there is no universe, there is no God. There is only That, which is indescribable.

You have to be very honest with yourself. Do I really want to become free? Am I really looking to awaken, to be liberated? What am I doing about it? Be honest with yourself. (laughter from kids nearby) Listen to those kids having a birthday party. Whatever they're doing, they're so happy. Yet at the end of the party they have to go home. They have to go to school tomorrow, or they have chores to do, and then they have to do things they don't like. Soon their minds start thinking about partying again. They make more parties. And they keep this up until they grow up. It never stops. Party after party after party. They become party animals, searching for happiness, searching for peace. Searching for everlasting joy. Yet, they do not understand that nothing outside can give you this. Nothing!

You have to jump within yourself. You have to learn to sit in the Silence, to quiet the mind. And it will come by itself. You do not have to pray for it or practice sadhanas, or, as I said before, do certain rituals or read certain books. You

simpy have to sit, quiet the mind by observing it, inquire, "To whom do the thoughts come?"
Be still, and know that I Am God.

Meditation and Self-Inquiry

Does meditation serve a purpose in the spiritual quest?
For the beginner it quiets the mind to an extent, and it makes you one-pointed. It makes the mind one-pointed so that you can concentrate on one thing at a time. It does help. But as you advance, it actually becomes a hindrance. For on whom are you meditating? To meditate you have to have an object and a subject. You are the subject meditating on an object. But in truth, in reality, there is no subject and there is no object. There is only the one Self, there is only Brahman. Therefore, you have to ask yourself the question: "Does Brahman have to meditate? Does God have to meditate?"

Does not meditation benefit us? The Lord Arjuna himself is shown in meditation.
For the person who believes they are separate from God, yes. If you believe you are separate, that Brahman is up in the sky or someplace else, that God is someplace else, that Shiva is someplace else, Krishna is someplace else, then, yes you have to meditate on these Deities. But when you remember that You Are That, Tat Tvam Asi, who is to meditate on whom? You have become Krishna yourself. You are Shiva, you are Brahman, you are That. All you have to do is to be aware of the Truth. But again, if you believe you are separate, then by all means, you have to meditate. This is why Jnana Marga teaches: *There Is Only the One and I Am That.*

There never was two of you. There never was God and you. But as long as you believe this, or perhaps nobody told you this before, then you have to meditate. You have to pray. You have to do all the rituals. You have to perform puja, and sing bhajans and kirtans. All these things are necessary when you believe you're separate from God. So, why not start from the top?

It's the Unmanifest that manifests the One. Is that correct?
Yes, same thing. I and my Father are one. If you have seen me, you have seen my Father. Same thing.

Sitting in the Silence is different from meditation?
Yes.

Like sitting in the chair with your eyes open looking out at your garden? Sitting with your eyes closed without an object, sitting there?
It doesn't make any difference.

Asking, who am I, and so on?
Of course you can always practice Atma Vichara, inquire, "Who am I?" And as soon as thoughts enter your mind inquire, "To whom do these thoughts come?" Realize the "I" is not you. And you look for the Source of the "I," which is in your heart.

But then the Source of the I will be slow to gradually start to remember that, like there is something lost and it comes back to us.
You can say that, yes. The "I" becomes the real I.

But as you remember it more and more, you're more aware of it, you remember it for longer times. And you forget everything else.

Yes.

In the meditations, when you sit down to meditate, do you try to stop the thoughts, or do you try to dismiss the thoughts?

Never try to stop the thoughts. If you try to stop the thoughts, they will become bigger and greater, and they will win. Because the mind appears to be very powerful. Yet in reality, the mind does not exist. There is no mind. There is no such thing as a mind. So when you sit in the Silence, you observe, you watch, you become the witness, you can do many things. You can watch your breath by practicing vipassana meditation, watch the feelings in your body, observe the breathing. Yet the better way is to still inquire, "Who am I?" You never answer that question. You just ask the question and keep still. When you keep still, thoughts will come into your mind. Simply inquire, "To whom do these thoughts come? They come to me. I think these thoughts. Then who am I?" Who am I simply means, what is the Source of the I? From whence does the I arise? You follow the I back to the Source, which is the Heart center. And one day, the I will disappear, and you will be totally liberated.

It is the "I" that makes you human. Everything in this universe is attached to the "I." Do you not say I feel this and I feel that? And I am this and I am that? All day long you're using your "I." All day long you're saying I am this and I am happy, I am sad, I am sick, I am well, I am tired, I am everything. But when you practice Atma Vichara, you become aware of this, totally aware that you're always saying I am this and I am that. And you question this by asking, "Well, who am I? Who is this I? Who gave it birth? From whence did it arise?" Just by asking this question, you will find peace.

In the past, sages such as Ramana Maharshi, Shankara, and others, have said that Self-inquiry is for mature persons. You have to be mature spiritually to understand Self-inquiry, to understand Advaita Vedanta. When I say to you that you are nothing, everything is nothing, and you get to nothing, people still believe that I am good for nothing. But I'm paying you a compliment when I tell you, you're good for nothing. This really means that you are good for no thing that the senses can perceive. Everything the senses perceive is false. No thing appears as it appears. Everything is a mirage, a dream. It's not what you think it is. So to be no thing is a great blessing. To be good for nothing is a greater blessing. Know who you are. Understand your true nature. Practice Self-inquiry. Be yourself. Awaken to your true Self. Yet most people cannot do this because they're so involved in the world, that this maya keeps them from seeking themselves as God, as Absolute Reality. And it is difficult for most people to do this. There has to be a way for the average person to come up to the point where they can practice Self-inquiry.

We'll talk a little bit about this. Most people usually call me and ask me how to alleviate their problems. How do I get rid of a bad marriage? How do I find another job? How do I remove illness from our life? How do I become a millionaire? And so forth and so on. What I usually say is, "Do not think of your problems, but think of God." Now, I'm not speaking of the God up in the sky. I'm not speaking of an anthropomorphic Deity. I'm speaking of Pure Reality, of Consciousness. When I mention God, I mean Absolute Intelligence. Think of

God whenever your problem comes along, or maybe you feel despondent. Maybe you feel out of sorts, or maybe you feel something is wrong. Think of God. "How do I do this?" you ask. "How can I think of God?" What we call God is invisible. Absolute Reality has no form and no shape. How can I think of God? I've gone over this once before. Who can tell me? How does one think of God? How does one meditate on God? I'll give you a hint. What is the first name of God?

I Am
Exactly. I Am is the first name of God. When you want to think of God, you think of I Am with your respiration. I Am is the first name of God. Close your eyes and try. Inhale and say, "I." Exhale and say, "am." Inhale say, "I," exhale say, "am." Doesn't that make you feel good? Just by saying I Am to yourself, it lifts you up. So the thing to do is this: Whenever you have a problem, I don't care what it is, I don't care how serious you think it is, whether it's personal or worldly, wherever it came from, the secret is to forget yourself. For the moment, forget about the problem for as long as you can, and do the I Am meditation. Every time the problem comes back to you, do the I Am meditation. If your mind wanders, bring it back again and do the I Am meditation.

When I explain this to some people they say, "Robert, but you tell us we have to get rid of our minds. We have to annihilate the mind, not think with it." This is true. This is the highest truth. But yet most people cannot do this. Remember Advaita Vedanta is really for mature souls. People who have practiced sadhana in previous lives. It's like going to school. Self-inquiry, Advaita Vedanta, is like the university of spiritual life. You cannot fool yourself.

There are so many people who try to practice Self-inquiry and they give it up. Then I tell them to surrender, surrender completely. That's the other way. Again this becomes difficult. They try it for awhile and they always revert back to themselves, your personal self. So I give them the I Am meditation. Everybody can do that. When nothing seems to work, go back to the I Am. It's really very powerful. Do not take it simple. I can guarantee you this. If you can practice I Am for one day, just one day, all of your troubles will be transcended. You will feel happiness you've never felt before. You will feel a peace that you never even knew existed. As you keep practicing I Am, your thoughts will become less and less. Your personal self will go into the background and you will begin to feel an inner Bliss. You will begin to feel that it no longer matters what I'm going through. It makes no difference, because it is God who is going through this, not me. And God has no problems. You automatically become happy, just by using the I Am meditation.

In the Bhagavad Gita it says, "Out of a million people, one searches for God. And out of a million people who search, one finds Him." It's sort of difficult. That's how it appears. But if you begin to use I Am as a meditation and you allow the I Am to go deeper and deeper, your bodily consciousness will disappear, and I Am will take over.

If you want to mix Self-inquiry, Atma Vichara, with I Am, that's permissible. You can use them both together. I'll explain how. Say you're using the I Am meditation. In between, thoughts keep popping up. Whether they're good thoughts or bad thoughts makes no difference, but thoughts keep interfering. You can now inquire, "To whom come these thoughts?" and you don't have to go any further. Just observe and watch.

When your mind becomes silent again, you go back to the I Am meditation with your respiration. When thoughts come again you inquire, "To whom do they come?" As you progress in this method, you complete the question. "The thoughts come to me. What is the Source of me? Who am I? What is the Source of I?" You begin to feel and see that the I that seems to have the problem is not you. You begin to feel, "I" have a problem. "I" am sick. "I" am angry. "I" have no peace of mind. And you begin to laugh. For the realization tells you, "I" has all these things, I don't. "I" is the culprit. "I" appears to want this and need that. So it is with desires, wants, self-aggrandizement. All of this belongs to the "I." Who is this I? Where does it come from? If the "I" isn't really me, then who am I? And you keep still.

Now you may go back to I Am with the respiration. You inhale and you say I. You exhale and you say Am. As you progress this way, you're going to find something interesting happening to your life. You're going to find there's more and more space between I Am. It will happen by itself. You will inhale and you will say I, and all of a sudden nothing will come out of that. Then you will exhale with Am. You will inhale again and say I. Remember you're not putting this on, you're not making it happen. It's happening all by itself. And the space between I Am is the fourth dimension of Consciousness. After waking, sleeping, dreaming. It is the state of the Jnani. It is your freedom. It is Pure Awareness. Pure Awareness is not the I Am. The I Am leads to Pure Awareness. And when you keep practicing, "Who am I?" alternating with both of them, there will be a greater space before you say, "Who am I?" again. That space is Bliss. You'll feel something you've never felt before. An inner joy, an inner delight. You will just know that the whole universe is the Self, and I Am That. As the months progress, the words will become less and less. You may start off with I Am, and then you will be in the Silence. You will not say another word. You will just experience the Silence. That Silence is Nirvana, Emptiness. It is no thing. It is the nothing I was talking about. You will just sit in the Silence.

The Nature of Mind

Does the mind exist in the real world?
It appears to exist. It's an appearance.

But it's not there?
There really is no mind.

It's just a belief?
The mind is a belief. It is really your thoughts. All of your thoughts are the mind. Your thoughts come from out of the mind. It is really the thoughts that you have to get rid of, to remove from yourself. So the mind is a conglomeration of thoughts. Thoughts about the past and worries about the future. This is all the mind is. When you really understand the nature of the mind, the mind will disappear. The mind is like a rainbow. The rainbow seems to be real, but when you get close to it, it doesn't exist. It's an optical illusion. Such is the mind. The mind is the same thing. The mind makes you believe you are a body, and that you have to go through experiences with your body. And the mind continues to fool you by making you believe there's karma, and reincarnation, and samskaras, and a whole mess of things that you have to get rid of. But when you inquire, "To whom does the mind come?" the mind will flee, it will run away, and you'll be free.

Robert, when you were referring to the mind in that question, what about things like, say, cooking and electronics, or driving your car on the freeway. Those things enter the mind.

When the mind is gone, then those things are spontaneous. What we call the Self, Consciousness, motivates you. You will do all those things spontaneously. All the things that you have to do will be done. But it will no longer be the mind doing this. It will be Consciousness, the Self.

So, those things and the mind are different things?

The mind is really Consciousness, but appears to be the mind like a dream. When you give up the mind, only Consciousness exists. And then you'll be motivated, guided by Consciousness.

So what would you call these practical things? That they're not mind, that they are just objects out on their own, inanimate objects?

What you call practical things is also like your body. As long as you believe you're a body, then there will be practical things for you to take care of. But when you realize that you're not the body, you're not the mind, then there no longer will be practical things for you to take care of. Yet you will appear to be taking care of them. They'll be taken care of better than you could ever do before. At the same time you will know beyond a shadow of a doubt, that it's not you that is the doer. You're not the doer. Yet everything will be done.

I don't understand how bhakti and puja and things of that sort perpetuate duality. But it also feels to me sometimes that Self-inquiry itself does the same thing. Sort of presupposes the questioner and that which is being questioned. And sometimes when I try to practice Self-inquiry, it actually feels annoying. Like I'm being mental when I prefer just to be silent.

Then by all means, you should be silent. Self-inquiry is good for many people. And there are many people who cannot do this. So by all means do whatever you have to do. Keep silent. Keep still. All roads lead to the same goal. All roads lead to the summit. Therefore, do whatever you have to do to become free and liberated.

Robert, when you talk about the Silence, you're talking about the mind being silent, right?

When I'm talking about becoming completely silent, the mind cannot be silent by itself. The mind is a conglomeration of thoughts. When you become silent, the mind slows down, until it finally disappears into the Magnificence from which it came. You can't really make the mind silent.

Thoughts, right?

There's only Silence, pure Silence.

The absence of thoughts?

Yes, you could say that. If you try to make the mind silent, you have a hard time, because the mind doesn't even exist. Therefore, what are you trying to make silent? You just want to be silent. The mind will take care of itself. What appears to be the mind will disappear of its own volition when you become silent, because it never existed. When you become quiet, quiescent, everything takes care of itself. The true Self emerges with all its splendor and beauty. And everything else that appeared will disappear. So it's a misnomer to say, "I'm going to kill the mind to make the mind silent." There never was a mind to make silent. Again, you just want to be silent. Forget about the mind. And if you become really silent, you'll see you never had a mind to begin with. You'll be of no mind. You'll be out of your mind!

Usually when people say to be silent, it refers to speech, but you're talking about much more than just talking or not talking.
Yes. What people are talking about is quieting their mind. I'm not talking about that at all. We're not trying to quiet the mind. We're trying to reach an inner silence which is Brahman. Another name for this silence is Brahman, or Absolute Reality. This is true Silence.
May you be in Silence the rest of your life and forever!

Robert, what are the most common pitfalls or tricks of the mind when someone is doing Self-inquiry?
Well, the main one is the mind will make you think it's real. It will tell you after a while, "Why are you wasting your time doing this? You could be busy doing something else, getting drunk, going to a movie, watching TV, going bowling. Why do you waste your time with Self-inquiry?" And then it will also tell you, "Look how much time has elapsed. And nothing has happened to you yet. Give it up. Go back to your old way of life." Your mind is not your friend. It will bring up all kinds of things. It'll start by bringing up fears, even fears of the past, fears of past lives, and you will wonder what's going on. You will see black spaces in your meditation sometime, and you will be frightened. You may see all kinds of negative conditions taking place in your mind, and you will be encouraged to stop asking for a while. Always remember, most people have

gone through this, and the way to succeed is to keep inquiring, "To whom does this come? Who sees this? Who is going through this?" It's always the I. Abide in the I and become free.

So, if you find yourself in the void, or blackness, as you said, then you inquire to whom this void comes?
Yes, and bear in mind that there is nothing that can hurt you. There are no devils, no demons, no anti-Christs. All of that is mental. And by inquiring, "To whom does it come?" they disappear.

Why does the mind seem to always go to the negative?
Because the mind is trying to save itself from annihilation. It doesn't want to be destroyed. Therefore it will scare you. It will cook up all kinds of schemes so that you will forget about Self-realization. After all, who wants to be destroyed? The mind wants to continue its nonsense. Therefore it sometimes brings up all kinds of negatives, to frighten you so you'll give up the practice. Sometimes it may show you wonderful things also. It will tell you, "You don't need this. Look what you've got! You've got all these beautiful people around you, and you've got everything you want out of life. This teaching is only for negative people." Your mind will do anything. It will play all kinds of games with you. Keep up the Self-inquiry.

Who Practices Sadhana?

The only way you can become totally free is when you surrender yourself totally, when you give yourself up completely. When you begin to leave the world alone totally and completely, when you stop reacting to person, place, or thing, and you start working on yourself, you begin to do some sort of sadhana, spiritual practice. You become very interested in spirituality. You're not doing it for any reason. You're doing it because you feel that you want to do it. You may begin by practicing hatha yoga, learning all sorts of postures, asanas. Then, perhaps after a few years, you become tired of bending yourself into a pretzel, and you begin the practice of raja yoga, mind control, ashtanga yoga, the eightfold path, prayanama breathing exercises. Makes no difference what religion you are, you start to search for the mysticism in religion. If you're a Jew, you start to read the Qabbalah. If you're a Christian, you start to read Christian mysticism. If you're Islamic you start to read the Sufi material. It all leads to the same goal.

If you're intense, sincere, you will reach a point that no matter what religion you're in you ask yourself, "Who is the one who is going through all this?" You finally get to the place where you can practice Self-inquiry. "Who is the one who has been doing all these things?" You start to introspect yourself. You start to think, "All of these years I have been practicing all these different methods. But who's been practicing? Who's been doing all this?" And one day something tells you, "I have. I have been practicing. I have been doing all these things." Something tells you to go searching for this I. What is this elusive I that has been practicing all these things for all these years, trying to perfect my body, my self, my personal self? And you start to be quiet. You begin to enjoy the Silence. You begin to sit for long periods in the quietness, and you search for the I by inquiring, "To whom does this I come? Where does this I come from? Who am I? What is the truth about myself?"

You begin to realize, as long as you are involved in doing things, then you are the doer. But if the I is removed everything will be done by itself. You begin to understand this, and you follow the I to its Source, which is the spiritual Heart, which is Consciousness.

Forget about those things. Don't even desire them. Just do the work and you'll be surprised. The more you want it, the more it eludes you. And that's natural, because you're chasing after yourself. You're trying to catch yourself, when you're already caught. So the more you chase yourself, the faster you are going to run away from yourself. Stop doing that. It's simplicity itself.

There is really nothing intellectual about it. You don't have to know certain words or certain phraseologies. You don't have to memorize certain text. You simply have to remember the I. Abide in the I. *That's all you have to do. Abide in the I. Hold on to the I.* Everything is attached to the I. Your body, the world, the universe. When you discover the source of I, everything else will go with it into the ocean of Bliss. Bliss is a natural outcome of your search. When you stop searching and you calm down and you put your books away, and you confront yourself and see what you are all about, that will bring about bliss faster than anything else than you can ever imagine or ever do. It's not in chanting mantras. It's not in being a good guy or a bad guy. It's not by doing penance. It's simply by observing your I. Abiding in the I. "Where did I come from?" When you say that, you're not saying where did my body come from. You're saying where did "I" come from. I.

I is separate from your body. Your body is attached to I. The I is not your body. I is separate from the world, but the world is attached to I. God is separate from the world, but God is attached to I. Therefore, when you ask, "Where did I come from," something happens to your mind. Your mind becomes weaker and weaker. And when your mind becomes weaker and weaker, the I begins to expand and becomes all pervading. Then the I becomes another word for the Self, and you begin to realize I is none other than the Self. I Am That. You become free.

It isn't hard and it isn't easy. It just is. Think about yourself for a moment. Watch what thoughts come to you when you think about yourself. Some of you are saying, "I'm hungry." Some of you are thinking of your needs. As soon as you think about yourself, you think about your body. But your Self is not your body. Your body is only a heap of rotten flesh, but that's not you. You are I. I Am. I am not this and not that. I Am. I Am. *There's nothing else, nothing else exists but I Am.* There's nothing to say about it. There are no speeches to make about I Am. There is only I Am. When you say I Am to yourself, what happens? Isn't there a quietness that comes over you, a stillness, because another name for I Am is Silence.

Now you see what I mean when I've told you all these times, you follow the I to the Heart. As you follow the I to the Heart you're going through the molecules, and the atoms, and the sub-atomic particles, going deeper and deeper, back to your Source. Back, back, to the Source, to the energy waves, to the void, and finally your entire body is totally dissolved and Consciousness stands alone. When I say Consciousness stands alone, I do not mean that Consciousness is something else from yourself. You have not died, you are just the way you were always. You're the same person, except something wonderful has happened to you. You realize with all your heart, with all your soul, with all your being, that you never were the body or the mind. You were never an ego. You have always been Consciousness. You are filled with Bliss. You now understand what the word Sat-Chit-Ananda means. I Am That I Am, Ultimate Oneness, Absolute Reality, Nirvana, they're all synonymous with Consciousness. You have overcome. You are free!

Nothing in this world will ever disturb you again. You laugh at death, for you have realized that you were never born. You have never prevailed as a body, and never die. You're always the same, Pure Consciousness. It makes no difference whether you possess a body or have no body. It's all the same to you. Others may look at you and they see your old self. Your family, your friends, see you as they did before, but you are not what you were before. You are Total Happiness. You are the Universe. You understand that all of this is the Self and I Am That.

Progress on the Path

A question I'm commonly asked over the telephone or in person is this: "Robert, how do you see the world?" How am I supposed to see the world? Someone tells me, "I know you see Consciousness, you don't see us." If I didn't see you, I wouldn't be able to function. Of course I see you. Someone else tells me, "You see bright lights and sacred images." Again, if I see bright lights and sacred images, I'd get run over by a truck. I see exactly what you see. Nothing. The only difference is this: I look at the world and I laugh, for I realize I don't know or I don't think.

I realize that the world is none other than myself. The world is Consciousness. It is not the world as it appears, but it's still a superimposition. Therefore a sage sees the world but realizes the world is Brahman, and is only an appearance. Whereas most people look at the world and they identify with the world. Therefore they have fears, frustrations, pains, arguments, wars, man's inhumanity to man. Only because they identify with the world.

A good example of this is the example we always talk about. The snake and the rope. That's unconditioned superimposition. Where you see the snake and you become frightened because the light is dim. But when you make the light bright again, you know it's a rope. And that rope can never fool you again. Whenever you walk by the rope, you know it's a rope and it's not a snake. The snake being the world and the rope being Consciousness. But then someone says, "That's a good example, but when I see the world it doesn't change for me like it changes for you when you turn on the light and see it's really a rope. The world remains the same to me whether it's dark or light or whatever. How do you explain that?"

So again the answer is this. You are seeing the world like water in the mirage. The water doesn't change. But when you first see the water in the mirage, you try to grab it and you grab sand. After that, you know it's a mirage but it always appears as the water. It doesn't change like the rope to the snake. You always see the water. Only you don't react to it any longer. When you walk by the spot where the water is in the mirage, you laugh, for you realize the water is not real. And so the sage sees the world exactly the same way. The world no longer fools the sage. It's like water in the mirage. He partakes of the world, but doesn't get fooled by the world. The world has no interest for him, for the identification is with the Self, with Consciousness.

Then a pundit comes over and says, "Well, those are good examples Robert, only look at it this way. When I'm in the world I can grab you, I can grab the lamppost, I can drive a car and I can feel things. Whereas with your example of the water in the mirage, you cannot feel the water because it doesn't exist. How do you explain that?"

So I guess I have to go to the dream world. In the dream world you are born, you grow up, you go to school, you become a doctor, and you get married, you have children, you get old and you die. Only you were a dream baby being born. And your dream baby is growing up to be a dream teenager. You're a dream doctor, and a dream person who gets married. And you marry a dream girl, and you have dream children. And you dream you get old and you dream you die. It's all going on in the dream. So you see, instead of asking all these stupid questions, and you can go on and on and on, Self-inquiry is the easiest and fastest way to cut through all the rigmarole and find out the truth for yourself. Because what difference does it make what I see? What difference does it make how I see things? Why should you believe me? About a dream world, about water in the mirage, about the snake in the rope. "Those are all great examples but I can't feel that," you say. "I'm identified with the world and I hurt because the world affects me," you say. "Things affect me. When I see man's inhumanity to man, I cry. When I see a funny movie, I laugh. When I get what I want out of life, I'm happy. When I don't, I'm sad. Therefore, these examples and all these things you talk to me about don't do me any good."

Now that's an intelligent observation. You should not accept book learning at face value. You should not accept anyone's experiences at face value. You should develop your own truth. I can tell you the world is Brahman, and that Brahman is Absolute Reality. Absolute Reality is Pure Awareness, and so forth and so on. What good does that do you if you're hurting? There are things come into your life that you take very seriously. And you don't understand that your social body is going through its karma, and it has absolutely nothing to do with you. You identify with the conditioning. That's the first truth you have to admit to yourself.

Do not try to psyche yourself out by remembering all these great truths.

That's not going to do it for you. You and I know many people who have memorized books by Nisargadatta, Ramana Maharshi, and by others, and who can recite these books backward and forward. But the first person who bumps into them, they become angry. As soon as they hear they are going to lose their job, they start crying and they get worried. It appears that books are doing them good only when things are going their way. Then they can quote from the books. But as soon as their world tumbles down on them, they throw the books away. And they do not believe a word they read. Until things start improving, then they buy more books. (laughter) Then something happens to them, and they fling the book across the room and say, "This is nonsense!" But then it gets better again, and they go out and buy another book. And it goes on and on like this. I'm probably talking about some of you. When will you grow up?

It's only what you experience that matters to you. It's not what you read. So what if you learn a truth you haven't learned before. So what if you say this teacher expresses it this way, and now I know it from this angle and that angle. I must remind you again. Knowing truth intellectually does absolutely nothing for you. You might as well take LSD. Because you only get psyched up. Then again, as soon as something comes your way that you don't like, you become an imbecile, angry, mad, upset. You want to know if you're making progress on the path? When was the last time you got angry? When was the last time that something mattered to you? When was the last time you thought the world was hurting you? When was the last time you became over-elated over something good that happened to you? That shows you you're still in possession of your human faculties. You have not transcended.

You cannot escape in a book. Many people, when they are upset and they don't want to think, will turn on the TV. But people on the spiritual path will open a spiritual book. It's like turning on the TV, except you are memorizing spiritual truths. I won't say that that's not any better than TV. Of course it's better than watching TV. But all the same, you can do that for a thousand years and you hardly make any progress. How do you make progress? By using books for reference only. By practicing the methods I share with you. By practicing Self-inquiry. By watching as you go through life's experiences and not reacting. Watching yourself become depressed. Watching yourself become angry. Do not deny it, but observe it. And if you observe yourself correctly in that calm way, you can ask yourself, "Who becomes angry? Who is feeling depressed?" And follow it through. Do this over and over and over again, as many times as you have to. One day, the anger will leave you, the depressions will leave you, your thoughts will leave you. And you'll just BE.

Until that happens, do not fool yourself. Maya is very powerful. Maya is apparent reality of the world. As long as you believe you are the body, then the world is going to be very real to you. This is why you work on yourself first. Remember, your body as well as all the universe is a manifestation of your mind. Therefore, when the mind begins to dissolve, so does your body and so does the universe. Also remember, when everything dissolves you do not see Consciousness. As I mentioned in the beginning, you do not walk around and see empty space. One person even told me he read in a book somewhere that a sage walks around in a fog and sees fog-like people. Where do they get these ideas?

I remind you again, the only difference between the sage and yourself is you see the world and you identify with it. You think it's real. A sage sees the world and he knows it's a superimposition upon Consciousness. So he identifies with Consciousness.

Robert, you were talking about books and how much progress you've made on the path. Many teachers and books talk about theory, but not much emphasis is really put on practice. In fact, if you look at many books, they go into all of the different theories and how one thing relates to another, and this and that. But not too much of any book really goes into actual practice of what they're talking about. It's why, I put this little thing together on vichara practice and your saying how much progress we've really made. Really, we can't know how much progress we've made because progress can be a very dubious thing. In one sense you're making progress, you may be aware of it. In another sense, you may not be aware of it. On one hand things may seem to get better and you may have a better understanding. On the other hand, things may seem to get intense, and you can't tell how far you've come until it's all over.

As you go through the vicissitudes of life, what you're saying is true. But if you abide in the I, your problems of the world do not affect you as seriously, and you will appear to sail through life more easily if you abide in the I.

But as you said, sometimes things intensify.

Things intensify, but to whom do they intensify? You abide in the I and you watch all these things you're going through. You'll find that you're not affected as you used to be. They're not as meaningful any longer. It's like being in a fire and you don't get burned as hard because you're abiding in the I.

Sometimes, though, you may be doing that and be unaware. You may think of yourself as being the same, when actually you can't tell.

Sometimes you can tell. But if you abide in the I, again you'll not be affected by those things and you'll watch those things come and go. You will rise higher by observing and not reacting. Therefore, the safe thing to do is to always abide in the I.

Some of you wonder why you don't make too much progress on your spiritual journey. That's not hard to see. Just take a look at your belief system. Look at the way you're living.

Some of you are afraid to make changes. You want your life to be the same now and forever. You know this is impossible. If you're afraid to make a change, life will come along and pull the rug from under you one day. And you'll have to make a change.

All the things that hold you back, your security blanket, think about this. What is your security blanket? Food? The opposite sex, or the same sex—whatever you prefer—or no sex? All these things keep you back. Just being involved in a movement, trying to make this world a better world in which to live, keeps you back.

Now, some of you new people will feel sort of strange when I say something like this. For you're saying, "Aren't we supposed to help the world?" You're supposed to find out who you are. Your first and main job is to awaken. And then you will see if you want to help the world. What world?

But first awaken. The more you become involved in peace movements, or anti-peace movements, or this or that, the more you get pulled into materiality. These are all commendable things. It's better than being a bank robber, I guess. So if you have to do something, help other people. There's no question about this. But remember the truth." I've got to find myself," you should say.

You do not have to find yourself at the expense of others, this is wrong. But be by yourself all you can. Realize that this is your life. It is not your husband's life. It is not your wife's life. It is not your children's life. It is not your relative's life. It's your life. You exist here and now. What are you doing with it? How can you allow people to make you angry? How can you allow people to tell you what to do? To make decisions for you? All the answers are within yourself.

But you have to turn within yourself. You have to sincerely turn within with a great passion, and find yourself.

The world appears very strong. People appear very real. Some of us always seem to get involved in all kinds of situations. Yet take a look at your life and see why you get involved. Honestly look at yourself. Do not be afraid to see yourself. See the things you do, the words you say, the thoughts you think. And you'll see why you're not making too much progress.

Now, if you really want to make progress, you will drop everything mentally. Remember when I speak of dropping everything, I'm not referring to your quitting your job, moving to India, stopping reading books, or watching TV. I'm not referring to this really, if that's what you want to do. I'm referring to mentally letting go of your reactions to whatever is going on in your body and the world.

Leave the world alone. Leave people alone. Do not try to change people. Or to make them see your point of view. There is no point of view. Every point of view is wrong. We want to get rid of points of view.

You have to sincerely want to awaken. And I kid you not, to awaken is simple. You just have to give up everything mentally. That's all. And consider the fact that everything is Consciousness. Everything. No thing is as it appears. This includes yourself.

There are many people who stay the way they are, and they are always talking about something outside themselves. They try to change the world. They try to see the world as Consciousness. They shrug people off. They become indifferent. This is not right.

You start with yourself. You take an honest look at your habits, and see the things that you're doing. Don't worry about other people. Remember you are creating others with your mind. Everyone who is in your life, you have created yourself. Otherwise where do they come from? You are the creator, and all the things in your life are your creations. You have done this unconsciously.

Karmically, you have attracted everybody in your life that's in your life right now. You think certain thoughts a certain way, and you'll attract those people in your life. If your mind is full of larceny, bad thoughts, you will attract people like that into your life. And then you will say, "It's a bad world. You can't trust anybody."

But it begins with you. You have to look honestly at things holding you back from your own realization. And you have to start working on yourself diligently, until the time comes when you no longer have to do that.

Surrender

There is really nothing to say. Words are superfluous.
The only reason I use words is so you can detect
the silence in the words.
Silence is truth. You cannot explain truth in words.
The words become meaningless, redundant.

The truth comes to you of its own free will
when you prepare yourself through deep surrender
to your Self,
giving up all attachment, giving up your body, your mind,
and everything that's important to you,
to the Self.
As long as you're holding on to anything,
the Reality will evade you.
The Reality only comes when you give up yourself,
when you give up your ego,
when you give up your needs, your wants,
trying to make something happen, desires.
When you give up trying to become Self-realized.
When you just give up.

Then something wonderful happens.
You begin to expand.
Not your body, but the Consciousness which you are.
You become all pervading, Absolute Reality.
It happens by itself.

To Whom Do You Surrender?

To whom should I surrender, Robert?
To your Self. The Self that is omnipresent, omniscient,

omnipotent. The Self that is all-pervading. The Self that is Ultimate Oneness, Pure Awareness, Sat-Chit-Ananda, Para-Brahman. Surrender to that Self, for you are truly That.

And you are amazed by what you have heard. You begin to do just that. While you are at work, while you're washing dishes, while you're watching TV, you always remember to surrender. And one day the inner guru pulls your mind inward to the Source and you awaken. You become liberated. You become your Self. Then you're free.

There is nothing in this world or anywhere else that can affect you or cause harm to come to you unless you believe it. The growth of the world is made up of mental beliefs. Everything that you behold is a projection of your mind, and because it keeps changing constantly, you cannot say this is reality. For instance, your body is not the same as it was ten years ago, or twenty years ago or when you were first conceived. How can you therefore say that your body is real?

The world isn't the same as it was twenty years ago. Everything has changed. Then how can you possibly say the world is real? Most of us are afraid to get into that subject, for we begin to feel that nothing is permanent, and this brings fear. If nothing is permanent, then who am I really? What am I? Where did I come from? What is the source of myself? These questions can only be answered by you.

There is something more beautiful, more grand, more wonderful, than you could ever imagine, that exists within you, which is the substratum of all existence. Yet in order to feel this joy, this bliss, in order to find total freedom from life's so-called burdens, you have to dig for yourself. You have to give up something. You can't stay the way you are, with the same disposition, the same values, the same preconceived ideas, the same concepts, and be free. You cannot do this have to do an about face and totally give up all your ideas about life, totally surrender your ego, your mind, your body, your preconceived ideas. To whom do you surrender this? To your Self. Your self is going to say, "to God." But who do you think God is? God doesn't want your problems. Why should you give God your burden? Find out who this God is, from where this God came, and you will soon realize that you have created God in your image. There is no such God, but it's better than nothing. It's good to know you have a big daddy somewhere, who you can cry to, who you can scream at, and blame for all your problems. Yet, as we grow, as we unfold, as we let go of all this stuff we've been holding on to, something happens; we become lighter. The burden seems to disappear by itself.

The only burden you've ever had is your mind. There is no other burden. See if you can stop your mind for a few seconds and see how peaceful you are. When there are no thoughts there are no fears, no worries. There are no anxieties, no desires, no wants, no greed, no hurt, no enemies. It is the mind, the thoughts, that cause these things to come to us. We actually create these conditions. We create our own reality. Think of the kind of life you are living today, your possessions, your friends, your loved ones, your employment. Do these things come to you through luck or chance? Of course not. You have created all things yourself. For you have believed in the false self, you have imagined you are a human being who has to go through experiences. You have been brainwashed since you were little to believe the things you believe today.

Liberation Exists Within Yourself

So, if you really want freedom, liberation, you do not go searching for this. It is nowhere to be found. For it already exists within yourself. You are already That, so where can you go searching for it? Who can give it to you? If you want water, you turn on the tap. You do not look at the tap and scream and cry, "I want water." You turn on the tap and you have water. Yet when you were a little kid, you didn't know how to turn on the tap. Therefore, if you wanted a drink, you would cry and make a fuss, and your mom or dad would open the tap and give you a drink. So can you drink from the spring of eternal life, which is your Reality. You have to turn on the tap. YOU have to turn on the tap. You turn on the tap by letting go of everything that you are. *Everything.* When I say everything, I mean everything. You have to turn yourself inside out. Can you imagine how you would look turned inside out? Wouldn't be a pretty sight.

Most of us believe, in Advaita Vedanta, that if you hear the right word, that if you awaken through the grace of a sage, you will be free. This is true in some cases. But these people that you have read about in the holy books, who were touched by the grace of a sage, these people have done their homework, prior to this happening. You have to want it yourself, and when you want it badly enough, something will happen to you. When you desire liberation more than anything else in life, this means you have begun to give up the rest of your stuff that we talked about. That's the only way to desire liberation. This is a legitimate desire, because you are not really asking for anything, you are giving up the stuff you don't need anymore: your anger, your pettiness, your bad disposition, your temper, your greed, all of the things we were carrying around with us so long.

This is how you desire liberation, by speaking to the Lord within you. This is total surrender. "Lord, take my anger, take my greed, take my bad disposition, take my temper," and you give it up totally. Once you do this, automatically you are liberated. So you see, it's not the other way around; it's not trying to find freedom, liberation, Self-realization, to add to what we already are. You cannot add one iota to what you already are because you are full up with your own garbage. You therefore have to empty the garbage can, turn yourself upside down, and empty yourself out, and it is then that you will find that you are already free.

And even as I talk to you about these things, some of you here are so full with yourself, small "s," with your ego, that you'll never, never, never, let go completely and give up all your stuff. For your ego has been telling you all these years if you do this you'll be nowhere. But isn't this exactly where you want to be? Nowhere! When you are nowhere, you are not somewhere, and in the nowhere there is nothing. This nothing is everything. This nothing is what we call Effortless Pure Awareness, Absolute Pure Reality, Sat-Chit-Ananda, Nirvana. It is what is left over after you have given up all your stuff.

Take Refuge in Yourself

What you really are you have to find out for yourself, and you do that of course, by stopping identification with the body. Do not react to conditions. That's being yourself. It's not knowing words, or paragraphs, or phrases. It's not by memorizing scripture and trying to impress others. It's by being yourself. To be yourself, you just have to stop the thinking process. Always remember it is your thoughts that keep you from yourself. Every thought that comes to you is your enemy. Even the good thoughts. For the good thoughts are just leading you on. It is your mind playing tricks on you. The good thoughts are trying to make you feel that this world is real, and you should strive after certain things, you should enjoy the world, and take it for what it's worth. But then you have to come under the law of change. And you become disillusioned because the things in your life are no longer the same after a while. Then you have to jump back into yourself and take refuge in your Self. When you take refuge in your Self you become happy. When you take refuge in your Self you have peace. When you take refuge in your Self you have harmony, you have joy.

It is a mystery to me why people would take refuge in the outside world, in person, place or thing, when you know the outside world is subject to the law of change, and is never the same continuously. So whatever you take refuge in becomes a disappointment, whether it's a person, place, or thing.

There was once a young girl who was brought up in a house of prostitution. This was her destiny at the time. She couldn't get away from it. But she used to pray to Ramana Maharshi, "Oh Lord, if I must go this route, be with me. I'm not praying to change my life, if this is my destiny. But I'm praying that your strength and your love will always be with me."

Now, across the street was a so-called Jnani. And he used to stand in front of the market place telling everybody they're Consciousness, Absolute Reality, preaching, screaming. This went on for years. Finally the time came when they both died and they went before God. God told the girl, "You have to go back to the Earth, and you have to be a Jnani." And he told the so-called aspiring Jnani, "You have to go back to the Earth as a snake."

The man said, "How come, Lord? I extolled your virtues to everyone. I told all the people they were Consciousness and they were Absolute Reality, and you send me back as a snake. What did I do?" And God said, "You have no heart. You come from the talking school. All you did with your life was to talk, talk, talk, talk, talk. But this girl gave me her heart. She surrendered to me. She didn't bemoan her fate. She just wanted me to be with her during her trials and tribulations. And I gave her the strength to carry on, so now she is free. But you still have a lot to learn. So you have to go back as a snake."

This makes us think. What are we really doing with our lives? We read lots of books, see lots of teachers, have a lot of head knowledge. But how many of us have given our hearts to God? And God is not far away. God is really the Self. But in order to contact that Self, you have to have a lot of humility. To feel God's grace means you have to surrender completely, have a lot of humility. You have to have the attitude, "I know nothing. You are everything." This kind of an attitude will set you free.

And yet, how many of us have an attitude like this? Many of us think to become a Jnani, to become Self-realized, we become proud, and you actually become more egotistical than you ever were before. We have a holier than thou attitude. This will never do it. There really is no difference between a bhakti and a Jnani. One surrenders to God, and they have no other life. They realize that whatever they do, it is God doing it. Therefore it is good. They never complain. They never think of their problems. They think of others and their problems rather than their own. And the other one realizes that the I is responsible for all their problems, and for their existence. So they trace the I back to its Source, to the Heart, and they become free. At that stage there is a merging of both bhakti and Jnana. So a bhakti is a Jnani and a Jnani is a bhakti. Therefore, if you see a teacher who thinks they are better than anybody else, and they seem egotistical, be careful. Most Jnanis never take on a teaching role at all, and they have very little to say. After all, what is there to talk about?

Just Being Is Enough

Just being is enough. Not being this, not being that, just being. Being at satsang. And whether I talk about ice cream or jellybeans it makes no difference. The words themselves have value, because the sound of the words are the grace that you feel. But the meaning of the words are only interpreted in your mind. That's why, whatever I say is taken differently by each one of you. For it filters through your mind. And your Consciousness and your Beingness mix with the words, and the words come out according to your way of life. But if you listen with no-mind, then you get the true meaning. In other words, do not put too much value on everything I say. But open your heart so the Grace portion of it may enter, and you may pick it up and lift yourself upward. How do you do this? Just by becoming still, by stopping the mental activity. And you may stop the mental activity by any method you know. If you like to do pranayama, do that. If you like to practice vipassana meditation, do that. You wish to observe your breath, do that. If you wish to practice Self-inquiry, do that. In other words, do whatever you have to do to stop your mind from thinking.

Vichara, Self-inquiry is only to keep your mind from thinking. That's all it is. All the practices of yoga lead to the place where you stop thinking. All of the higher religions are to make your thoughts one-pointed. And when your mind stops, you become your Self. You're free.

There are no rituals you have to go through really. You don't have to chastise yourself and try to get rid of your guilt feelings, samskaras, or anything else. Identifying with an empty mind will do the job for you. But the empty mind is not realization. It is the step before realization. Realization is not an empty mind. Realization cannot be explained. Suffice it to say that realization is beyond everything and anything you can ever imagine. But if you achieve empty mind, then you're on the way to realization. At that stage the guru within yourself will pull you inwardly, and you will awaken to your Self.

Be No Thing

So, number one, you have to develop humility. You have to open your heart to loving kindness. Number two, you have to forget about yourself and your problems as if they never existed, and help others. Give of yourself to others, because there is only One Self, and I Am As That. Number three, you have to stop quoting teachers and telling yourself that I am Brahman, I am no-mind, I am Consciousness, for that really inflates your ego.

You have to stop comparing yourself with anybody or anything. In other words, you have to become nothing, and that hurts some of you. Because you say, after all, I've gone to school for fifty years, I've got a profession, I'm doing this and I'm doing that. And now you tell me I have to become nothing.

Well, Consciousness is nothing, it is no-thing. What you call God is nothing. So if nothing is good enough for God, it should be good enough for you, too. Can't you see now that when you say to yourself, "Well, I'll never be nothing, I'm somebody, I've studied for years, I'm somebody important...." Can't you see now that this is what holds you back? Every sage has come to the point where they've thrown away the scriptures, thrown away the books, thrown away their body, thrown away their knowledge, and thrown away themselves with a small "s." When you get rid of all that stuff, then you become your Self.

Surrender Is Mentally Done

Can you see now why it takes so long for some people? Because they're holding on to something. They say I can let go of this, but I can never let go of that. I don't mean you get to the point where you don't care. I don't mean where you quit your job or leave your family or go anywhere. You have to do all this mentally. You do all this in your mind. You use your mind to do all these things. And then the mind turns within itself and disappears into the Heart. So take a look at your life and see what's holding you back. What are you attached to? What do you think is important in this world?

You cannot have both. You cannot mentally be attached to person, place and thing, and awaken at the same time. If you want liberation, you have to pay the price. And the price is letting go, giving it all up, surrendering. Having perfect faith that all is well. Not trying to interpret what "all is well" means. Just realize that everything is in its right place, just the way it is. Don't interpret it. There are no mistakes. As you begin to dwell on this, as you begin to dwell on these things, automatically you will come to the place where you will realize the last thing you need to go is the I. Everything has been attached to the I. But you see how long it takes to get there? You have to do everything else first. This is why it's dangerous for some people to just teach jnana marga by itself. For egotistical people become greater egotists. It builds up your ego. You have to have humility first and go through all these things we discussed. If you really want to do this, you will.

You will not do this by taking action, but by sitting in the Silence and surrendering your mind and your body to your Self. I Am will take care of Itself. You see, I Am is your real nature. Therefore you do not have to try to bring it about. All you've got to do is to realize that this stuff that's holding you back has to be given up. Everything has to go, your whole belief system. What are you holding on to? Think, what's in your mind that is so strong? Fear? A job? All these things are meaningless if you want to awaken. You will still have your job. You will still do whatever you came here to do. I have to emphasize this because we always believe—and the question that I get from most of you is that—"How will I function if I do what you say?" I keep telling you, have no fear, you will function. You will function much better than you can ever imagine. It's hard right now working with your ego, to think "How can I function without a mind?" but you will.

Here is something that cannot be explained in words. When you get to the Ultimate State, you become human like everybody else. That's why it's difficult to know what a sage is, because a true sage appears no different than you and I. The Ultimate State is functioning like everybody else, except there is something inside, there's something that makes you understand that you are like the mirror, and your body, your affairs, and everything else in the universe is a reflection. You become both. It appears that you act out your humanhood, but you're not human. And this is the most difficult state to explain. For it is beyond words. It is beyond thoughts. It is beyond reasoning.

You cannot be reasonable to become liberated. It's beyond every human faculty. That's why you can't think about it, and you cannot try to explain it. And you can't even discuss it. All you can do is to do whatever you have to do to get rid of all your stuff. That's all. And everything else will take care of itself.

Renunciation

You have absolutely nothing to give up.
Nothing to surrender, nothing to let go of.
You are already liberated.
How can you believe that you have to let go of something
that never existed?
You believe that you have to let go of your attachments.
How can the Self have attachments?
You think you have to surrender all of your fears,
all of your depressions,
all of the things that have been bothering you.
Surrender to whom? Those things are not yours.
They do not belong to you.

You are Pure Reality. You are the Imperishable Self.
Never were you born, never did you prevail,
and never will you leave.
You are the One. The All-Pervading One.
Consequently, you have absolutely nothing to give up.
For you had never anything to begin with.

It's really egotistical to believe you've got
something to give up.
There's nothing you have to surrender.
It's only the ego that believes that something
has to be surrendered,
something has to be given up, you have to let go of something.
Who is the one who had something to begin with?
There is no one.
There is only the One Reality, and you are That.

The One Self

You come to sit with me in the Silence. In the Silence is where all the power is. In the Silence is where all the answers are. Happiness comes to you all by itself. Joy comes to you. When you sit in the Silence you remember who you are. We come to see we are all one Self. What does this mean? It means we are not separate, we are one, One Self. Think of that. We are all the One Self.

The One Self expresses Itself through choiceless, effortless, Pure Awareness. Choiceless, effortless, Pure Awareness. This is what you are, Pure Awareness. Think about this. You are Pure Awareness, choiceless, effortless, Pure Awareness. What do we mean by Pure Awareness? Pure Awareness simply means that you are All-Pervading Consciousness. Your essence is in everything. You are aware that the whole universe is a direct product of your thinking, of your mind. It is only aware. You are aware of the trees, of the mountains, the sky, like boundless space, Pure Awareness. You are aware of reality, the truth of yourself. Yourself is Pure Awareness and you are That. Ponder this. The Self is Pure Awareness and you are That.

Attachment and the I-Thought

If you only knew what this meant to you. You are totally free, completely free—effortless, choiceless, freedom. Everything else is an illusion. Everything else is an illusion, the world, universe, personal God.

Everything else is an illusion. So where do all these things that look so real come from? Where do all the people come from? Where do all the things come from, that you see all day long? Where does everything come from? From the I-thought. The I-thought produces the small self. That's what makes you think you are a body and a mind, that it's your condition, that you have problems. You have to work through things. The I-thought does all these things for you. It ruins your life completely. It hides reality, and produces a world. Therefore, you come back to the Self. You have to somehow transcend the I-thought. And this is done by forgetting all the knowledge that you have up to now. All the knowledge that you know. Everything you've been taught since childbirth has to be given up. All your beliefs, all your dogmas, preconceived ideas, they all have to go. When they're gone you rest in the Self, and you will be unconditioned, choiceless, awareness.

We have something we own. A person, place, or thing. We cannot get it out of our mind. We're attached. Because of this attachment we go through many lives, it appears. And we go through many experiences, simply because we are attached to something. It can be mental or physical. Even if you hate someone. If you hate someone or something with a passion, that's attachment. You will come back to this earth or to another planet similar to this earth again and again and again. And you will meet this person that you hate so much under different circumstances again and again and again. One time he may be your daughter, he may be your mother, he may be your husband, he may be your wife. But that person that you despise so much will meet you again and again, and do things to you in order to upset you. And you will hate again and again. You will never be free until you understand.

The understanding is to turn within, to forget about the person, but to see your own reality. To trace the I-thought to the source. After all, it is the I-thought that hates and loves. That has attachments to person, place or thing. When the I-thought is transcended, only the Self remains. Then your karma is finished, your body is finished, your God is finished, and you're home free. But as long as you allow a person, place or thing, and maybe your own body that you're attached to, your own mind, that's person, place or thing also—as long as you deeply feel those things—you will never become free until you let them go.

Whatever you're no longer attached to, gives way. Whatever you're no longer holding on to, no longer holds on to you. And as you let go of your opinions toward person, place and things, you find that you're growing, you're evolving. You're beginning to become something that is ineffable. Something that cannot be explained. Something that is so wonderful, you'll never dream that something like this existed. Yet it does.

You have to reconcile yourself with the whole universe. The mineral kingdom, the vegetable kingdom, the animal kingdom, the human kingdom. When you have become friends with the entire universe, you will not have to do Atma vichara. You will not have to trace the I or worry about the I. Just the reconciliation with the universe will free you. After all, when you love everything, unqualified, what else can you do? There's nothing else. *The total love of the whole universe kills the ego.* For it is the ego that plays the other games with you. That makes you love someone special or hate someone special. That makes you despise certain animals and eat them. That makes you think poison ivy is worse than the rose. That causes you to qualify life. A sage sees everything as equal. Nothing is worse or better than any other thing. And just by hearing this, allowing it to go into your Heart, feeling it, will lead you to an awakening. Think of the problems you think you have. Why are they a problem? What difference do they make? There is nothing in the world that's that important, for you to want to feel badly, or where you want to get revenge, or you're afraid that something will happen to your body. You're concerned about a loved one. You're worried about the world situation. When you're like that, you are assuming responsibility for these things. After all, you didn't ask to really get born. You didn't ask to get born to the family where you were born. Into the nationality, into the religion that you were born into. In the city and state and country that you were born into. The Power that takes care of that knows how to take care of you. Don't you see, there isn't anything you have to do to help. In other words, God doesn't need your help. All you have to do is to take a deep breath and say, "Take it God. I'm finished with it. I will never worry again. I will never be upset over anything again."

Now where are you coming from? What do you see when you wake up in the morning? You worry about your life, it's not going where you want it to go? You think you have to find a teacher someplace far away? And the teacher will give you something that you need. A special book that you can read, that will enlighten you and make you happy. Give you some thing that you can do, become peaceful, relaxed, that will last. None of these things ever last. For a while, for a few moments, for a few days, a few months, a few years. Then you revert back to what you were before, because the mind has never been destroyed.

Your job is to destroy the mind that thinks about these things. That's why you're here. To destroy the ego completely. That's the only way you'll be free, totally free forever—the only way. Ponder these wisdoms I'm speaking to you and see if I'm not right. Every teaching is of the mind. Every teacher that you chase, every teaching that he gives you or she gives you, is from the mind. Only from the mind. If there is no mind, you'll have nothing to look for. And the mind wants to search and look. But if there is no mind, who's left to look, who's left to see? So life goes on with the seek and the object of the seek. This is how we're made to see the objects, and identify with the objects. I'm saying transcend the seer and the objects both. By inquiring to whom does the object come to? Who sees this object? What is its source? You must ask this question repeatedly all day long. What is the source of my misery? What is the source of my happiness?

Will your mind try to be judgmental? Catch yourself. Ask, "To whom does this come? To whom does this judgment come? It comes to me. I think this. But am I really the I that thinks this? Am I an I? Where did I come from? Who am I? Who is the thinker?" And go beyond. Keep going beyond everything that comes to your mind. Go beyond all the answers. Until you're left in total peace. When there are no more answers, you're totally free and peaceful.

As long as you are looking for answers, you can have no peace or happiness. Always remember, this world is not a world to improve, even if you are trying to make this a better world in which to live. You can't do this. It will only be for a few days, a few months, a few years. This world is not a world to be improved at all. It's a world to be gotten rid of, *in the mind.* It starts in the mind. It begins in the mind.

Don't think that if some day the world will be a better place in which to live, you'll be happy. It will never happen. Since the beginning of time, man has tried to improve this world, to no avail. Things sometimes seem to improve for a while, but it will become worse than ever before. Why? Because this is the way of this world. You have to have friction in this world in order for it to survive. If there is no friction in this world, this world would disintegrate totally. You'd have no world. It's good and bad, right and wrong, up and down, forward and backward. In order for a jet plane to fly, there has to be the same amount of power pushing it back, resisting. This is how the plane flies; it has to have resistance. If there was no resistance it wouldn't fly. It wouldn't be able to get off the ground. So it is with our life. In order to achieve something, there has to be resistance. Think about this. All you wish to achieve in life, you have to have resistance in order to achieve. If there was no resistance, there would be nothing to achieve.

This is why I say to you, Advaita Vedanta has nothing to do with this world whatsoever. You try to make yourself a better human being, or a more competent person. This just makes you more worldly. You've got to get off this planet totally and completely. And when you get off this planet, you have to fly away to some place like Mars, where you go deep within and touch Reality. It's what's comprehensible, what happens when you touch Reality. It's more beautiful than you can ever understand or appreciate. So stop searching, stop looking, stop being what you are, what you think you are. Stop doing everything you do *mentally*. I know you're concerned what's going to happen to you if you stop thinking. You'll always be taken care of. You'll get all the things you need.

Again, think what is the worst thing that can possibly happen to you? You can die. There is no such thing as death. You all know this. You can lose a fortune. You came into this world without a fortune and you're going out without a fortune. Have no concern about these things. Karmically you have and you are going through the experiences you have to go through. But that's for your body, not for you. Do you not see by now that you're totally free? Your real nature is Absolute Goodness, Parabrahman, Absolute Reality. You are the Self, the All-Pervading Self. What can you possibly fear? What can anyone possibly do to you? You are free. You are whole. You are complete. And there is only one of you. There never was you and me. There is only the One. And that One is Absolute Reality. You are that One. You are the body of Bliss. Wake up. Get rid of all those feelings that are beseeching you to do all these stupid things. Awaken. Be free. Simplify your life. Have no fear. Fear is another thing that you become attached to and it keeps you back.

Never believe that you have something important to think about. All things are not important. No matter what you may think about it, it's not important. As long as you have to think of something, it's not important. Yet you say to yourself, "How can I function without thinking?" Think of what you said. "How can 'I' function without thinking?" Not *you*, but "I." What you're really saying is, how can the I function without thinking. What I are you referring to? The ego I has to think to exist, but the I Am Consciousness is self existent. There's nothing to think about. So whenever you're thinking about something, realize it's the I-consciousness, the I-ego so to speak, that does the thinking. If you go beyond the I-ego and go back to the I Consciousness, your thoughts will stop. There will be no thoughts. For again, what is Reality to think about? Reality is Reality. It's All-Pervading, Omnipresence. There's no room or space for it to think. It is a power which knows Itself. The power that knows Itself is Consciousness, the

Absolute Reality. It can only know Itself and nothing else, because nothing else exists apart from the Self. There is no duality in the Absolute Reality. Duality only appears to exist at the human level. It's an appearance. It's not true. It's not real. You can say this to yourself.

Look at the world. The world is a cosmic joke. It appears to be real. The good things, the beautiful things, the horrible things. They are all imposters. The world is a world of duality. For every good there has to be a bad. It has to balance. For every bad there has to be a good. For every up there is a down. For every forward there is a backward. We can never understand this world. It's too complex. Get out of it. Not by committing suicide, but by transcending the mind and body, and awakening to your real Self. That's how you get out of it. Stop feeling sorry for yourself. Stop paying so much attention to your thoughts, to the world, to your body. Let come what may. Surrender totally to your Self. Your Self is God, Consciousness. Begin to identify with the I Am, not with conditions. Leave conditions alone. As I told you before, you are not responsible for anything. Get rid of your guilty feelings.

Mentally, you have to feel in your heart the Oneness of Eternity. And until we mature and this comes first in our lives, we will only go so far on the spiritual path. Where your heart is, that's where God is. Today, think, "What is this thing I'm attached to?" What is so meaningful for me in this world? And realize it is that which is keeping you back. Let go of it mentally, by turning within, and realizing that "I" feel this. I feel I need this. Where does the I come from? Follow the I thread to the source and become liberated.

When you follow the I to its Source, then all of your troubles, your problems, your life, your world, become dissolved in the Source. Until that happens, realize that you are not the I that has problems. That's the point. It is the I that sometimes feels depressed or worried or hurried or upset or fearful. It is depressed I that feels that way. Yet, that's not you. You are not the personal I. Even though you are following the I, you are following a mirage, an optical illusion, for you are not the I. You are Absolute Reality, Nirvana, Sat-Chit-Ananda, you are not the I. If you are not the I, then who has the problems? Who has the sickness? Who has the doubt? Who has the suspicions? Who has all these worldly problems, that most human beings have? "I" do, but I am not the "I." Yet "I" has the problem.

Do you see what I mean? "I" has the problem. Not me, but "I." In this case, "me" is Absolute Reality, Pure Awareness, Consciousness. Therefore, this is the best psycho-therapy that's ever been invented. For you can step back and watch the I having the problems. You can understand and realize intelligently that the real me, the real Self, can never have a problem. It's impossible. Yet "I" feel the problem. You immediately catch yourself and realize yes, "I" feels the problem. You see, not me, but "I" feels the problem. Then you forget for a while and you say, "I feel depressed." And you catch yourself and you laugh. You say, "I" feels depressed, "I" feel out of sorts, not me, but "I." Then after a little while you forget again, and you say, "I feel sick." Then you remember. You say "I" feels sick. Not me, but "I." You do this all day long. Finally, what will happen is that you will separate your Self from I. You will no longer look at your body as I. You will no longer look at your mind as I. When you realize that I is everything in the universe, I must also be the body and the mind. You then realize that you are not the body and you are not the mind, but "I" is. I is the body and I is the mind. I is all the problems. You separate yourself. You watch. You observe I having all these problems, and pretty soon you're having a good laugh at yourself. You'll feel freedom. If you practice this, I can assure you that you will feel a freedom that you never felt before. You will feel Omnipresent. You will feel an indwelling bliss. You will come to see that the body does not exist as a body. You will look at yourself and see the body, but you will laugh. You will know it's not your body. There is no body. It's like the water in the mirage. There is no water. It only appears so. That's the way the body is. You appear to have a body, but you don't really. "I" has the body. And I doesn't really exist. Do you see this revelation now? There is no I, there's no body. Then what gets old and dies? What gets sick? What becomes depressed? And the answer is, nothing. There is no one to get depressed, there is no one to die. There is no one to have mental anguish. There is no one left to do anything. You're home free.

You Are Not the Doer

When you feel this way, there is nowhere to go, because everywhere you go, you are the Self. No thing makes you happier than another thing. It's all the same. You no longer differentiate between objects. All the objects become like a piece of clay that you have taken to make objects out of. But you realize it all comes from the same piece of clay. That's how it is with your life. There is no one doing anything. There is absolutely nothing to do. When I say there's absolutely nothing to do, I do not necessarily mean you're going to sit still and sit in one chair all day long. This appears paradoxical.

Your body will appear to be doing this. And yet you will know beyond a shadow of a doubt that there is no one doing anything. Think about that.

This is a very important point. You will appear to go to the movies, if you have a job to go to work, to come home, to get married, to get divorced, to go swimming, to do whatever you do. Yet you will know, no one is doing anything. How can that be? How can you appear to be doing something, yet nothing is being done. The sky appears blue, and yet upon investigation, there's no sky and no blue. So you appear to be doing something, but there is no doer. There is really no one who needs to do anything, or does anything. Space and time have been eliminated. You are in an entirely different dimension where you appear as if you are moving, working, experiencing, and there is nothing being done. I admit that state is difficult to think of, yet it is the truth. No one has ever done anything.

There is only One, and that One is All-Pervading and Omnipresent. There is only One. And if that One is All-Pervading and Omnipresent, where is there room to do anything? Think of it this way. Look at it this way. If you were the only one in the universe, and you were the size of the universe, all of the planets and the stars and the moon and the earth, people, places and things would be within you. You would have no space to do anything. Yet everything is being done within yourself. It's the same thing. This is really the truth about you. You are the microcosm and the macrocosm. When you are working in duality, in ignorance, you appear to be a small human being, and you look around you, and you see billions of human beings just like you. You argue with them. You fight with them. You love them. You do all kinds of activities with fellow human beings. But as you work on yourself, and as you begin to rise in Consciousness, something tells you there is only One. There is not you and I. There's only the I. And the I doesn't exist. Therefore, there is no thing that you can comprehend that exists. There is no such thing as existence. There is no God that creates the universe. There is no being that causes anything to happen. The highest truth is, nothing is happening.

Separate from the "I" and Awaken

So you say, "That may be true, Robert, but I'm suffering. I have mental anguish. I appear to be ill. I have difficulty with people. Why?" Simply because of wrong identification. You are identifying with the apparent existence. As long as you identify with existence, you're going to appear to exist. And if you exist, you're going to have problems. For every human being that's born has a problem. There are no exceptions. As long as you believe you are born, you've got a problem. Therefore, somehow you have to get rid of the notion that you were born. You have to get rid of the notion that you exist, and you have to get rid of the notion that you've got a problem. In other words, you have to wake up. You have to wake up to your Reality. No birth, no death, no problem. Nobody dies, because nobody was born. I can go on and on like this, but if you're not experiencing what I'm talking about, how can you believe me? I know some of you here have had a glimpse of this Reality, so you know it's so. But most of you have not. How can you accept this? You have to experience it within yourself. That is the only way you can ever wake up.

Do not experiment in the world. How do you experiment in the world? When you believe those trees are beautiful. Beautiful sunset, beautiful sunrise, beautiful flowers, beautiful people. As good as it may sound, this keeps you back from awakening. Why? Because you are identifying with an external cause that does not exist. You do not realize that the beautiful tree comes from your mind. The beautiful sunset is in your mind. All of the beauty and all of the ugliness that you perceive, is all within your Self. You are that Self. So the person who wants to awaken when they look at beauty, they realize they are projecting it. They are both imposters. Two sides of the same coin. And you start to inquire, "To whom has this come?" Think about that. When you behold all the beauty outside of the window, instead of being in awe and admiring it, ask, "Who sees this?" In other words, the beauty that you see out there really comes from in here. You are the beauty. It only exists out there because you exist over here.

When you are in deep sleep at night, who sees? There are no trees. There are no flowers. You are in deep sleep and yet you are awake. Deep sleep is the closest thing to Self-realization there is. Do you ever wonder why, when you come out of deep sleep you say, "I feel good"? There is no one who comes out of deep sleep who feels bad. You may have a bad dream. But I mean when you are really in deep sleep and you wake up, if you catch yourself, you'll see you feel good. You feel great. You feel wonderful. It's only when you start to think, that the feeling changes. Check it out for yourself. Why? Because deep sleep is really bliss. Yet it is unconscious bliss. Liberation is conscious bliss. Liberation is when you're awake and you're conscious. You're not conscious of anything in particular, you're just conscious. That's liberation. So when you see anything external from yourself and you get involved in it, catch yourself. Realize it's coming out of you, and question, "To whom does it come?"

I know there are many of you who like to go hikiɪ climb mountains, like to become part of nature. That's ∪ᴋ, ⅄uι do not believe that these things are external from yourself. These things are yourself. You are That. When you question, "To whom does this come?" you again realize, "It comes to me, I perceive it." Then you remember that you are not I. "I" perceives it. Yet in reality, you are not the perceiver. You are not the witness. "I" perceives it. "I" is the witness. This is a very important point, and I want you to understand it because it can change your whole life. Whatever you see in the world, you are to realize that "I" perceives. But do not look at I as being the self. You have to catch yourself and say, "I" perceives. This does not mean that you perceive it. It is "I" that perceives it. When you separate yourself from the I, all is what? Consciousness. It is only when you believe that you are I, that your humanhood comes into play. But as soon as you perceive that I is the universe, you have separated yourself from I. And then Consciousness comes into play, you have awakened. In other words, when you can separate from your I, you will be awakened and liberated.

Play this game every day. Whatever you see, whether it is your body or your mind, or other people. When someone does something to you that you don't like, the worst thing you can do is react. Can you see why, now? Because when you react you are affirming your humanhood and your ego becomes stronger. But when you no longer react, the ego becomes weaker and weaker and weaker. The I and the ego are the same. I know most of you believe when you see the bad things of life, man's inhumanity to man, all the dastardly things you see on TV, you want to separate yourself from that, but it's the good things also. You are not the good things and you are not the bad things. You are no thing. You are not trying to exchange bad for good. Play the game with yourself. Whenever you think of a beautiful sunset, catch yourself. Ask yourself, "To whom has this come? It has come to me. I perceive it."

The "I" Does Not Belong to You

Before you ask, "Who am I?" remember to realize that you are not the I. The I that perceives is not you. In other words what you must do from now on, is when you refer to I, you're not talking about yourself. Can you remember that? Whenever you use the word "I" you want to catch yourself and say, "I is not me. Me is, Who am I?" Me is the question, "From what source does the I come?" But the I has absolutely nothing to do with you. If it has nothing to do with you, this means that you do not have to struggle to give it up. If the I really belonged to you, you would have a fight on your hands. For you would be looking for all ways to remove the I. But when you remember that the I does not belong to you, there's nothing to fight. You simply realize you are not I. Then, "Who am I?" If you practice this in the way I've just outlined, when you say, "Who am I?" you will have a completely new revelation. You do not say "Who am I?" until the very end. Until you come to the realization that the I is not me. Therefore, everything that's attached to the I is not me. My problems, my house, my family, my birth, all attached to the I. And since the I does not exist, nothing exists. If nothing exists, then who am I?

Remember, never say, "Nothing exists and I am Consciousness" because you don't know what you're talking about. It's just words. Never say, "The I does not exist, but I am Sat-Chit-Ananda." Those are just words for you. You have to inquire, not make a statement. Do not make a statement. This is not a metaphysical class where you make affirmation. Affirmations are kindergarten. That's just to improve your humanhood. What you're trying to do is get rid of your humanhood, not improve it. Everything is a question. I am not I? I am not the body? I am not anything that is attached to the I? Then who am I? If you've gotten this far, then when you say, "Who am I?" you will be in deep Silence, and you've come a long way.

So let me succinctly recapitulate. Starting tomorrow morning when you get up, whatever you see, say to yourself "That's not me." Whatever you feel, whether you feel wonderful or you feel depressed makes no difference, say to yourself "That's not me." Whatever you hear, whatever you feel, whatever you touch, whatever you smell, say to yourself "That's not me." But then admit "I smell it, I taste it, I touched it, I feel it, but that's not me. It is the I that is going through the experience of the senses, feeling, touching, tasting, smelling. But I am not the I. Then who am I?" What I want you to do now is to close your eyes, and practice this on yourself. Go through the whole thing. Look out the window and look at the trees how beautiful they are and realize the trees are not coming from nothing. They come from "I." So the beauty of the trees is "I." I have nothing to do with it. But "I" does. So who am I? Practice this on yourself.

Be Still, Be Yourself

You see, the beautiful thing about all of this, you are already enlightened. You are already Self-realized. But you refuse to believe it. How do you refuse to believe it? By completely believing everything else. By feeling the world. By allowing all conditions to annoy you, to bother you, to react to them. This hides your reality as if you were hypnotized. And you believe there's a world with others. Believing there is a world that you have to overcome, conditions you have to transcend, and you have a battle on your hands.

The truth is you have nothing to transcend, nothing to overcome. Silence is your reality. Stop thinking. Be silent. Be quiet. Allow the mind to become quiescent. Never mind what's going on. What is going on is always going on, and will keep going on when you've gone. Do not concern yourself with this world, or get caught up in it, and it will be like the world will come and go. Sitting back from the world, you remember who you really are, what you really are. You have absolutely nothing to do with this world. I know it sounds strange when I say this, but you have absolutely nothing to do with this world. Nothing. This world doesn't belong to you at all.

For you are not here at all. There are no mistakes. Where are you? You are nowhere, yet you're everywhere. Why ponder these things? Why think about these things? Just be your Self. Refuse to acknowledge the world, and worldly things. Know yourself as Pure Awareness, effortless, choiceless, Pure Awareness. Know yourself this way. When you first awaken in the morning and get out of bed, say this to yourself: "I am choiceless, effortless, Pure Awareness." And keep still. You'll be surprised how good you feel. "I am effortless, choiceless, Pure Awareness." Yet you think you're somebody else. You think you are a male, or female, you have a name, you have a profession, a program, and you refer yourself to these things. But I tell you, you are not these things at all. Drop these things. Get rid of your pride, your ego. So you believe you have to make things happen, you have to get ahead of people. What has to happen has already happened.

It's so easy to become peaceful. It's so easy to become loving, blissful, happy. You just have to reject all those thoughts that come to you—all those thoughts, all those feelings, all the emotions. Just reject them. You reject them by not giving them power. You give them power every time you let them feel something inside of you. When your thoughts take on a feeling nature you give them power. But when you refuse to take on that feeling nature, the thoughts disappear. In other words, you are the one that gives them power. You are the one that creates your condition, be it good or bad. You are the one who sees the world the way you see it. See only yourself, see only Reality. See only emptiness. It's really very simple to do this. Just sit the way you're sitting now and observe. Do not analyze, don't try to change your thoughts, do not fight your thoughts, just observe them, watch them, look at them, and when you're ready you can ask the question, "To whom do these thoughts come?"

Otherwise, just sit and look at your thoughts. Let your mind do whatever it likes. Let it become as nasty as it wants! Let the mind tell you all kinds of things—scary things, happy things, wrong things, right things. The mind is only here to make trouble for you, that's all. But when you do not allow the mind to make trouble for you, it disappears! And how do you do this? By not reacting to your thoughts. By not allowing them to feel anything. Where do these thoughts come from? Nowhere. They are called false imagination. All thoughts are false imagination. False imagination is like the water in the mirage. That's where your thoughts are. They appear to come to you but they don't exist. If they were real you'd be able to grab them, hold on to them, save them, put them in a box, store them away. But you cannot do this, which proves that they have no substance. How can they frighten you?

Always remember the idea is to stop thinking completely. Nothing functions mentally at all. Yet some of you still believe if you stop functioning mentally you will become a vegetable, you wouldn't be able to function. This is not true. What you were will not function. But what you become will function very well. You will always appear to function. Yet there is no function-er. You are not what you seem to be. No matter how many times I tell you this, you're still thinking, thinking, judging, judging, coming to conclusions, trying to work out your life. You have to let go. Totally, absolutely, completely. You have to let go so completely that you will feel no body, no mind, no pain, nothing. That is the only time you will make progress. Do not think about this. The thoughts cannot help you. There are no thoughts that can help you realize the Self. It is only a total completely letting go, giving up. What do you give up? You give up the ego, the mind, your opinions about things. That's all you give up.

But yet a tree seems to appear, it turns into a beautiful tree as it grows. So will you appear. Yet you'll know you're not the appearance. You will know that you're totally free and you are Omnipresence, All-Pervading. The whole universe is taking place inside of yourself. And if you're no self, there's no universe. You are beyond the no-self, where there is a no no-self.

You're beyond the no no-self, where there are no words to describe it. Yet it is so beautiful, so blissful, so joyous, that if you have had a taste of it, you'd never return. You'd never want to go back to humanhood. This is why there have been many who have been touched slightly by this realization. They have been touched by truth. And they can remember there's something there, even though they're back to their human self, so it appears. They never forget that touch. And these people are the ones who strive forward to go all the way, and to realization.

What does it mean to go all the way? It means to look at your life as a picture show. All the experiences are images on the screen. It means not to regulate your life at all in any way, but to observe it and watch it. To look at it intelligently. To see the emotions that come into your mind. To observe the fears, the arrogance, and not to do anything about them. But to look at them, look through them and become free. Only by looking through them can you become free of them.

Think of an emotion that you have that bothers you. Perhaps you have a bad temper, a fearful disposition, whatever. First you have to see it. Then you dive deep, deep, within it. And it will totally and completely disappear. It will never bother you again. When you try to change things, they all appear to be fine for a while. Then you'll find yourself in the same position you were before. Different people, different places. You don't want to change anything. You want to be still and look. As you become still and look, what you're looking at will look back at you. As you look at the world without interpretation, as you look at the world without attachment, what the world is will be revealed to you. The world will be revealed to you as no thing. As an image on the screen of Consciousness. You will become radiantly happy for no reason whatsoever. You will find the peace that you never dreamed existed.

You have to want this. You have to love this. You have to want this more than anything else in this world. When I say ın anything else in this world, I don't mean it in a "I ıve it sense and I want it." I mean to feel and believe anu ı.ow that you are That. And you want That to be uncovered for you by going deeper all the time. By letting go of all the things that seem to be happening in life. Continuing to dive deeply within the Self. You dive deeply within the Self to the extent that you give up the stuff that you've been carrying around for years. There is no one who cannot awaken. Since your real Self is already awake, there is nothing that can keep you back but yourself. By the self I mean your mind, your thoughts. Your thoughts are the only things that keep you back. You have to look at these thoughts and not allow them to do anything to you. Do not allow them to frighten you. You have to remember to practice Self-inquiry. To inquire to whom do these thoughts come? To always think in your mind, there are no thoughts. All these thoughts are a mirage.

So you come to sit with me in the Silence. Be still. Know that you are effortless, choiceless, Pure Awareness. Know this deep in your heart. As soon as thoughts come to you, ignore them. Let the thoughts come, let the thoughts go. Pay absolutely no attention to the thoughts, and they'll disappear of their own volition. But you try to change them, and the power of them will become so much stronger. Remember, don't try to exchange good thoughts with bad thoughts, or bad thoughts with good thoughts. Whenever thoughts come to you just ignore them. Sometime in the morning, just scream it out at the top of your voice, "I am effortless, choiceless, Pure Awareness." That'll send the message home, who you really are. And go through the day like this.

Be still! If you can only be still enough, you will feel this unalloyed happiness within you arising. And you will just become happy for no reason whatsoever. But it only comes when you're still, when you're quiet, when you're peaceful. Do not be two different people, one who comes to satsang and is quiet and one who argues in the world all day long with people, and finds everything wrong in the world, gets angry, gets mad and upset. Be one person. All pervading Consciousness. *Be That.*

Never allow yourself to believe that something's wrong in your life. Catch it before it starts. And say to yourself: "I am effortless, choiceless, Pure Awareness." Whatever comes up, say that. Know the truth about yourself. God has no problems. Neither do you. For you are That.

I know the teaching sounds absurd to most people. And yet this is the teaching that has been propagated by rishis, sages, since the beginning of time. This is it. This is your opportunity to awaken. Why not use it? Do not let another moment go by where you are believing and thinking something is wrong somewhere. Everything that is happening in this world today has happened before. Different times, different people, different places. All of these things have happened before previously. They have always happened in this world. This is the nature of this world.

There are so many people who want a beautiful world in which to live, where there is everlasting peace and tranquility, where there is joy and abundance. Yet these things are temporary. This is not the way of this world. It's interesting, when you stop thinking of joy, when you stop thinking of sadness, when you stop thinking of good things and bad things, again something wonderful happens to you. For you are no longer attached to anything. Yet in this non-attachment, you feel love, and kindness, beauty and joy, in a totally different way. Why not awaken now? Will you do this for me? Wake up. Do me a favor. Stop playing these games.

Have mercy on yourself. Stop those thoughts that make you angry or make you upset. Forget about the past. If you are not the mind, not the body, how can you be the past? Never mind the body, the individual. You don't have to worry about the past. You don't. For there was never a beginning, there was never an end. You were never born, you can never die. You do not prevail. Don't try to analyze what I'm saying or figure it out. Just be it. When you say to yourself, "I am effortless, choiceless, Pure Awareness," this transcends the past, transcends the future, it transcends everything and awakens you to the Self which you are now. Awaken to that Self right now! Awaken to it! Awaken to it, right now! To your true Self. Be still silly mind, let the true sun shine forth!

Now let us close our eyes for a few moments. Say to yourself, "I am choiceless, Pure Awareness. I am effortless, Pure Awareness. I am choiceless, effortless, Pure Awareness." And keep still and watch. Observe. Watch your body disappear, the mind disappear.

Trust in the Power That Knows the Way

You see, you live in a universe which is self-existent, self-abiding, self-sufficient. This means that all of your needs are met from within. *All of your needs are met from within.* But this will only happen when you accept it this way. If you think that your needs have to come from a person, place or thing, you've always got a fight on your hands because you're hoping to get a better job or get some money in the bank or that someone will come along and help you with some problem.

These are all erroneous thoughts. If you could only learn to rely on the Self, miracles would take place in your life! If you can only learn to rely on the Self. How do you learn to rely on the Self? By trusting life. Trusting life just the way it is. I'm not saying to trust certain people, or to trust certain conditions, certain situations. I'm saying just to trust life. To trust life you go beyond people, places and things. You trust the substratum of all existence. You trust Consciousness. In other words, you feel and believe in your heart that there is a Power that knows the way. You came out of it. So you're That also. For you are It. You are that Power yourself. And you feel good about it. This is what I mean when I say, trust the Power that knows the way.

There's nothing to fix in your life. Nothing to change. Nothing to accomplish. Nothing to do. Except to abide in the Power that knows the way. It's so simple, yet it's so hard for some of us. And it's hard because we allow the thoughts to come to us and spoil everything. You have to control your thoughts, control your thinking. When you are free from thinking, you will always abide in Consciousness, which is the Power that knows the way. And soon you'll find yourself becoming happier and happier every day. Peaceful. Harmonious.

What can really disturb you and make you sad, make you afraid? Only something that you think may happen to you. But if you're living in the eternal now, if you exist this moment—and you do—in this moment is there a problem? There's no problem in this moment. It's only when you begin to think of tomorrow or the next week or the next week that you think of problems. But if you learn to stay centered in the moment where nothing is happening, this moment will become the next moment. And the next moment will become the next hour, the next day, the next week, and the next year.

This is how to live, from moment to moment. But what do we do? We stretch out those moments to days. We like to see the future. We think something's going to happen to us tomorrow or the next day or the next day. But nothing can ever happen to you unless you allow it. You allow it by believing it, by thinking about it. You give it power by fearing it. But I say to you in truth, there's nothing to fear in this whole universe. There's no fear. Fear doesn't exist. Only the Self exists. Only the Self exists. Catch the meaning of those words. Only the Self exists, and I Am That. That's a profound statement.

There Is Only One Reality and You Are That

All is well. All is well. All is perfectly well. Never forget that. Do not think about it. Do not try to analyze it. Just accept it in your heart. All is well, period, end. Most of us are here because we want to become Self-realized. We want to experience moksha, liberation, awakening. There are three points that you should always remember. If you remember these three points, you will be already awakened. You have to remember these three points in your heart. By assimilating these three points, by digesting them, by becoming a living embodiment of these three points, you will become Consciousness, Pure Awareness, which you already are.

The first point is this: WHATEVER BEFALLS YOUR BODY OR YOUR MIND, REMEMBER THAT IS NOT HAPPENING TO YOU. Whatever appears to happen to your body or your mind, whether you have cancer, AIDS, the D.T.s, bubonic plague, whether you are the strongest person on earth, whether your mind feels depressed, disillusioned, or your mind feels happy or reassured, it is not happening to *you*. You have absolutely nothing to do with that. Makes no difference what's going on in your life. You can be materially relatively the happiest person on earth, or you can be miserable, sick. It has nothing to do with *you*. It has absolutely nothing at all to do with you. This is your body and your mind, not *you*. You are Brahman. You are Nirvana. You are the Absolute Reality. The goings on in your body and your mind have absolutely nothing to do with you. This is the first point.

The second point that you must always remember is that: ALL OF YOUR KARMAS, YOUR SAMSKARAS, YOUR SINS OF OMISSION, COMMISSION, THE SINFUL ACTS THAT YOU ARE RESPONSIBLE FOR, NONE OF THESE THINGS CAN TOUCH YOU IF YOU CENTER YOURSELF IN THE HERE AND NOW. In other words, the Here and Now is Omnipresence. The Here and Now is All-Pervading, Omniscient, the Here and Now is Consciousness. The Here and Now is Boundless Space, Effortless, Choiceless, Pure Awareness. When you hold on to the Here and Now, when you identify with Here and Now, the past is no longer valid. There is no past, there is no future in the Here and Now. There is I Am. There is the Ultimate Reality, Ultimate Oneness, and You Are That. When you are living in the Here and Now, your karmas do not exist any longer, samskaras stop dead in their tracks, sins are abated, you are born again, so to speak. You become the new man, the new woman. You are free.

The third point you must always remember is that: YOU HAVE ABSOLUTELY NOTHING TO GIVE UP. Nothing to surrender. Nothing to let go of. You are already liberated. How can you believe that you have to let go of something that never existed? You believe that you have to let go of your attachments.

How can the Self have attachments? You think you have to surrender all of your fears, all of your depressions, all of the things that have been bothering you. Surrender to whom? Those things are not yours. They do not belong to you.

You are Pure Reality. You are the Imperishable Self. Never were you born, never did you prevail, and never will you leave. *You are the One. The All-Pervading One.* Consequently, you have absolutely nothing to give up. For you had never anything to begin with. It's really egotistical to believe you've got something to give up. There's nothing you have to surrender. It's only the ego that believes that something has to be surrendered, something has to be given up, you have to let go of something. Who is the one who had something to begin with? There is no one. There is only the One Reality, and *You Are That.*

If you can remember these three points, by assimilating them, by digesting them, by becoming a living embodiment of them, that's all you have to do. If you remember these three points, you do not have to practice any sadhana. You do not have to do mantras, or meditations of any kind, for you will already be awakened. Again, it is the ego that has to meditate. It is the ego that has to do sadhana. Are you the ego? Who are you? What are you? Where did you come from? What are you doing here? Where are you going? The answer to all these questions is: *I Am. I Am. I Am not this. I Am not that. I Am. I Am That which has always been, I am That which will always be. I Am That I Am. Am.*

Your swarupa is Absolute Reality. You are not the person that you identify with. The person who goes to sleep and wakes up, goes through experiences, worries, thinks, frets, sometimes happy, sometimes sad. That is not you. No longer think of yourself as that person. When you get up in the morning, take a deep breath and realize the truth about yourself. First thing upon awakening you can say to yourself, *I Am Brahman. I Am the Imperishable Self.* Bullets cannot kill me. Fire cannot burn me. Water cannot drown me. I Am That. And rejoice in your true Self. Feel the happiness in your Heart. Feel your Reality, in the stillness, in the quietness, when there is no mind, no thoughts, no words. Who are you then? You just *are.*

If I say anything else, it will be redundant. There are so many words. So many stories. So many teachings. Yet if you only remember the three points that I shared with you, that will suffice. Why talk any further than this? The more words you hear, the more confused you become. Actually, the first hour that you sat in the Silence was the best time for you. There are certain words, very few words, that you have to hear, and then there is the Silence that you should always be in. It is interesting that the words that I speak to you are really the Silence. Those are the words of the Silence, Truth, Infinite Truth, Reality, Consciousness, Bliss, Pure Awareness, Ultimate Oneness, all this is the Self. And *You are That.*

God

When you are without thoughts,
when you are without needs, without wants,
without desires,
then you are God.
You are the Universe.
You are Divine Love.
You are Beautiful.

What Is, . . . Is God

A devotee of Ramana Maharshi, who had been with him about twenty-five years, had a son who died and he was grief stricken. So he begged to have an audience with Ramana. Now, Ramana rests from twelve to two. He agreed to see his devotee. When the devotee entered the hall, Ramana was reclining on his couch with his eyes closed. And the devotee started to cry and tell him all his troubles, how much he loved his son. And then he asked Ramana, "What is God?" Ramana didn't answer. He kept still for about fifteen minutes. Then he opened his eyes and he said very softly, "What is, is God." What is, is God. It's like when someone asks the question, "Is the world real?" The world, by itself, is an illusion. But God, as the world, is real. As we progress we find that there never was a God, so there never was a world. But for the sake of talking, because God is, the universe is.

Everything from the lowliest microbe to the fullest galaxy is God in expression. Everything is God. Every leaf, every piece of clay, every star, every planet has no basis for its existence by itself. Because God is, everything else is.

That's what Ramana meant when he answered, "What is, is God." He was trying to explain to the devotee, your son is dying, that is God. Your son is living, that is God. There is no real difference. Only in your mind. We differentiate only in the mind. If the mind were made quiescent, quiet, there would be no differentiation between death and life. We make the differentiation because we think. It's a mental concept that someone dies, and that's bad, but someone lives and that's good. There's no such differentiation.

There is only God. And everything that exists, everything, is God. There can be nothing apart from God.

But then I say that God doesn't exist, except in your mind. That is the reason that, in reality, no thing exists. Do you follow that?

As long as you think, there will be existence, person, place and thing. But when you stop thinking there's no room for existence, because there cannot be the Silence and existence. Everything that appears to be opposes the Silence. The Silence is Consciousness, Absolute Reality, Sat-Chit-Ananda. The Self exists as Itself, yet when you begin to modify it you say, well, God exists. God is the first modification of Consciousness, and it's God's job to create the world and then to dissolve the world and then create the world.

Who gave God that job? Henry? Henry didn't do it. Who did? Why would God want to create worlds, universes, and then dissolve them, and after a period of time bring them back into existence? Yet, this is what we read about in all the scriptures. This information is for the ajnani, for the man steeped in ignorance. You have to explain to this man how the world became existent, or he will not be satisfied. You therefore go into all the modifications. There is the Self and the Self is Consciousness. Consciousness modifies itself, and you have God. God modifies Itself and you have existence.

Ramana realized that if he explained this to the devotee, the devotee wouldn't understand. If he told the devotee that only the Self exists and your son didn't die, because he was never born, it would be too much for the devotee to comprehend. Therefore, instead, he said God is. What is, is God. It made the devotee feel better, for he realized that his son was in God's hands, and all is well.

But yet, if we have a questioning mind, we question, "Where did God come from and why does God appear as all these things? What is Its purpose?" Most of us know there is no purpose. No thing exists the way it appears. Your real nature is Pure Awareness. Pure Awareness is the Universal. There is no place for anything else. In other words, you cannot have existence as it appears and Pure Awareness. Otherwise you would have diversification, as the appearance shows you. There's a beautiful tree, there's the sky, there are flowers, there are animals, there are insects. If Pure Awareness or the Self is self-contained, how could there be anything else? Where would the room come from?

It's just like space. When you have a room filled with furniture what happens to the space it takes up? And then you take the furniture out of the room. Has the space changed? Nothing has happened to the space. The space is the same whether the room is filled with furniture, or not. And so it is with reality. Reality exists. The Self exists as the Self. But it appears as if there are things in the universe, as if there were a universe. There are people, there are animals, there are planets. There's the vegetable kingdom, the mineral kingdom. All this appears as real. You therefore have to ask the question, "To whom does this appear? Who sees this?" You know by now it's the "I." *The "I" is the culprit.* If it weren't for the "I" there would be no universe, there would be no God, there would be no creation.

So Ramana couldn't tell this to the devotee, because the devotee wouldn't understand. He therefore said, "What is, is God." The world appears to exist. The world by itself could never exist. So the next step is to say that God exists as the world. But I say to you there is no God and there is no world, and nothing is as it appears. The appearance is called false imagination. And whose fault is it? The "I." Blame the "I." Whenever you make a mistake, say it's the "I's" fault, because there are no mistakes. It sounds funny because it's true. If you did not identify with "I," no thing would exist. Things only exist because you identify with your "I."

Now, the grand secret is to follow the "I" back to its source. If you really follow the "I" back to its source there is no God. Where would God come from? Even as I talk about the word God, some of you are still thinking about a figure up in the sky, an anthropomorphic type of deity. Who created Him? It's the same old question: If God created the universe, who created God? There is no verbal answer, for it goes beyond thought. You'll know the truth about this question when you quiet your mind. When the mind is no longer in existence the answer will reveal itself, for you will be the answer. Otherwise there's no answer. But I can assure you there's no such thing as God. There's no such thing as creation, and there's no such thing as the universe. So there's no such thing as the world. And there's no such thing as you. There's no such thing as "I." What is left? *Silence!*

Who Worships God?

I realize that many of you are bhaktas, and I'm taking away your enjoyment. I'm taking away your God that you worship, be it in the form of Buddha, Krishna, Jesus, Moses, whomever you like to worship. But I speak at many levels. As far as a Jnani is concerned, it is virtually impossible for a God to exist separate from yourself. But yet, such people as Nisargadatta Maharaj, Bhagavan Ramana Maharshi, and many other Jnanis did bhakti. Ramana used to pray to Shiva in the form of Arunachala. Nisargadatta also prayed to Shiva. So the question is, why did they do that? And the answer is, for the sake of others.

To get to the stage where God does not exist for you any longer is a very high transcendental stage. I do not expect you bhaktas to give up your worship. As you know, on Sunday we have puja and we have chanting. To whom are we chanting? To Hari, to Ram, to Shiva.

I must again tell you as long as you believe you are the doer, that you are the body and the mind, do not fool yourself into thinking you're not. For if you weren't, you wouldn't react the way you react to situations. So as long as you believe that things are real, then you have to pray to God, because God does exist for you.

You can call God the law of karma. In reality karma does not exist. Yet how many of us have such reality? Therefore, the best thing for you to do is to practice the Jnana practices, but keep doing your puja. Do not give it up. If you're doing japa, whatever practice you have, keep it up. But practice Self-inquiry. And as you practice Self-inquiry you will notice something very interesting happening to you. You will notice that little by little you begin to give up your worship, slowly but surely, until the day comes when you become the object of your worship. If you've been worshiping Krishna, you will see yourself as Krishna, and so forth. If you try to act like a Jnani before your time, you will have a lot of problems, for you will develop an "I don't give a damn" attitude, and that's not what we're talking about.

I'll give you an idea of how a Jnani acts. There was once a Jnani who lived in a little shack on the mountain by himself. He was radiantly happy. He was coming back from his walk, and he saw some thieves breaking into his house. He crept up by the window to see what they would take, and of course, he owned nothing. There was just a torn blanket on the floor. So the thieves started to curse, and one said to the other, "This guy has nothing here. Let's just take the blanket and leave." So they took the blanket.

The next day he intuitively perceived that the two robbers were caught by the police. So he hurried down to the police station to see what would happen. When the sergeant saw him he said, "Come in. Are these the men who stole from you?" And he said, "Yes." So the policeman asked him, "What did they take?" And he said, "They took my hat and my shirt and my pants and my shoes." And the two thieves started screaming, "What a liar this man is. He didn't have anything. He just had a torn blanket." And the sergeant said, "Is this true?" The Jnani said, "When I put the blanket on my head it becomes my hat. When I put it around my shoulders it becomes my shirt. When I tie it around my waist it becomes my pants. And when I walk on it, it becomes my shoes." Of course the sergeant laughed and he said, "Shall I press charges?" And the Jnani said, "No." The two thieves became his disciples.

The meaning of that story is, because you're a Jnani it doesn't mean you don't have compassion. A real Jnani has more love and compassion than anyone else. But it's not attached to anything. And he'll be the first one to run to somebody's aid, to help somebody. It sounds like a contradiction, but it's not. For while the Jnani carries a body, the body becomes under the Jnani's jurisdiction, and becomes an instrument for good in this world. Therefore, you can never judge a Jnani, for you have no idea what a Jnani is. You can see a Jnani praying to God, just as ardently as a bhakti. Yet the Jnani knows there is no God, but does it for the sake of others.

So when I tell you there is no God and there is no universe, and there is no world, and there are no people, there's only Absolute Reality, do not take it too seriously. See where you're coming from. Be true to yourself. Do not fool yourself. Whatever you're into, whatever you're going through, if you sit in the Silence and practice Self-inquiry, things will begin to stir within you. Things will begin to happen. You will find that your feelings change, your reaction changes, you become less selfish, you develop loving kindness, you understand what this universe is all about. And you're at peace.

Robert, do you think that worshiping God, or believing in God impedes realization?

On the contrary, worshiping God makes you pure. It makes you pure enough so that you can follow the I back to the source. Whereas, if you did not worship God, you would just know everything intellectually, and you would have a hard heart. Worshiping God softens you up, makes you mellow, kind, causes you to become one-pointed, and lifts you higher. So, by all means, worshiping God is good. But what kind of

God will you worship? Worshiping God in the form of a Satguru, or in the form of a Buddha, or a Christ, whatever, is even better.

Why so?

For if you worship God without form, the energy is not as strong. For what kind of a God are you worshiping? An invisible God that has no form, no shape. Therefore you have doubts. You're not too sure. And the energy you send out is not that strong. But when you worship God as form, you can give that God all of your energy or totally surrender to that particular deity. That's the purpose of worship. To finally totally surrender your ego, your pride, your body, your affairs, your life, to that deity. And then you become that deity itself.

Is it better, Robert, to focus on one form?

Yes, of course. For you become one-pointed. It causes your mind to become one-pointed. And then your mind becomes your servant. And finally the mind disappears. It's like the sun. When the sun spreads its rays all over the place, it's not as powerful as if one ray of the sun moved to a certain place. A fire would start. That's how powerful it is. But when the sun dissipates its rays they're not as powerful. In the same way, when you worship many deities, you dissipate your energy and the worship is not as powerful.

Even if you think of them as more or less representative of the same consciousness?

That's hard to do. You can't worship Buddha, and Christ, and Muhammad, and Krishna at the same time.

I thought you could in the sense of them all being the Christ Consciousness.
So how will you worship them? How will you do that?

As a unit.
How can you do it? What will you think of?

The underlying consciousness that they all represent.
If you can do that, that's good, that's wonderful. But I still think you'll think of each one and dissipate your energy. Whereas, if you have one, they will eventually all merge into Oneness. In other words, if you worship Krishna, if you worship Krishna correctly, eventually Buddha, Christ, Shiva, everyone, will become Krishna. So it's better in the beginning to worship One. Then the whole universe will become that One.

Is God All Pervasive?

There was once a holy man who died and went to heaven. He approached the Pearly Gates and knocked. God came out and asked, "What do you want?" The holy man replied, "I am your servant. I have come." God said, "Sorry, there is no room for you here. You can't come in. Goodbye."

The holy man sat down and started to gaze in silence to ponder this. "Why won't God let me in? I've been good. I've practiced the scriptures." He pondered this for six months. Finally, he said to himself, "I've got the answer." He knocked on the door and God came to the gate. He said, "Let me in. I'm your humble servant. The one who has chanted Your name for centuries, who has bowed to You, who has prayed to You."

God said, "I'm sorry, there is no room for you here." Again, he closed the door. This time the holy man became completely upset. He didn't know what the problem was. He had been a good person, a holy person. Why won't that guy let me in? He said to himself, "I'm going to sit here forever if I have to, until I come up with the right answer."

Centuries passed and he pondered. Remember, he was dead anyway, so it didn't matter. (laughter) After this long period of pondering why he hadn't been let in, he paused and asked himself, "Wait a minute, who is this I who wants to get into heaven? Who is the I that chanted God's name? Who practiced the scriptures? Who am I?"

All of a sudden, he started laughing. The answer came. He got up and knocked on the door of heaven. God came to the door and said, "Who is this?" The holy man said, "It is Thou." God opened the gate and said, "Come in, my son. There never was enough room in here for both Me and you."

So it is with us. We claim we want to be Self-realized. We don't realize we are already Self-realized. We just have to let go of the belief that I am the doer.

It makes no difference what you have done in the past, so far as Self-realization is concerned. Once you know the truth, you become free. The truth is, there is no past. There never was a past. The universe has no foundation. There is nothing to hold it together. Therefore, there is nothing you have done that can keep you out of heaven, so to speak.

This does not give you license to go out and do evil because it doesn't matter, not at all! As far as you are concerned, as long as you believe you are the doer, and the body/mind phenomena, everything you do has to be accounted for. The law of karma will get you. As long as you believe you are human, you can't get away with anything.

As long as you believe you're a human, a personal .,
there is a personal God. This is where prayer comes in. You
can pray to that God and you will be helped. Your personal
God will take care of you if you surrender and submit. When
you submit, you are giving up your ego. You are saying, "I am
nothing and you are everything." This will help you. One day
you will awaken to the fact that the God you have been praying
to is none other than yourself.

How can this God be separate from you? Where would he
live? What would be His nature? You begin to understand that
"I am That." You find freedom in yourself. You begin to see that
God is not within me, but that I am in God. What I had called
God is Consciousness. I am conscious. I am aware. I exist. I Am.
There is nothing else. You begin to see yourself as omnipresent.
You are no longer limited to your body or to the personal I.

Your job is to keep the mind from wandering. The mind
has to be held by you. Your mind is not your friend. It makes
you human. It makes you believe you are a body, separate.
When you see that the body is an emanation of the mind, that
it has no existence whatsoever except in your mind, you also
begin to see that the body of the universe is the same as your
body. It is a manifestation of mind. This brings the beginning
of freedom. Bondage begins to break up. You look at the world
and realize the world is the Self. I am that Self. There is
nothing else.

You have an idea of what God is. Can you imagine God
having fear? Can you imagine God complaining about how
things are going, or judging this or that to be right and wrong,
or saying, "I'd rather have this than that"? There is no duality
in God. The universe is ultimate Oneness beyond concepts.
The mind cannot comprehend it.

Even if the word "God" comes after I Am, your mind is playing tricks. Ask, "To whom does the word 'God' come?" I Am will suffice. That is all you have to be. I Am. Everything else is superfluous. Whatever idea comes into your mind, inquire as to whom it comes. Listen to the Silence. Listen to I Am.

Can I remember what you said?

There is something within you that remembers. Something within you knows. If you sit still, put a smile on your face, these things will come forth. That's an interesting question. A sincere student has an open heart, and the highest truth is revealed. My words may sometimes not even be remembered by the brain, but the Heart never forgets. And when you rest in the Silence, you sit still, you remain quiet, something begins to work within your Heart as you become a living embodiment of the Reality, of the Truth, of the Self. Always spend time by yourself, sitting alone in the Silence, being quiet. Be still and know that I Am God.

Many years ago when I was working, I seem to have spent a whole day with my inquiry. One day I just did, and I didn't do anything with what I did. In spite of myself, everything that would have been a problem resolved all the way home this way. And when I got home I thought I would lie down for a moment, and I did. I turned around and that blazing attribute through strength of intensity—the totality of it—absolutely frightened me and I turned right back. I think I was probably not ready for it.

You have nothing to do with it, and you have nothing to say about it. When it happens to you, it will happen totally and completely. You got a glimpse of it and apparently you got a good glimpse of it. But who are you to say that you're not ready for that?

Well, because I turned around the other way.

You speak as if you're an authority on God (laughter), that you have something to do with it. When God is ready for you, God will take you over completely. And you'll have absolutely nothing to say about it whatsoever. But that was a good experience. If that happens again, surrender to it. Surrender totally to it, and have no fear. That's beautiful. Nothing can ever hurt you. That's all Bliss. It's all Love, Joy.

That's what I mean by, can I really remember this?

It will remember you.

It will remember me? I had nothing to do with it.

No.

When you die what happens?

When you die what happens? What do you want to happen? Who dies? The ego dies. The body dies, but you never die. You'll live forever. Nothing really happens. I know you've heard all kinds of stories about going to different realms and planes of existence. This is all part of the dream. You create these things yourself. You create all these different planes. The subtle plane, the mental plane, the causal plane. All these things you read about in the Yoga text are of the mind. They all belong to the mind. So you believe in these things. You go according to what you believe. It's all created by you. You create your world after you die.

But the ultimate reality is, no one ever dies and there's nowhere to go. You're already Here. This is it. You are Eternity. You are Fathomless Space. You are the essence of the whole universe. You are the sky, the sun, the moon, the flowers, the animals, the insects, human beings; you're everything. This is your real nature. No one ever dies.

When our lady friend said she had this experience, then she turned back or couldn't handle it, does that mean the mind just can't handle all that kind of new energy or a new perception? The mind can't handle it, so the mind has to be coaxed slowly into accepting Reality?

No, no, on the contrary. All these experiences come from the mind. Reality is Reality. And this is your very nature right now. So what is there that can't handle Reality, since it is your nature? This is what you really are. The thing you're dealing with is the mind. The mind makes all these experiences up and makes you believe you can't handle it, it's so much for you. This is why you work on destroying the mind and inquire to whom does the mind come? Who is this mind? What is this mind? Where did it come from? Who gave it birth? And you'll experience there is no mind. Once you know there is no mind, there is no longer the experience you've got to go through. All experiences cease. But be aware that all experiences have come from the mind. In reality there are no experiences. The life you're living now is an experience. The false life we all live, this is the experience I'm talking about. It is all of the mind. And the average person believes in the mind so strongly, that when they seem to drop the body, they go forward in a plane of existence that they've created for themselves out of the mind. And then they come back and take on another body. It is all from the mind. So rather than go through all these things, transcend the mind and be free!

How long does it take to get another body to do it? Is that a stupid question? How long does one, after they die before they . . .
Why worry about this? Why be concerned about another body. There are no bodies. Try to find out who you really are. That you never were a body to begin with, and be free!

God Is All There Is

It's good to be with you again. It is wonderful to be with you again. I always enjoy coming here, for I feel there is only One, and we are all that One.

There is only the One Brahman, the One Self, the One Reality, and we're all That. Therefore, I will make Our confession. The I Am confesses to you. Not my confession or Henry's confession, or Dana's confession or anybody's confession. Our confession. The confession is not coming from a person, it's coming from the One Self, it is the One Self.

Close your eyes. I Am boundless space, infinite like the sky, I Am. Not a person, place or thing, but I Am. I Am choiceless, effortless, Pure Awareness. I Am Parabrahman. I Am Sat-Chit-Ananda. I Am Ultimate Oneness. I Am Absolute Reality. I Am Nirvana. I Am infinite like the sky. I Am Absolute Consciousness. I Am That I Am. I Am. I Am. I Am.

There are some who want to awaken with all their heart and with all their soul. Yet they always forget that they have to get rid of the stuff that's keeping them from awakening. The concepts, the preconceived ideas, the dogmas, the belief system that we've had for so many years. This has to be given up.

We must develop loving kindness, compassion. If you are I Am, then you must practice ahimsa, non-violence to any living thing. For if you admit and confess I Am Absolute Pure Awareness, I Am Parabrahman, this is All-Pervading, this is Omnipresence. Therefore the trees, the animals, the mountains, the Universe, everything, is I Am. When I use the word I Am, do not believe or think it applies to the human body. There is no human body. The human body does not exist. I Am Consciousness exists, and the I Am Consciousness is everything.

Everything is holy. Everything is sacred. Do not believe that some things are sacred and some things are not. Everything is sacred, even man's inhumanity to man, the dastardly situations that appear in the world. It's hard for the human mind to understand these things, but everything is very sacred. *Everything is God. God is all there is.* There is nothing else. So how can there be an evil situation someplace and also be God? This is duality. And we know and understand that duality does not exist. There is only the ONE, and the ONE is everything that exists. You consequently have to start feeling this in your Heart. For your Heart center is Omnipresence, All-pervading. It includes the whole universe.

There is nothing to be angry about, nothing to be upset about, nothing to be depressed about, for the whole Universe is God and nothing else. You are not your body or your mind. We still make the mistake in believing that when you say I Am Brahman, you're referring to your body. Your body can never be Brahman. The body is an illusion, a mirage. There is only Brahman, only God, nothing else.

What Is Dharma?

We have to be in our own dharma. Dharma means the right path. You are in your dharma now, whatever it may be, for there are no mistakes. The dharma that appears that you're in, is the result of karma. This is why I always say you are in your right place, right now. This is your dharma, this dharma to totally transcend and transmute everything and become free. When there is no karma, there is no dharma, there's nothing. But while you are searching, you have to be thankful for the dharma that you're in. Do not feel that something is wrong, or you're out of place, or you should be something else. I know people tell me many times, "Robert, I feel so spiritual I really don't belong here on this earth." (laughter) If you didn't belong here on this earth, what are you doing here? Why are you here? As long as you are here and you feel that you're here, then you belong where you belong. This is your dharma.

There is an interesting story that illustrates this. There was once a holy man sitting under a tree meditating. He had his hands open and a female mouse fell into his hands. A bird had apparently dropped the mouse. He felt sorry for the little mouse and because he was a great siddha, a being of great powers from his years of meditation, he turned the mouse into a lovely young girl, and took the girl to his house. His wife was enthralled with this. She was unable to have children, and she was so happy to have this little girl. They both loved her very much, and brought her up to be a fine young lady.

One day the wife said to her husband, "Husband, it's time for our daughter to get married. Where can we find a suitable husband for her?" And the holy man said, "I know, I'll ask the sun." So he went outside and he called the sun and he said,

"Mr. Sun, our daughter is of the marrying age and we're looking for a suitable husband. Can you help us?" The sun said, "Certainly, I will marry her myself." How would you like to get married to the sun? The husband was thrilled and he said, "Oh! What great joy has come over me that the sun would pick my daughter to be married to." And he ran in, and he told his wife and he told his daughter. His daughter said, "No, Dad, I don't want to marry the sun. There's too much light, I'll be burned. Find me a different husband." So the holy man went outside, he spoke to the sun again, he said, "Mr. Sun, our daughter does not wish to marry you because she will be burned with your light. Can you think of anyone else more powerful than you, who can marry my daughter?"

So the sun thought about it and then he said, "The cloud is mightier than I am because many times the clouds hide me and I don't appear, and I can do nothing about it. So the cloud is mightier than I am. Ask the cloud." The holy man beseeched the cloud and said, "Mr. Cloud, I have a daughter who is of the marrying age, and I'm looking for a suitable husband for her. Can you help out? Do you know of anyone who should marry her?" And Mr. Cloud said, "I will. I'll marry your daughter." And again, the holy man became overjoyed with this. Imagine a cloud marrying my daughter. (laughter). This was a good thing. He ran in the house and told his wife and then told his daughter. The wife and the husband were so happy. But the daughter said, "Chill out, Dad. I don't want to marry that cloud. For when it rains, I'll get soaked. Get me a better husband." So, again, the holy man went out to the cloud and told him the story, "Can you think of anyone else?" And the cloud said, "Well, how about Mr. Mountain? There is a great mountain here that is mightier than I am. Because when I flow around the mountain, I can't go through it and I have to flow around it. And there's nothing I can do about it. So the mountain is very powerful."

The holy man beseeched the mountain, "Mr. Mountain, can you think of someone who can marry my daughter?" And the mountain also said, "Well, I will." So again, the holy man was very happy about this. A mountain marrying his daughter. What could be better? He ran into the house, told his wife. She was overjoyed. And he told his daughter. Again, she didn't want to marry the mountain. She said, "Come on, Dad, I can't marry this mountain. The mountain has cactus growing all over it. And when we embrace, I'll be pinched with cactus. Think of someone else." So the holy man went back to the mountain and told him the story, and said, "Can you think of anybody else for my daughter?"

The mountain said, "Well, the only one I can think of who is more powerful than me is this little mouse that lives in the bottom of me. Because he bores holes and has a nest inside of me, and I can do nothing about it. And since he bores holes in me, he must be more powerful than I am. Ask the mouse." So, the holy man went to the mouse and said, "Mr. Mouse, I have a daughter of the marrying age, I'm looking for a suitable husband, can you help me?" And the mouse said, "Yes, I will marry her myself." He was overjoyed. Imagine, a mouse marrying his daughter. He ran and told his wife, and they both went and told their daughter. The daughter thought about this and she said, "Yes, I will marry the mouse. The mouse is very cute. I will marry the mouse. But father, can you do something for me? Can you please turn me into a little mouse also?"

So the holy man turned her into a little mouse, and they got married, and they lived happily ever after in the mountain.

Now, what is the moral of the story? I'll give you three choices:
(a) Everyone's daughter should marry a mouse.
(b) This was her dharma originally, for she was a mouse. She had fulfilled her dharma and become free and liberated.
(c) If you marry a mountain, a cloud, and a mouse, you will have children that become freaks and you'll be able to put them in the circus and make one million dollars.

So which one is the right answer? (b), of course. This story tries to bring home the fact that your dharma is what you have to live out. If you try to change it, years will pass and you will make all kinds of mistakes, and go through all kinds of problems. Whatever your dharma is has been presented to you by karma. Therefore, do not fight it. Bless it.

This is sort of difficult to understand sometimes. For you have the impression that if you live in a condition that is horrible, terrible, you have to stay there and not change the condition. This is the ultimate truth. This is exactly what you want to do. And you know why. For you have within you the conditionings that are at the level of your experience. This means that if you change your environment, or if you change the condition, the samskaras and the conditioning that you have inside of you will just put you back in that kind of a position with different people, different environment, but you have not risen from that condition. Therefore you have to experience the same thing over and over and over and over again.

We find this happening in people who get divorced, get married, get divorced, and get married. They always think they're going to get something better. But they always seem to have the same problem. Just new faces, new people, same problems. So if you have a horrible marriage, or if you're not living with the person you love, do not try to change this, for you have not changed yourself. Merely know the truth. Work on yourself and never react to the condition. This is the freedom you've got from dharma and karma. When you begin to see the truth in yourself, automatically you will be picked up by the Power That Knows The Way, and you'll be placed in a position or place where you are supposed to be at this time.

This is why I tell you so often, there are no mistakes. It appears complicated to the finite mind, but you are in your right place, going through those experiences that are right for you at this time. Only if you are thankful and you bless the position you're in, do you become a higher being, do you lift yourself up, and finally you find liberation. But it begins and ends with you.

Never pray to God for release of your problems. Never pray to God to change your life, and to give you something better. This is wrong prayer. If you have to pray to God, pray to God to give you the strength and the wisdom and the courage that you need to be able to handle the situation that you're in. This is correct prayer. Do not try to change anything. Be yourself. Work on yourself. Begin to see things in a new light. See your situation differently. There are no bad things, there are no good things. But thinking makes it so. Stop thinking of the extremes, good and bad, right and wrong. Rather look at yourself in the moment. Stay centered. See yourself as a Divine Being, an Infinite Being, totally free and liberated. Do not feel sorry for yourself because you are in a position and in a situation you don't like. This just holds you there more. And again as we mentioned before, even if you run away from a situation, you will attract some of the circumstances elsewhere.

Running away is never the answer. Changing yourself is the answer.

Take a look at your own life and see if it is not true what I'm saying. The changes you've gone through in your life. I know so many people who have left their home and family and gone to India to meditate, to find gurus, teachers. They have come back very depressed, even suicidal. For they've given up everything. Remember, there's nothing you have to give up. Only mentally do you give up attachment.

Always look at the world as a reflection of you. You are the world. The world can be nothing without your approval. It sounds strange, but true. You have to stop identifying conditions apart from yourself. I know it seems hard to do. When you see the riots we've just had, the murders, the looting, it seems really difficult to realize you are one with this. But think about this. Why should you only think you are one with the good things? If you are One, you are One with everything. Never just the good things that you enjoy and you like and bring into your life. You are All-Pervading, Omnipresent, and you are One with all there is.

The correct way to observe this is to look at everything in the world intelligently without any comments, without any reactions. Do not be for or against anything. Train yourself to observe, to watch, to look without any reaction. You may start training yourself with the small things. Work on the small things first. As an example, if you go outside and you have a ticket on your car for over-parking, catch yourself reacting to this by not reacting at all. Simply see the situation, look at the situation, have no comment, no reaction. Pay the ticket and forget it. Do not think this is good, this is bad, this is outrageous, this is wrong, I don't deserve it. If you didn't deserve it, it wouldn't happen. Say you stub your toe. Instead of cursing the chair, getting upset, feel the pain, observe it, watch it, and let it go. Everything that takes place in your life, this is the way you should react. Someone cheats you, and you're thinking of taking them to court to sue them. Think about this carefully. Is this what I really want to do? And then your ego will say, of course you do, you were cheated. Your business partner cheated you out of $50,000. So you want to take this person to court to sue them. Say you did go to court and you won the case. You think this is good. But something will happen to even it out again. You'll have to go to court again and again and again. Sometimes you will win, sometimes you will lose. There are people like that you know. I'm thinking of a particular woman right now who makes a habit of going to court at least once a month. She is always suing somebody for something. Sometimes she wins and sometimes she loses, and she's a nervous wreck. She's not a happy woman.

If you begin to understand that everything is in its right place, how can somebody do something to you? No one can hurt you. What is rightfully yours, no one can ever take away. So why worry? Why be upset? It makes life so much easier. You start to worry and you become upset because in your finite mind, in your ego mind, you're thinking, "Well I've been cheated out of $50,000, this is all the money I have. I'm going to go to the poorhouse, I'll become a homeless person," and your mind keeps playing tricks with you. Telling you all the bad things that are going to happen to you. If you can only laugh at yourself and stop thinking of those things, you will find that you have risen higher in consciousness, and you're in control of the situation, and all is well. Never allow your mind to play tricks on you, to play games with you, and tell you about all the things that might happen. And then fear comes in and you start running around, crying, trying to correct things, trying to make things good, while you keep thinking about all the bad things that are going to happen to you. These things we are talking about are very important, for it keeps you back from thinking of truth and reality. It keeps you back from moksha, from liberation, for you are spending all your time involved in the material world. I'm not saying you should give up thinking about your business, or thinking about your family, or thinking about things in your life. But make them short and sweet. Think a couple of minutes about these things, and leave them alone.

Self-Inquiry and God-Realization

And go back to your spiritual Self, thinking about who am I? What is my real nature? Who was I before I was born? Where did I come from? We're talking about "I," not you. See I caught some of you didn't I, for when I was saying, "Where did I come from? Who am I?" you are going back to your humanhood, to your personal self. Learn whenever you say the word "I," you're not thinking about your personal self. When you forget it, you are thinking about your personal self. But when you remember, I Is God. I is Pure Awareness, Absolute Reality. Even when you forget this and you are involved in conversation, when you are using the word I, you are thinking about your personal self. Remember to catch yourself. Keep catching yourself all the time. This is how you grow. This is how you mature. Never allow a day to go by when you do not work on yourself in this manner. A situation is presented to you good or bad, do not get excited. Observe the situation, keep your cool. Realize the situation comes to me. I am experiencing this. The personal I is experiencing this predicament. Not me, the real I is not going through this, but the personal I is going through this. To the extent that you do not feel the condition or situation that you are in, to that extent is the personal I not working any longer, and the real I comes along. You begin to feel higher, spiritual, sacred. This comes by itself. All you've got to do is to let go of the personal I by not reacting to the condition, and automatically the real I comes along, for you are really the real I. This is your real nature. This is your swarupa, God, Brahman, Consciousness.

Can you imagine what would happen if you thought about this all day long, without forgetting? Why, you'd be enlightened in no time. Now perhaps you can see the reason that is keeping you back. Yourself. You are keeping yourself back. Why? Because you are involved in the material world, in your mind. Remember I'm not saying you have to give up your job or not do things in this world. You've got a body and the body is going to do things. But mentally, you have to not be attached to what you are doing. Your body will know what to do and will do everything that is necessary for it to do. Be your Self.

Stand Naked Before God

Again, what I'm saying is this. Every position that you find yourself in, every situation that you find yourself in, with whomever you find yourself, the positions that you have or don't have, whatever you may be in this world, is your right place at this moment. Bless this, love it. I know it sounds hard when you think of a horrible condition and you say, "I must love it?" Let me explain again. The reason you love it, is because *God is all there is.* Try to remember this. *There is nothing but God.* Therefore if you hate something, you're hating God which is your Self. It's all coming out of you. *You are That.* You must learn to trust and love your Self, your precious Self. When you become despondent, depressed, hateful, feeling sorry for yourself, this is what blasphemy really means, for you're feeling this way about your Self. Can't you see? There's only your Self. If you think something is horrible, you're speaking about your Self. You look at a situation, you watch it, you observe it, you never react, you leave it alone. And then you'll be given the power that you need to handle it, to go through it, without thinking, without thoughts, without any commotion, without any noise. These are the things you must work on.

Be that Self. Never be frightened again by anything. If I can make this perfectly clear to you, never allow anything in this world to ever frighten you.

Allow things to unfold as they may. Remember, you just watch and observe. Hold on to the truth. Happiness will come of its own accord. When you hold on to the truth, when you do not react to life's conditions, person, place or thing, when you leave things alone and you stop fighting life, you're not giving up.

In the Western psychology we're told you never give up. We are taught to keep on fighting. But I'm telling you there is nothing to fight. And the only thing you're giving up is your ego. Western psychology has never gone beyond this. Therefore, they do not know of life beyond this. Western psychology works on the presumption that you are a body and a mind, so naturally they tell you never give up, fight to the end. Stick up for your rights. But in the highest teachings of the truth, we learn that you have no rights. You're giving up your body, your ego, your mind. And when this happens, you go beyond psychology. Something happens that psychiatry, psychology are not aware of whatsoever. And that is, you rise to a higher dimension where there is happiness, peace, compassion, love and joy, that is naturally yours. You begin to feel these things instead of the things you felt before, prior to this, when you were fighting life, when you were sticking up for your rights, when you were trying to get even, when you were working as an ego. You were never able to feel happiness or joy or peace. Only sometimes when you won, when you got your point across, when you won an argument, when you won a fight, when you sued someone and won. You felt happy for a while, but it didn't last long. And you have to go through it again and again. But this is as far as the world goes. It doesn't know anything but this.

What I'm saying to you is, let go of everything. Do not hold on. Stand naked before God, without any crutches, without anything to hold on to. When you can do this, from this moment on you will begin to rise. And you will become aware that you are not the body or the mind or the world or the universe, but you are effortless, choiceless, Pure Awareness. You are boundless space, infinite like the sky. You have become everything, and everything has become you.

There comes a time in everyone's life when they have to stand naked before God. By standing naked I mean no scripture, no fancy words, no preconceived ideas, no spiritual intellectual knowledge. But to be totally naked, in humility and humbleness. Therefore when you can forget about your scripture, forget about everything you've learned, and become totally empty, you will then become full.

Self-Realization

*There is nothing you can think of in this Universe
that can tell you what you are.
It is beyond words and thoughts.
You can never with your finite mind
understand who you are.
So do not try to do this.
It works in reverse.
It is when you actually stop thinking about who you are,
or wanting to know who you are,
And you stop analyzing, and you stop trying to figure it out,
that the truth about you is revealed.*

*It is beyond all of the thoughts and feelings
that you ever had.
It has absolutely nothing to do with you
as you are now.
It is the substratum of all existence.
You may call it God if you will.
Do not think of yourself as an
anthropomorphic deity,
apart from God.*

*Because God is, you are.
Therefore, what God is, you are.
There is no separation.
Awaken to this truth.*

There Are No Mistakes

Most people are home watching the presidential debates. We ought to have Jnani debates, where all the Jnanis in the world show up. Whoever shows up loses, of course. (laughter)

If only people understood the first principle of Self-realization, which is simply this. Whatever is destined to happen is going to happen, no matter how you try to stop it. And whatever is destined not to happen will never happen, no matter how much you try to make it happen. Wouldn't it be wonderful if the politicians understood this truth? There would be absolutely nothing to worry about, nothing to fear, nothing to conquer, nothing to win, nothing to lose. Everything is unfolding the way it should. Everything is in its right place. There are no mistakes. Everything is lovely and beautiful just the way it is.

If you can only understand this in your own personal life. What you're supposed to go through in this experience, in this incarnation, has already been planned for you before you came into this body. Yet you have absolutely nothing to do with it, because you are not the body. As long as you think you are a body, you think you're somebody, somebody important. Or you think you are a failure, whatever you think about yourself. If you would only turn within and see the one Self, then you would never worry about what is going to happen to you at all. For you would realize, there is no you for anything to happen to. You are total freedom right now, total liberation, complete Awareness. Yet, you do not believe me. You still feel inclined to be a body, a doer. Think of the experiences you went through today, and see if you do not believe that you are a doer. How many times did you become angry today? How many times did you feel slighted today? How many times did you feel fear, or something is wrong somewhere, or you're not in your right place? This shows you that you believe that you are a body. And as long as you believe that you are a body, why not just let go and stop fretting and worrying about your body.

The Power that knows the way will take care of you. The One who makes the sun shine, the grass grow, the apples grow perfectly on apple trees. The food that sustains us, nourishes us, everything has been lovingly provided for us. Have faith.

Trust the Power that knows the way. This is a first step. To have total faith and total trust in the Infinite, the One. You may call this God if you want to. Makes no difference what you call it. It is within you. It is without you. It is everywhere. Always turn within. That is where all the answers are. Without is a dream. Within is the Self. In reality there's no real without, there's no within. It's a figure of explaining this. You have to turn within because you think you're living without. When you turn within, the within will eventually disappear and the without will eventually disappear. Everything will disappear when you begin to turn within. Yet when you awaken, everything will appear the same as it is now, except you will not be a part of it. You will see things that you do now, but you will no longer be fooled. The world will no longer fool you by telling you this is right, and this is wrong, and this is good, and this is bad. You will be finished with all this.

You introvert the mind upon itself. When the mind is introverted upon itself, it disappears, for it never existed. But when the mind is extroverted, then you're alive and well in the world. It comes with all types of experiences.

In school they taught you to be extroverted, to have an outgoing personality. Well what has it done for you? It made us all into a bunch of idiots. Look at the world in which we are living. See what's going on. Look at our figureheads. Government officials, state officials. These are all extroverted people. We have been told that to be introverted is to be a loner, and never get anywhere. Where do you want to get? If these people only realized that the world in which they are playing is all karmic. In other words, everybody is in their right place, where they are supposed to be. There are no mistakes.

So these people do not believe they're not the body and the world does not exist. But they believe there are bodies and there is a world and a universe. They should accept the fact that karma is the ruler of the universe. And everything that appears to be is karmic in effect. This is why I always say there are no mistakes. For you are where you are supposed to be in accordance with the law of karma. But do not keep thinking about getting rid of karma, for you'll have a battle on your hands. You have to grow out of this and see that karma never existed and does not really exist. So just wake up. Awaken.

Why not awaken to this truth? Why not awaken to the fact that there is nothing that you have to become? There are no goals to accomplish. You are to believe everything is preordained, and it's been mapped out for you. Or, you believe that you are just a victim of circumstance going through many experiences to learn a lesson. It's really funny to me when people tell me, "something happened in my life, but I guess that's the lesson I have to learn." Or, "that's my karma." Forget about karma. Forget about lessons you have to learn. No one has to learn any lessons. No one has to go through their karmic experiences. Put an end to it all. Drop it all.

After all, for whom is there karma? For whom are there experiences? Only for the I-thought, for the mind, not for you. You are bright and shining. You are the Absolute Reality, Brahman. Yet even those words are superfluous, redundant. What do these words actually mean to you—Absolute Reality, Brahman? They are just names that are given to the Absolute Reality, to the Self. Yet everything has to go. The Absolute

Reality has to go. The Self has to go. The reason it has to go is because you're thinking about this with your finite mind. And every answer you come up with is erroneous. Always remember, the finite mind can never know the Infinite. It's impossible. And there's absolutely nothing you can do about it. Consequently, the wise person becomes silent, quiescent.

Most of us have a mind set, and it is very difficult for us to change this. This is the only thing that keeps us from seeing Reality. As long as your mind is set, it is in accordance with the universe and the world, and you see things as they appear to be, but not as they are. You look out the window and you see a beautiful tree, a beautiful sky, woods, a lake. That sounds great. You look in the other direction you see rioting, man's inhumanity to man, destruction, earthquakes. How do you reconcile this? Look at your own personal life. You have good times and bad times, and it's from this you know what you want to experience. You want to experience the good times, not the bad times. Yet what you fail to understand is, where there are bad times, there are good times. And where there are good times, there are bad times. You cannot have one. You can never have one.

And to give an illustration of this, is the story of the two frogs. Once there were two frogs. They inadvertently jumped into a vat of milk. There was a fat frog and a skinny frog. And they couldn't get out. They were swimming around, the sides were slippery, and the fat frog said to the skinny frog, "Brother frog, there's no use paddling any longer. We're going to drown, so I might as well give up." The skinny frog said, "Hold on brother, keep paddling. Somebody will get us out." They paddled for hours. Again the fat frog said, "Brother frog, I'm becoming very tired now. I'm going to just let go and drown.

There's no way that anybody can ever get us out of here. It's Sunday, nobody's working. We're doomed. There's no possible way we can ever get out of here." And the skinny frog said, "Keep trying. Keep paddling. Something will happen, keep paddling." Another couple of hours passed. And the fat frog said, "I can't go on any longer. There's no sense in doing it, because we're going to drown anyway. What's the use." And he let go, he gave up. He drowned in the milk. But the skinny frog kept on paddling. Ten minutes later he felt something solid beneath his feet. He had churned the milk into butter and he hopped out of the vat.

So it is with us. We go through so many experiences in life. We think there's no way out. We believe we're human and we're caught in maya. We've got to go through certain experiences, and suffer, and be happy, and do all kinds of things. But when I share the truth with you, that there is no maya, there's no universe, nothing is the way it appears. It is only your mind that creates these conditions, and your mind doesn't exist.

You don't believe me. You want me to talk about karma and reincarnation. You want to get into all kinds of facets of the universe. You want eloquent lectures about how we're going to be saved. Yet there is no one to save. For no one ever existed. Yet you do feel human, don't you? You do go through experiences, don't you? If you'd only learn to sit still, to be quiet, to stop reacting to the universe, to the world, to the situations, to life. We give everything a name, that's the problem. We say this is cancer, this is poverty, this is an earthquake, this is a million dollars, this is a new home, this is a new car, this is a war, this is a dog, this is a cat. We have names for everything. What if we forgot about those names? And we stopped seeing things as something? What if we just observed things, watched things, without giving them a name, without coming to a conclusion? What do you think would happen? You would transcend everything.

Remember again, why do you wish to awaken? Because you're sick and tired of this world the way it is and the changes that take place. Everything happens here. It unfolds. You have happiness, you have sadness. You have good, you have bad. When you awaken, you will never experience these things again! You will be in total bliss all the time. And you will keep silent, you'll keep quiet. There will be nothing to explain, nothing to discuss, nothing to prove. You have become the immutable Self that you've always been. The mind can never know these things. The mind only knows itself as a body, as a doer. Therefore, you have to transcend the mind, transcend the thoughts, transcend the world, transcend the universe, and enter the Silence where there is total bliss and peace and harmony.

This is your life. You always have the freedom to make the choice. You're always free to make the choice, always. The choice you make depends on what you know. Right now.

Actually, the only freedom you have is not to react to conditions and to turn within, to see the truth. Everything else is preordained. Whatever appears in your life is destined to be. It is your reaction to what appears that matters to you, what is going to happen to you next. It is your reaction to life's experiences that come to you, which determines what is going to happen to you next, by the way you respond to it, by the way you react to it.

Right This Moment You Are Totally Free

Do not be in conflict with your thoughts and the Self. When there is no conflict, there are no thoughts. Thoughts only appear because there is conflict. By conflict I mean you're worrying about getting rid of your thoughts. You're doing sadhana, meditation, pranayamas, japa. All of these things cause conflict. For aren't you saying, "I'm doing these things to become liberated. I'm doing these things to become free." These are the conflict, because you're already free and liberated. Therefore, when you give yourself the information that you have to do something to become liberated, there is immediately conflict. This is the only problem you have. It is your conflict. And this conflict comes from programming when you were a child, from samskaras, from previous existence. Things that you took with you, the habits that are inside of you, that you believe you are. This is where the conflict comes from. For it tells you, I'm just a human being. I'm just a frail body. I have to suffer sometimes. Sometimes I have to be happy. This is all a lie. There never was a you that has to suffer. There never was a you that has to be happy. There is no one in you who needs to be happy. There is no one in you who needs to be miserable. They are both impostors.

So every time you try to exchange negative conditioning to positive conditioning, you are causing conflict. This is the reason psychiatry and psychology do not work. Because they are trying to make you normal. Who wants to be normal? How boring. The truth is, do not wish to be anything. There is nothing you wish to be. There is nothing you have to become. There is no future for you to become anything. Right this moment you are the One. And there never was another. Right this moment you are totally free, without thinking a thought, without trying to make anything happen.

You're not even trying to change your thoughts or stop your thoughts. For how can you try to stop something or change something that never existed to begin with? Can you see now why you are in conflict? You're trying to correct something. You're trying to become something. You're trying to do something. And something does not exist. Also, what you're trying to correct does not exist. What you're trying to change does not exist. You get nowhere. This is why I tell you so often, leave everything alone. Have no opinion for or against. Do not be judgmental. Be nothing and you'll be everything.

Why do most of you come to satsang? As long as you have a reason, it's the wrong reason. There should be no reason. There shouldn't be any valid reason why you come to satsang. For if you think back on what I've been referring to, you will see every reason is erroneous. For the reason you're trying to come to satsang doesn't exist at all. You say you come to satsang to become enlightened, to know the truth. Who has to know the truth? Who has to become enlightened?

You come to sit with me. You can always sit with me wherever you are. I'm trying to tell you, do not look for reasons why you do something. When you start giving up all reasoning, all ambition, when you start surrendering all of your so-called power, your human power that you think you have, this is when the mind begins to slow down. The mind will never slow down by trying to make it slow down. I don't care what method you use. When you are using vipassana meditation, or you're using breathing, whatever method you're using, you're using your mind. It is your mind that you're still using. That's why you can never get anywhere. You must use your mind, no matter what you do.

Therefore, stop doing anything. I know many of you have been practicing sadhana for twenty-five years, forty years.

Practicing many forms of meditation, going to teachers, reading many books. And what becomes of you? You may get a good feeling, then it goes away and you're back where you started from. The only thing that you should do or must do, is not to be in conflict with anything. Do not be in conflict with anyone or anything. When you're not in conflict with anything, the mind begins to surrender itself and goes back into the Heart, and you become your Self. This is the easiest thing that you ever had to do. It's simplicity itself. It's simplicity itself, because there is nothing you have to do. There is nothing you have to become. There is no one you have to change. *You are That.*

Do not analyze what I am saying. Do not even agree with what I'm saying. Just be open. Open your heart by remaining still, silent. Allow the thoughts to come, and try not to stop them. Do not judge your thoughts, analyze your thoughts, or try to change your thoughts, or try to remove your thoughts. This will put you back in conflict with your thoughts. Do not even observe your thoughts. Do not even be the witness to your thoughts. Why? Because in reality there are no thoughts. The thoughts that you think you are thinking are an illusion. It is false imagination. Don't you see, everything that you're thinking about is false. There is no thinker and there are no thoughts. So why have you been practicing all these exercises all of your life? It's like a person in the ocean going in search of water.

Awaken, be free, be yourself. You are the joy of the world. The light that shines in darkness. You are a blessing to the universe. Love yourself always. When you love yourself, you love God. Forget about the past. Never dwell on the past. Remember, time and space does not exist. If time and space does not exist, then there cannot be a past or a future. For the past and the future is about space and time. And if there is no time and space, there cannot possibly be a past or a future. So who thinks about the past? Who thinks about the future? Even to say the I does, the I-thought does, this again is mostly for beginners. Self-inquiry is very important, don't get me wrong. But the day has to come when you go beyond Self-inquiry. When you just realize and understand that there is no I-thought at all. It never existed. Therefore you do not have to get rid of it. There is nothing to get rid of, because nothing exists. You are total freedom, right this instant, right this minute.

Leave Everything Alone

Whenever your thoughts dwell on the past, do not become angry with yourself. Leave them alone. Do not observe them. Do not watch them. Do not be the witness to them. Just leave them alone. They will disappear of their own volition, due to the fact that they never existed. This is an important point. This is the reason why you leave everything alone. Now if things existed, if there were such a thing as negative thinking, karma to get rid of, then you'd have a job on your hands. You'd have to do all sorts of things to remove your karma, your past sins. You'd be working continuously. Practicing all kinds of japa, mantras, everything, to remove all of these thoughts of the past. But I say to you, since these things never existed to begin with, why do any work at all? Oh, it's OK if you like to work, but I'm very lazy myself, and the less work I have to do, the better. I know it's difficult for some of you to think that you have to do absolutely nothing to become free because you're already free. For you've been brought up that you have to work, work, work to get ahead. Why do you want to get ahead? Ahead to what? To whom? Everything must change sooner or later. Everything must dissolve and return to the elements from whence they came. And new forms are always being born, so to speak. So what kind of goals are you trying to achieve? Your goals will vanish when everything else vanishes, sooner or later.

Think how many civilizations we've had on this planet. Many civilizations, and they've also passed us where we are today. But where are they now? They're gone. Dissolved into the nothingness from whence they came.

So it is folly to try to improve yourself, or to try to achieve anything. It is folly to try to change something or to become something. Just Be. You may ask, how do I just Be? By asking, you're not being. To just Be is to just Be. Not to be this or to be that. Or to try to discover how to just Be. Just Be, without trying to understand what that means. Without analyzing. Without pondering.

Just Be. Just Be. Just Be. Just Be.

Who Becomes Enlightened?

Do not look for results. Because it's your true nature, sooner or later the results must presume themselves. But it comes without your help. You cannot help God. God does not need your help. Just be yourself. It's difficult to be totally honest with yourself, yet this is exactly what you have to do. Forget about being a Jnani or enlightened, or having Self-realization. I get too many calls like that. People are calling me from all over the world telling me that they are Self-realized.

So now I just say, "Good, what do you want me to do?" They want the confirmation. So I was thinking of printing certificates (laughter) and mailing them out. "This is to inform you that you are now Self-realized. Congratulations!"

It's interesting to note that many people throughout the world are beginning to be attracted to Advaita Vedanta, the non-duality principle. More than ever in the last two years or so, many people who have never dreamed would be involved in Advaita Vedanta are being involved in Advaita Vedanta. Now the amusing and interesting thing to me is that a good eighty percent of these people become teachers. New teachers of Advaita Vedanta are popping up all over the world.

I received many calls during the week, and you'll see why I'm smiling when I explain it to you. Just this morning I received a call from somebody in Texas with whom I have been corresponding. And he told me, "Robert, I read your transcript for a month straight like you said and I am enlightened now," (laughter). So I said, "That's wonderful. What makes you think so?" He said, "I stopped quarreling with my wife, I feel more peaceful, and I don't give a damn about the world. (laughter) But I have a question. What do I do now?" (laughter) What can I say?

There are many people who are going around claiming they're enlightened, more than ever. It really makes no difference to me, but it's amusing. It's interesting.

First of all, what does the word enlightenment mean? I'm not talking about a dictionary definition. To the path of Jnana, what does enlightenment mean? The answer is, there is no such word. No one becomes enlightened. There is no body, no I, no me, there is no thing that can ever become enlightened. The word enlightenment is used by the ajnani, by students.

Absolute Reality, Choiceless Awareness, Sat-Chit-Ananda, Parabrahman, those are all words that do not exist except to the student in order to explain that there is a state beyond the so-called norm. A state of total transcendence, and we give a name to this: enlightenment.

When this actually happens or transpires in a person, the I has been totally destroyed, totally annihilated. The me no longer exists, and to that being, there is absolutely no one who became enlightened. That being is resting in his true nature, in nothingness, absolute nothingness.

No one can become enlightened. No one can be liberated, for the you that thinks it can be liberated doesn't even exist. There is no you. There is no person. There is no human being who is a human being one day and the next day becomes liberated. There is only the liberated Self, and you are That.

There is not you as you appear. The appearance of you which you think you are is false. This is why I say all of your problems, all of your nonsense that you go on with, all your worries, all your cares, all your emotions, they do not exist. They never have existed and they will never exist. It is all the game of maya, the leela. It doesn't exist. No one in this room exists. There is no you and there is no me. There is only the Self. And when the self becomes the Self, it is no longer the self. For there never was a real self to begin with. This is the reason why I emphasize, stop thinking. Your thoughts pull you deeper into maya, into illusion. Do not think of enlightenment or awakening, or being liberated, or finding a teacher who can help you. You are beyond help. No one can do anything for you.

Actually what happens is this. You begin to realize you are not your thoughts, you are not your body, you are not your mind, you are not the world, you're not even liberated. You are nothing. As you begin to think this way, whatever has to happen in your evolution will transpire without your doing anything. If you are meant to be with a teacher, you will be with a teacher. If you are meant to be by yourself, you will be by yourself. Yet, you have absolutely nothing to do with these things. Remain in the no thought state. Leave the world alone. Leave people alone. Do not come to any conclusion. Do not judge anyone. Everything will take care of itself.

The worst thing you can ever do is to search for enlightenment, for liberation. This keeps you back. It keeps you back because there is a self that is searching. There is an I that is searching. There is a me that is trying to become something, and the whole idea is to remove something from your consciousness. Therefore, the process of realization is removal, not adding. Removing this and removing that. Removing all concepts and all preconceived ideas. Removing all of your thoughts, no matter what kind of thoughts they are. Good thoughts, bad thoughts, they all must go. And what is left will be nothing—no-thing. You are that. You are that no-thing.

Doesn't it feel good to be nothing, instead of believing you are thoughts, and you are human, and you have a job to fulfill, and you have a mission. There are many spiritual people you know who think they have a mission. They have come to save the world. They can't even save themselves, and they're looking to save the world. The world will go on the way it's going on without your help, for or against. Leave the world alone.

There is a Power and there is a Presence which I like to call *The Current That Knows The Way,* that takes care of everything. It is all part of the grand illusion. And even in this illusion which appears in front of your eyes, there is a Presence and a Power that lifts you up. It will lift you up as high as you can allow It to. Until It lifts you up completely out of your body, out of your thoughts, out of the universe, to a completely new dimension.

You'll appear to be the same person as always to people, but you'll not be that person any longer. For that person is gone, no longer exists. You have become Brahman. You have become all-pervading. You have become your Self without trying to do so.

You must always have gratitude for the way you are. Do not feel sorry for yourself. Love yourself just the way you are. By loving yourself just the way you are, you will transcend those things that have appeared to annoy you, to bother you, to cause you pain. They will all go. You'll no longer be aware of them. Let go of everything. Have no desires whatsoever. Dive deep within the Self. Do not react to the outside world or to your body. *All is well.*

When you are without thoughts, without needs, without wants, without desires, then you are God. You are the universe. You are Divine Love. You are beautiful.

Freedom

When you are aware that you are Consciousness, then you are everywhere and you're everything. When you realize you're everything, you become master of all. When you become master of all, you can do anything you like. Now what I just said does not give you license to go and do anything you like, and make a fool out of yourself or hurt other people. Remember how this goes. When you awaken to the fact that you're Absolute Reality, that you are Pure Awareness, that you are Consciousness, then you become everything. When you are aware that you're everything, you become master of all. Then when you are master of all, you may do anything you please. First you have to awaken to yourself. You have to understand your true nature, your swarupa. You have to realize who you are. When you understand that you are Consciousness, then you understand that you are everything. For Consciousness is not limited to yourself, your personal self. Consciousness is All-Pervading, Omnipresence. Therefore you know you're everything. You are the planets, you are the trees, the leaves, the bedbugs, the cockroaches, you're everything. The whole universe is you. When the whole universe is you, of course you are master of all. And then you can do anything you like.

But the paradox is, when you become that state, there is nothing you need to do. There's absolutely nothing you want to do, for you are all things. When you realize you're all things, what is there to do? It is only when you are limited to your body, or when you believe you are the body itself, then you want to do things, you want to achieve things, become things. When you realize you're Consciousness All-Pervading, you're already those things. You're everything in the universe. You are the universe. The whole universe emanates out of your Self. You then become God, and all the gods and goddesses will come to you with folded hands. For you have become That. So remember, I'm not giving you a license to do things as a human being. As a human being you have to behave yourself, be compassionate, loving, kind, helpful to others. But as Consciousness you have become others. You have become the epitome of compassion, of loving kindness, of bliss.

Consequently there's nothing to do. Do you follow that train of thought? If you're everything, what is there to do? Everything is already being done and has been done. So you keep still.

The question arises, "If everyone becomes free in this world, how will the world function?" People always ask me this. I have told you, do not concern yourself with this world. There is One that takes care of this world. When you merge with the One, you will understand this. So you do not have to keep running around, trying to improve world conditions any longer. Everything is as it should be. This is something you have to comprehend totally. Everything is in its right place. Everyone is where they belong, karmically speaking. There are no mistakes. None have been made, none are being made, none will ever be made. There is no past, there is no future. There is only this moment in which you live. In this moment ask yourself, "Who am I?" and see where you go. Remind yourself every day that you are not the doer. You are not the body nor the mind. Keep reminding yourself daily that you are Parabrahman, beyond Brahman. You are Choiceless, Effortless, Pure Awareness. You are Nirvana, the Ultimate Reality, the Ultimate Oneness.

The Three Virtues

There are three main virtues that you have to acquire
in order to become liberated.
There are three virtues that are most important,
most important for you to achieve,
before enlightenment.

Every enlightened person on this earth,
everyone who's been liberated has had these virtues.
You cannot be liberated without them.

The first one is compassion.
The second one is humility.
And the third one is service.

Compassion

What is compassion? Actually compassion is when you are reconciled with this entire universe. There's nothing in this whole universe that you are against. Think about that. Compassion means reverence for all of life, everything is alive, there is no such thing as dead matter. Everything has its own life. When you have reverence for life, you respect everything, you have no animosity towards anyone or anything. I'm not only talking about human beings, I'm speaking of the mineral kingdom, vegetable kingdom, and animal kingdom, the human kingdom. Have you ever heard of a sage or a liberated person, who was at odds with anything in this world? You have to come to terms with yourself.

Too many Advaita Vedantists, non-duality people, go around shouting, "I am one with this, I am one with that, everything is Absolute Reality," and yet they have so many bad habits. It's sort of paradoxical. So many times I tell you everything is karmic, everything is preordained, everything that has happened to you is preordained, you do not lift one finger that is not preordained for you to do. Yet, at the same time I'm telling you that you have to give up certain things, and develop higher qualities, which is right. For you would say to yourself, "If everything is preordained, why should I care about what I do, how I act, how I live, everything is supposed to happen anyway." This is true on one level, but then again, you have the total freedom to turn within and not to react to life's situations. You have that freedom. So, everything's preordained, and at the same time you have the freedom to turn within and find out to whom preordination comes to, by lifting up into a higher state of consciousness and becoming free. Therefore, compassion is very important.

I use myself as an example. I go to lunch with many of you, I enjoy going to lunch with you. But I do it out of a great compassion, a great compassion for you, because this gives you great pleasure. When I'm at lunch with some of you, you always see me taking a handful of vitamin pills. Before I came to Los Angeles I never took a vitamin in my life. But some of you heard about a so-called disease I may have, so you bring me vitamins and minerals, and pills and everything else. So I take these things for your sake, not for my sake, because of great compassion.

Approximately two years ago, someone came to my home at about four p.m. one Friday evening, rang the bell, I opened the door. There was this guy standing there with a big smile on his face, as if he'd known me all my life. He explained he met me once in 1958 in Bangalore in India at Papa Ram Dass' ashram. I didn't remember him. He also told me he came to my classes in Denver in 1975. But he felt so good about this, I told him I recognized him, I remembered him. He was passing through, so he came to see me. He wanted me to initiate him in Advaita Vedanta. I explained to him that I do not do initiations, I'm not a guru or a yogi or anything like that, and besides, you cannot get initiated into Advaita Vedanta, for it is non-duality. There has to be the initiator and somebody being initiated. There has to be a subject and object. And since there's no subject and no object, how can I initiate anybody?

But he didn't take no for an answer. He started beseeching me, he came a long way to see me, and I must initiate him. I explained to him again that I do not do this, I do not believe in this, and it has nothing to do with Advaita Vedanta. Why doesn't he go find a yogi or somebody like this who does initiations? The next thing he did, he took out $200 and put it down and said, "Here, initiate me!" I took the $200 and put it down and shoved it back in his pocket and explained to him I do not take money from someone I do not know, to be initiated. Finally, he got down on his knees and grabbed my legs and started crying, so what could I do? I was in a dilemma. So I told him OK. I put my left hand on his head and my right hand on his chest, and I said, "In the name of Advaita Vedanta you are now initiated into Pure Awareness." Now something happened to him. It's the first time I had seen anybody's hair stand up. It's as if a surge of electricity went through his body. And he stood up and smiled, and I was actually able to see myself as him. He really had been totally transformed. And he said goodbye and left, and I never saw him again.

Now, what is the purpose of this story? It has no purpose. It's just a story I add into this teaching, so time can pass faster.

I thought it was going to have to do with compassion.
No, no compassion at all, it had nothing to do with anything, it doesn't belong here at all. It's to make you see and understand that you have to break up your linear thinking. But to get back to compassion, you have to have compassion. I did actually have great compassion for this person, but I never use that word. It's a word to make you sort of understand what it is, to explain all these things.

Compassion is very important. Think of the times in your life that you could have had compassion and you didn't. For your thoughts interfered, and you came to the conclusion, based on the thoughts that came to your head. For instance, you see a homeless person who asks you for a couple of dollars or whatever. It makes no difference why he wants the couple of dollars, whether he wants to buy some whiskey, or he wants to buy some bread, or what he wants to do. It is your duty to help anyone who comes into your atmosphere. Anyone who comes into your life must be helped. It is no accident that this homeless person came to you. Do not turn him away, for by turning him away you are turning yourself away. This is compassion. Reconciling yourself with the whole universe, all of the kingdoms, animals. We should have a great compassion for every animal on this earth, whether they are ants or cockroaches, or goats or sheep or cows. If we had a compassion like this would we eat meat? We have to have a great compassion for the flowers, vegetation, everything that exists. We have to have a great compassion for all of the minerals on this earth, everything! This is reconciling ourselves with the entire universe. This is important.

Some of us wonder why we have been on this path for a long time and we do not seem to make much progress. It is because our compassion is not big enough.

Humility

Next we go to humility. Humility is very, very, important. Everybody wants to win a point, win an argument, win a fight, and yet if you have humility, it never comes into your mind to win or get even. Humility is karmic. Karma is like stepping on a rake and it hits you in the head; cause and effect. The cause is you stepped on the rake, the effect is the handle hits you on the head. This is our karma. Everything that goes around comes around. You step on the rake, but the handle doesn't hit you immediately, it may hit you years later or another incarnation, but you will get hit on the head. So there is immediate karma, and there's future karma. The only way to get rid of it is to have tremendous humility. Say somebody slaps you. The first thing our ego will tell us is to beat them up, slap them back, shoot them, kill them, get even with them. But if we're wise, we'll understand the reason we were slapped on the face. And of course, somewhere, somehow, this is the karma returning to us, and if we retaliate, we are setting new karma in motion, which will return to us later.

Therefore, anything that has ever happened to you in any area of your life, no matter how it looks, you are in your right place. No one is picking on you, no one is trying to do anything to you. No one is trying to hurt you. If you cooperate and do not react and do not retaliate, and send out a message of love and peace, then you transcend that karma and it will never come back again. But if you retaliate and you try to win the battle, you may appear to be winning the battle this instant, you may appear to be getting somewhere, but the fruits of your actions must return sooner or later. Therefore, you are playing games with yourself and you'll never get anywhere; you'll keep repeating the situation again and again and again, with different people, you may move to a different state, be involved in different situations, but you will find the same problems.

Therefore, whatever seems wrong in your life, whatever seems terrible, do not look at the problem in itself as a problem. Rise above it, realize no one is to blame for it, you have no enemies, no one is trying to hurt you. This is humility. You're not a coward, you're not a wimp. You have risen above that kind of thinking. That kind of thinking does not exist. That's why the story of Ramana Maharshi, when he went for a walk in the jungle one day, and he inadvertently stepped into a wasps' nest, and the wasps started stinging him, he didn't even pull his leg out, but he spoke to the wasps and said, "I deserve this, I invaded the house where you live and I deserve what you are doing to my leg, and if you want, you can attack the other leg." When he got back to the ashram from his walk, he was bitten all through the leg and had to put ointment on it. But he wasn't fazed one bit. He had a perpetual smile on his face, with the realization, "All is well."

Now look at your lives. Think of the things that bother you every day, that annoy you every day, the things that make you angry, that make you upset, that make you want to retaliate. Get rid of this.

Service

The third virtue is service. Our mission on this earth is to be of service to humanity. As you are trying to unfold, as you are trying to raise yourselves to a higher state to be liberated, to become totally free, be of service all you can, without looking for anything in return. Serve everyone you meet. Ask people what you can do for them to make their lives happier and brighter. Be of total service to everyone. It is written that the first shall be last and the last, first. If you try to put your ego up front, and you want fame and name and recognition, you will be beaten down all the time and you will have all kinds of problems that come with achieving fame and name.

In truth you are not the doer, the body, you are not the mind, you are total freedom. You are already liberated. But this is intellectual with some of us. Therefore, practice these three virtues and you will be amazed how fast you become free.

The Four Principles
of Jnana Marga

Feel in your heart that . . .

(1) Everything, everything, is an emanation of the mind.

(2) I was not born, I do not prevail, and I do not die.
There is no cause.

(3) Everything is egoless.
No thing has an ego or a cause.
No thing exists.

(4) Have a deep feeling of what Self-realization is,
by negating everything that it is not.
Not this, not this . . .

A Vision

I want to let you in on a little secret. There are no problems. There are no problems. There never were any problems, there are no problems today, and there will never be any problems. Problems just mean that the world isn't turning the way you want it to. But in truth, there are no problems. Everything is unfolding as it should. Everything is right. You have to forget about yourself and expand your consciousness until you become the whole universe. The Reality in back of the universe is Pure Awareness. It has no problems. And you are That.

If you identify with your body, then there's a problem, because your body always gets into trouble of some kind. But if you learn to forget about your body and your mind, where is there a problem? In other words, leave your body alone. Take just enough care of it. Exercise it a little, feed it right foods, but don't think about it too much. Keep your mind on Reality. Merge your mind with Reality. And you will experience Reality. You will live in a world without problems. The world may appear to have problems to others, but not to you. You will see things differently, from a higher point of view.

I had an interesting phone call this week. Someone asked me, "Do Self-realized people dream, or have visions?" Now, in order to have a dream or a vision, there has to be somebody left to have it, and yet, if you're Self-realized, there's nobody home. There's nobody left. So it's a contradiction, as truth is. All truth is a contradiction, it's a paradox.

The answer is, sages do dream sometimes, and have visions. But they're aware of the dreamer. In other words, they realize that they are not the person dreaming or having the vision. But as long as there's a body there someplace, there will be dreams and visions. Even though there's no one home, there will still, once in a while, be a dream or a vision.

As an example, Ramana Maharshi often dreamt and had visions. Nisargadatta dreamt and had visions. And they were both Self-realized. But again, the question is, "Who dreams? Who has the vision?" There's no ego left, as long as the dreamer is separate from the "I." I can only speak from my own experience. There's no difference to me in the waking state, the dreaming state, the sleeping state, or the vision state. They're all the same. I'm aware of all of them, but I am not them. I observe them. I see them happening. As a matter of fact, sometimes I cannot tell the difference. Sometimes I don't know whether I'm dreaming, or awake, or having a vision, or I'm asleep. It's all the same, because I take a step backward, and I watch myself going through all these things.

So, for some reason lately, I've been dreaming about the Queen of England. She was coming to satsang, I don't know why, for about three nights in a row. But I did have an interesting vision this morning, about four o'clock, and we'll spend the rest of the time discussing it, because I found it very interesting.

As many of you know, I have had a constant vision, periodically, of myself going to Arunachala, the sacred mountain where Ramana Maharshi lived. And the mountain is hollow in the vision. And I go through the mountain, to the center, where there's a bright light, a thousand times brighter than the sun, but yet it's pleasing and calm, and there's no heat. And then I meet Ramana, Jesus, Ramakrishna, Nisargadatta, Lao Tse, and others. And we smile at each other, we walk toward each other, and melt into one light, and become one. Then there's a blinding light and an explosion. And then I open my eyes. I've shared that with you before.

But this morning for the first time, I had a very interesting vision, which I'll share with you again. I dreamt I was somewhere in an open field, a beautiful field. There was a lake nearby, trees, a forest. And I was sitting under a tree, in this open field. And I had on the orange garb of a renunciate. I must have been a Buddhist.

All of a sudden, hundreds of bodhisattvas and mahasattvas come from the forest and start walking toward me. And they all sit down in a semicircle around me, in meditation. And I wondered what I was doing. Then I realized that I had become the Buddha. And we all sat in silence for about three hours.

Then one of the bodhisattvas got up and asked a question. He said, "Master, what is your teaching?" It was not in English. I don't know what language he spoke. But I understood it quite clearly. And without hesitation I said, "I teach Self-realization of Noble Wisdom." And he sat down.

We sat for about another three hours in silence, and then another bodhisattva got up and asked a question. "Master, how can you tell when one is close to Self-realization? How can you tell one is about to become Self-realized? How does one tell?"

And this is what I'd like to discuss today. How can we tell if we're on the path correctly? I gave four principles, which I really never do in the waking state. I never have a teaching. But I was giving a teaching, so I'll share it with you. I explained four principles, where you know that you're close to Self-realization. Of course, we're all Self-realized already.

Anyway, I explained these four principles to all the bodhisattvas and all the mahasattvas. Then we sat three hours in meditation and they got up and walked back into the forest. Then there was a flash of light, and I opened my eyes.

Principle Number One

You have a feeling, a complete understanding, that everything you see, everything in the universe, in the world, emanates from your mind. In other words, you feel this. You do not have to think about it, or try to bring it on. It comes by itself. It becomes a part of you. The realization that everything you see, the universe, people, worms, insects, the mineral kingdom, the vegetable kingdom, your body, your mind, everything that appears, is a manifestation of your mind. You have to have that feeling, that deep understanding, without trying to.

So you ask yourself, "What do I think about all day long?" Of course, if you fear something, if you worry, if you believe something is wrong somewhere, if you think you're suffering from lack or limitation, or sickness, anything, then you're out of it completely, because you're not understanding that all these things are simply a manifestation of your own mind. And if you worry about these things you become attached to false imagination. That's called false imagination. You've been attached to habit-energy for many years, and all these attachments and beliefs come from habit-energy.

Everything your senses show you is an emanation of the mind. You're projecting a picture, just like you project a moving picture, and everything you see right now, in this room, comes from your mind. You may say, "How can we collectively see the same thing?" That's because of the habit-energy that we're brought up in. So collectively we seem to be seeing the same thing, the same picture.

It's like watching a TV show and becoming one of the characters, when you know that you're not even in the TV. But you believe you're one of the characters in the TV show. So it is with the world. Do not get involved. I don't mean you become passive. I mean your body does what it's supposed to do. Remember, your body came to this earth to do something. It will do something without your knowledge. It'll take care of itself. Don't worry. But do not identify your body with yourself. They're different. Your body is not yourself. And I'll prove this.

When you refer to your body, what do you say? Don't you say "my body"? Who is this "my" you're referring to? You say "my finger," "my eye." Who are you referring to? You couldn't be talking about your body, because you're saying it's "my" body, like you own it. Who owns it? This proves to yourself that you're not your body. So do not identify yourself with the body and the world.

Therefore, the first principle, to see how close you are to Self-realization is: You are not feeling that you are identified with the world. You're separate. And you're feeling happiness, because your natural state is pure happiness. Once you identify with worldly things, you spoil it. The happiness disappears, it dissipates. But when you're separate from worldly things, happiness is automatic. Beautiful, pure happiness. It comes by itself. So that's the first principle.

Think about that! Everything in this universe, person, place or thing, everything, your body, your thoughts, creation, God, everything you can think about, everything, and I mean everything, is a projection of your mind. If you really understand this, how can you have a problem?

But you may say, "Well, my rent's due on the first, and I don't have any money, so how can this help me?" You would be amazed at what it does for you. Do the trees lack for leaves? Do the flowers fail to bloom? If you could realize the truth, that everything is an emanation of your mind, you would become your Self, and your Self is Omnipresence. It includes everything for the survival of your body. Think about that. Your body comes from your mind. But as long as you believe your body is yourself, and you understand that it comes out of your mind, it will be provided for, just like leaves are provided for the trunk of the tree.

So this teaching is quite predictable, and it can be used to improve your humanhood, not by trying to improve your humanhood directly. That's where you've got problems. But by forgetting about your humanhood, and realizing everything is a mental projection, again, what happens? When you realize that the whole universe is a manifestation of your mind, you become Omnipresence. And in the Omnipresence is contained all of your needs, and all of your needs are met from within. But, when you start worrying or thinking about it, you spoil it. Then you have to do human things to take care of you. But if you leave the humanhood alone, and go back to the understanding that it's all in your mind, you automatically let go of your mind and the Self takes over, bringing the right people into your life, the right situation, the right address.

Remember again, your body came to this earth because of karma. And it's going to go through whatever it has to go through. But you've got absolutely nothing to do with that, because you are not your body. But if you think about it, you spoil it. Subsequently, allow your body to do whatever it came here to do. Do not interfere. Do not fight. Simply observe. Do not react. You will be OK.

See, the secret is to think about these things as soon as you open your eyes in the morning. As soon as you open your eyes, what do you think about? You think about food, you think about your day, you think about work, you think about money, you think about friends, relationships, but you do not think about your mind being a projection of all the things that happen. Therefore, you have to think about the right things in the morning as soon as you awaken. Don't wait.

How do you work with these principles? As soon as you open your eyes in the morning—I'll speak in the first person—you have to say to yourself, "I feel and realize and understand that everything, everything—say everything twice—is a projection of my mind." Think about what that means. Forget about the other three. Work on that. "I feel that, I realize that, I understand that everything is a projection of my mind."

Then you may think about any problems, if you have any, and you say to yourself, "If everything is a projection of my mind, where do these problems come from?" You then realize, "Why, they came from me. I projected them. I created them." Then you say, "Who is this I that created them?" Now you're getting to the meaty part, to the substance. "Who is the I that created all this illusion in my life? Where did the I come from? Who gave it birth? My mind. Where did my mind come from? The I. They're both the same. The I and my mind are the same." It's a revelation. You think along these lines. "Where did the mind/I come from and to whom does it come?" You follow it deep, deep within yourself, and if you do it correctly, you will realize there is no I. There is no mind, so there are no problems. It will be over, and you will start laughing. You will actually start laughing at yourself. You'll start to think, "I fear this and I fear that." Once you get in that consciousness, something will happen to actually physically relieve you of that problem, or what you think is a problem.

As long as you believe in your mind that there's a problem—whether it is little or big doesn't matter, they're both the same—as long as you believe you've got a problem, you'll have a problem and it will grow and you can't change it. It may appear that you change it, but it turns into something else of a worse nature when you try to work with the problem itself. You never try to work with the problem, but ask where the problem came from. That's the problem. The birth is the problem. Because you believe you were born, you have the problem, and you can go on and on and on.

That's how you work with the principles. I feel, I under-stand, that everything, everything, is a projection, a manifesta-tion of my mind. Whose mind? My mind. Whose mind? Mine. My mind. Who am I who has this problem? And as you ask yourself this question, you will begin to feel better and better and better. You will actually begin to feel better, and as you begin to feel better, the problem becomes less and less important, and it will vanish. This is great psychotherapy. It works. If psychiatrists gave this to patients, they wouldn't have to give them any drugs.

It should be like second nature to you. When it's second nature to you, then you're going to find true happiness in your life, and reach your goals. But when you have to think about it first, it means your mind's impressed with something else. You've got other thoughts that you're thinking about most of the time. The first principle, again, is that everything, and I mean everything, the universe, the world, your body, your fears, your problems, your happiness, everything that you can think about, everything that your senses behold, is a manifes-tation of your mind. It's a mind quality. When you close your eyes, it goes away. When you sleep you transcend it. But when you are awake, the world exists. The world only exists because your mind exists, and your mind exists because your ego exists.

Therefore, when you begin to work on yourself, and you begin to realize that everything comes from your mind, you stop fearing, and you stop worrying, for you realize it's of the mind. And as you begin to change your mind, transcend your mind, annihilate your mind, bliss, happiness, peace, love, joy, truth, come all by themselves. It is the mind that is your enemy.

What is your mind? It is a conglomeration of thoughts about the past and the future. You worry about the past, and you worry about the future. That's all your mind is. It is not your friend. Therefore, ignore your mind. Do not believe what it says. Simply watch it, behold it, become the witness to it. But just to realize that everything is an emanation of your mind, that alone sets you free.

So, again, I ask you, "What do you remember?" You remember your personal problems, you remember your needs, and you think you're human. You think about the body continuously. That's why there is trouble with Self-realization. So you've got to investigate your mind, and watch it all the time. See what it's doing to you. Watch how it controls you. It makes you emotional, it makes you believe something is wrong. It makes you angry. All these things come from the mind. The idea is to be aware of this. The awareness alone leads you to the light; just being aware of that, alone. You don't have to know any book knowledge. Just be aware of what your mind really is.

That's how you conquer your mind. By being aware of it, and no longer responding to it. No longer to react to the mind. Something that usually makes you angry, before you would respond, and you'd want to win the argument, but now your reaction is no reaction. You simply smile and you watch. When your mind sees there's no response, it will become weaker and weaker, until it disappears. It's just like arguing with a person. What happens if you stop arguing? The person goes away. They don't know what to think. They just won't have anything to do with you. They just leave. So when you stop responding to your thoughts, your mind will go away, and become weaker, and weaker, and weaker, until there is no mind.

You understand, you feel, that everything is an emanation of your mind or it wouldn't exist. All existence, from the smallest nothing to the greatest cosmic galaxy—it all comes out of your mind. However, even if I tell you this, you still feel that something is real, don't you? You feel that something is real. You may say the sun is real. You may say that God is real. You may say that an atom is real, but you do not comprehend that you are creating these things. They're all a projection of your mind. If you didn't have a mind, you would not have these concepts. That's why we have to annihilate the mind, to kill the mind. No mind, no concepts.

And you have to practice Self-inquiry, by realizing everything comes out of your mind, asking yourself, "What is my mind? Where did it come from?" And you will realize that "I" is the mind, "I" is also the mind! Because you say, "I think," don't you see? "I think," and the mind is thoughts. So we get back to the "I" again. We always come back to the "I." Subsequently again, if you want to remove your mind, you remove the "I." You ask yourself again, "If the mind is I, then where did I come from? What is the source of this I? Who am I?" You always get back to the "I." Everything leads to the same thing, doesn't it? All the processes we use lead to the same thing. To "I."

The first principle: The whole universe is a projection of my mind. Then you say, "My mind. Who is 'my'? I'm referring to 'my' mind." And then again you tell yourself, "I am referring. I'm back to 'I' again. I am referring to my mind." Again you go back to, "Where did this 'I' come from? Who created it? What is its source? Who gave it birth?" And you keep questioning this way, again, and again, and again. And, as I said before, with most people, one day there will be like an explosion, and the "I" will blow itself to pieces. And you'll see light, tremendous light.

You'll become light. The light of a thousand suns. But that's not the answer. You have to go through the light, into Emptiness, into Nirvana, into Absolute Reality, which is called Parabrahman, Nothingness.

That Nothingness becomes Everything.

Principle Number Two

You have to have a strong feeling, a deep realization, that you are unborn. You are not born, you do not experience a life, and you do not disappear, you do not die. You are not born, you have no life, and you do not die. You have to feel this, that you are of the unborn. Do you realize what this means? There is no cause for your existence. There is no cause for your suffering. There is no cause for your problems.

Some of you still believe in cause and effect. This is true in the relative world, but in the world of reality there is no cause. Nothing has ever been made. Nothing has ever been created. There is no creation. I know it's hard to comprehend. How do I exist if I was not born, I have no life, and I do not disappear in old age? You exist as I Am. You have always existed and you will always exist. You exist as Pure Intelligence, as Absolute Reality. That is your true nature. You exist as Sat-Chit-Ananda. You exist as Bliss Consciousness, but you do exist. You exist as Emptiness, as Nirvana, but you do exist. So don't worry about being non-existent. But you do not exist as the body. You do not exist as person, place or thing. Do you feel that? If you have a strong feeling about that, then you're close to Self-realization.

Now go to the second principle and work on it just like the first. The second principle is: I perceive, I feel, I understand that I was never born. I am Unborn. I do not prevail. My existence does not exist, and I will never disappear.

Can you say I perceive or understand that I am unborn before the mind fully accepts it?
Whatever you can work with to let yourself know that you perceive or understand or feel.

Would it be more honest to say I am beginning to perceive?
There is no beginning. You can say, "There is something within me that perceives, or there is something within me that knows I was never born, I do not prevail, and I will never disappear. I am that one that knows. Start working on that.

What does this "I was never born" mean? I am unborn. It sounds like a contradiction because you believe your father and mother gave you birth. This appears to be true. Who gave them birth? My grandmother and grandfather. It goes all the way back. Who gave them birth? You go back to the beginning, way to the first man and woman and where did they come from? Who started this? Who started the human race? Who started the idea of birth? Now don't answer, because the mind will create answers, Adam and Eve, God. Somebody told you that. But is it true? Where did God come from?

Go back to the beginning. It is like asking what came first, the chicken or the egg? The tree or the seed? The man or the woman? Who made them? You will realize they don't exist. Nothing gave you birth. The whole origin of birth is false, it is a dream. It does not exist. Therefore, I do not exist the way I appear to be.

Then go back to the first premise. Who am I? You always go back to Self-inquiry. Who am I that exists? If I am not the body, am I my thoughts? I can't be my thoughts because they keep changing and changing. Then who am I? Keep silent for a while. You know it's working when you start to feel a quiet, loving feeling. You start to feel a peace you have not felt before. You start to feel that all is well.

If you do this often enough, you will feel a happiness you never felt before, and you won't care if a bomb is dropped on your head. You would feel this happiness because you would know you can't die. Right now these are just words. You will actually know, some day, that you can't disappear. Nothing can kill you. Kill is just a word. It means something that you have accepted. We make up words and put feelings behind them. Listen to the word, kill, kill, kill, kill, kill. It sounds ridiculous. The word itself has no power except the power you give it yourself.

When the mind is silent, then reality comes of its own accord. When you are thinking and thinking, the world has got you and you become worldly again. Self-inquiry causes the mind to be quiet.

After you work on that, you go on saying, "I do not prevail." You say to yourself, "You mean that my entire existence since I was a baby until I die, means nothing?" Then you say to yourself, "I have just proven I was not born. If I was never born, how can I prevail? What prevails? Who prevails?" You will see that it is the mind that prevails. The mind wants existence, wants strength, wants power. It makes you believe you are the body. Ask yourself, "To whom comes the mind? Who gave it birth? What is its source?" then keep still. You will begin to laugh because you will begin to feel, even if only for a moment, that there is no mind. You will actually feel no-mind. In the beginning it may last for a moment or two. As you practice every day, those moments of no-mind will become even greater.

Go on and say, "I will never disappear." Now you laugh again, because you realize that which never existed disappears. I am no-mind, so how can I disappear? This becomes very meaningful for you and as you do it every day, you become stronger and stronger in mindfulness, and something happens that's so beautiful that I can't describe it. You feel such love, such joy, such harmony, such bliss. Then you carry on.

Have a deep feeling, and a realization, that you are unborn, that you do not prevail, and you will never disappear. You will never die. Think about that. Just to think to yourself that you are unborn. There's no cause for your birth. Cause doesn't exist. There's no reason for your birth. You never are born. And as far as your existence is concerned, it's not there. You do not prevail from birth to death. There is nothing going on. *Absolute nothing.* And you do not get older, you do not disappear, or you do not die. Think about that. How free you'll become when you understand what this means. It's a beautiful feeling to know that you were never born, that you've always existed, but not the way you think you are. Your life as it is right now, whatever you think you're doing, however important it may be to you, is totally meaningless. Why? Because it'll be gone soon. So whatever you're getting into, whatever excites you, is only for a time.

Take Elvis Presley. People still remember him. But will anybody remember him five hundred years from now? Take your great classical musicians, concertos, Bach, Schubert, Rachmaninoff, everybody else; they're important to you right now, but five hundred years from now nobody will remember them at all. Everything will be so different it'll be like you're in another universe.

So the point is, if you get too involved in those things, you're missing the mark, because you're not understanding your real nature. You're not understanding who you really are. You should be searching for the meaning to yourself. And spending eighty percent of the time doing that. I know it's not easy to do for some people, because they seem to be involved in life. But yet, you can do it. It doesn't matter. You don't have to set aside a time for meditation. You can do it while you're driving your car, while you're at work, while you're playing music. Just be aware of yourself, of who you really are, and realize the rest is a projection of your mind. We're not born. We have no existence. In between the time we're born and when we die we really have no existence. And we do not die. There's no disappearance. To be aware of these truths sets you free. Just to be aware of them.

So how would you summarize it? That we are non-existent, or that we have no beginning and no end?
Both are right. We have no cause.

So you're saying that existence implies a relative cause, and existence only takes place in a relative world, and we're not really a part of that.
Yes, exactly.

And non-existence?
Non-existence also does not exist.

But then couldn't you say the mind doesn't exist? I mean you say that everything that exists. . .
Nothing that you can explain exists.

But earlier you said that everything emanates from the mind.
Yes, you're projecting the picture.

But then you have a mind.
You don't have a mind.

I think he means everything in the earth plane world.
In the relative world. In reality there's no mind. That's how the picture appears. The mind projects the whole universe. So if you get rid of the mind, there's no universe. We have to kill the mind. And the whole universe is annihilated, because it's the mind that projects the universe, and tells us all these stories.

Think for a moment of all the problems that you believe you have. Think of what's bothering you. You can tell me your story for four hours. This is wrong and that's wrong. It's all a projection of the mind. So by getting rid of the mind, everything stops, and beauty and joy and bliss ensue. But you're covering the beauty and joy and bliss when you worry, when you fear, when you think something is wrong someplace.

When you say you are unborn or you will never die, would that be the same as saying nothing exists?
Yes, it is. Nothing as you think or as it appears, exists. It appears to exist, but so does a dream. A dream appears very real. But is there a creation in a dream? Is there an end? Everything just begins, and ends when you wake up. The world is the same.

You should not say nothing exists, because even "exists" is an idea.
It's an idea. That's got to go at the end. In the beginning, when you're finding yourself, you realize that I exist. "I Am That, I Am" means I exist. Same thing. But then you find out who is the I that exists, and you follow it through. And that's

got to go. Everything has got to go. Now the average person will think, "If everything goes, what's left?" What's left is Everything. You are left, as your Self, and that's beyond explanation. Then you turn back to yourself and you become humble, compassionate, loving, because you are aware that you are the whole universe. And you can say, "All this is the Self, and I am That."

Is that an experience?
That's an experience. It's beyond experience. It's a revelation that stays with you all the time. That can be called Sahaja Samadhi, when you abide in the Self all the time. But that's ineffable, it's beyond words.

The experience doesn't matter how deep?
There's no such thing as deep. Deep is a mind concept. You're either That or you're not.

See, if you remember these things it will carry you across the ocean of samsara, into the land of Self-realization. But you have to think of these things all the time. The second principle is this: You are unborn, you do not prevail, and you do not disappear. In other words, you were never born, the life that you're experiencing does not exist, and you do not die. You have always been. What I am saying is, there is no cause for anything.

As an example, we speak about creation. How did creation begin? What is its cause? Of course the Bible will tell you Adam and Eve. That's a nice story, if you like stories. But if you're talking about reality, it just began out of nothing. What came first, the seed or the tree, the chicken or the egg? You can say to me, "I was born. My mother and father gave me birth."

Well, go all the way back. Who was the first mother and father, just like what came first, the tree or the seed? It's perplexing. The best way to explain it is, take a look at your dreams. How do you create a dream? Does it start with a beginning? As soon as you start dreaming, there's no creation. The dream just starts. Everything is already there. The trees, the sky, the earth, the flowers, the grass, people, insects, birds, flowers, everything just appears. Does it die in the end? You just wake up, and it's all gone. What we're doing now is living the mortal dream. We believe in our bodies, in our existence, as it were. We believe the world is real, the mind is real, our experiences are real, and we get involved in them, like we get involved in a movie. You know you're not the movie. You watch the movie, it ends, and you go home. The more you get involved in the world situations, and in yourself, the small self, your body or mind phenomena, the more you get pulled into ignorance.

You have to loosen yourself from this maya. And thinking every day that you are unborn, you have no personal life, and you do not exist, and you will not disappear, just thinking about these things does something to you. You begin to feel different. You begin to feel alive. But not as a body. As Omnipresence. You begin to understand what Moses said, when he said, "I Am That I Am." You begin to feel free, untarnished. Your past is dissolved, because it never existed to begin with. You have no past. There's no cause. It's all a manifestation of your mind. As you think about this, you become totally free.

Principle Number Three

You are aware and you have a deep understanding of the egolessness of all things; that everything has no ego. I'm not only speaking of sentient beings. I'm speaking of the mineral kingdom, the vegetable kingdom, the animal kingdom, the human kingdom. Nothing has an ego. There is no ego. And do you realize what this means? It means that everything is sacred. Everything is God. Only when the ego comes, does God disappear, what we call "God." Everything becomes God. You have reverence for everything. When there is no ego, you have reverence for everybody and everything.

So you have to be aware of the egolessness of all things. Animals have no ego, minerals have no ego, vegetables have no ego, and humans have no ego. There is no cause, so there cannot be an effect. There is only Divine Consciousness, and everything becomes Divine Consciousness. So if you look at your fellow man and animals and everything else as being egolessness, you will see them as your Self. Can't you see that?

It's the ego that causes separation. When I am full of ego, I become strong within myself. I become totally separate. So the more you like yourself as a person, the bigger your ego is. You say, "Well, I'm not supposed to like myself?" You're supposed to love yourself, but what self are we talking about? We're not talking about your body self, because that comes and goes. We're talking about your permanent Self, that has always been here. And your permanent Self is me, is you, is the world, is the universe, is everything. That's your permanent Self.

Egolessness. That's the only time when you can love your fellow human beings, when you have no ego. That's how you can tell where you are, if you're close to Self-realization. That's principle number three.

Something in me feels, understands, the egolessness of all things. All these principles are alike. Did you come to that conclusion yet? They all have the same source, nothing, but you have to work with them until you get there. I feel and understand the egolessness of all things. You say *all* things, not just some things, but *all* things, from the greatest galaxy to the minutest atom. Nothing has an ego. If it has no ego it has no source, because if it has an ego there has to be a source, and just by realizing this great truth you become free immediately. It blows your mind. It's like a Zen koan. All of a sudden something snaps in your mind, and your mind is gone because it has no source, since there's no ego. It never existed, and you feel so good.

Everything is egoless. Not only human beings, but everything. Mountains, trees, the sun, nothing has an ego. That means it has no existence. So where did it come from? When you have a dream, where does the dream come from? Same place. From nowhere. From false imagination.

I don't understand the expression "false imagination," because the word imagination implies a certain falsity.
You're imagining a false world and a false ego.

That's sort of a paradoxical saying.
Sure. It's all paradoxical. Because it doesn't exist. But that's how we imagine it. This is the reason I always go back to the sky is blue. Somebody takes me outside and says, "Look at the beautiful blue sky." And I agree with them, but I know deep inside that that's not true. There's no sky and there's no blue. It doesn't exist. Or the oasis in the desert. The water. It doesn't exist. It's a mirage. The world's the same thing. The universe only exists in the dream state. It's like a dream.

Can you say I Am is not the body?
Yes, you can say that. That's why I tell you not to use that

too much, because you make it too personal. You're still into yourself as an individual. When you read in textbooks, "I am not the body, I am not the mind," they're referring to the universal body and the universal mind. There is no body, nobody, no-o-o body. (everyone laughs) Nobody exists. That sounds ridiculous to the average person.

Now you may say, "What does all this do for me?" It does everything for you if you are creative in music, art or anything else. You'll become a better musician and a better artist without wanting to, without going after it. Your body will do what it's supposed to. There will be no karmic attachment. As an example, if you are a great artist or a great musician or a great carpenter, or a great loafer, or a great homeless person, and you go after it humanly, this is what is holding you to the earth, and you're going to have to come back again and again and again, because you made yourself earthbound, don't you see? Everything that you attach yourself to pulls you back to the earth, whether it's good or bad. If you hate something, it's the same as if you love something. It pulls you back to the earth. You've got to let go. It's just you're letting go because you know, "I am my brother, and my brother is me. I am everything."

Egolessness is at the basis of everything. Everything has no ego. Now I'm not just talking about sentient things. Everything. The mineral kingdom, the vegetable kingdom, the animal kingdom, the human kingdom, and so forth. There is no ego behind it. That means there's no cause for its existence. And just to understand this perfectly makes you live in the moment, all the time. It gets you centered. Think what that means to you personally, that there's no ego in back of anything. There's no cause for anything to exist. Like the dream again, is there a cause for the dream? All of a sudden you find yourself dreaming, and everything exists. Where did it come from? It came from the mind. It's a dream. And the only way to get out of the dream is what? To wake up! So this is also a sort of a dream. It has no substance. Everything is transient. No ego in back of it.

I don't quite understand there being no ego and there being no cause as being the same.

The ego is what makes something real. The reason your body is doing what it does is because of your ego. That's the cause of your body function, the ego. So if there's no ego, there's no lack, there's no limitation, there's no sickness, there's no death, there's nothing like that.

Are the ego and the mind the same, or are you making a distinction?

They can be synonymous, in a way. Take for instance, you've got a sickness of some kind. If you realize there's no ego in back of it, there's no cause, where did it come from? It didn't come from anything, so it doesn't exist.

So, could you also just say nothing exists?

But is it meaningful for you when you say that? See, it has to be meaningful for you. If you say nothing exists, your mind and your ego will come and fight you and say, "What do you mean? Look, the chair is solid. It exists." So you become disappointed. But when you understand the entire principle, that everything is egolessness, everything, then you just exist in the moment, like that (snaps his fingers). You exist in the second, in the moment, and in that moment all is well, and everything is unfolding as it should, in that moment. But as soon as you start to think, then there's a cause.

So the only cause is the thinking process.
Exactly. And you may think it's hard to do, to think like that, to be like that, but it's not. Just by remembering the egolessness of all things will wake you up. And you will become free.

You have to have a deep realization, and a deep feeling, that no thing has an ego. No thing has a cause, again. There's no reason for anything to be. No thing really exists. You are not a sinner. You are not an evil person. Your past is dead, forget it. You're born again, now, and all is glory and joy. This is what it means to be born again, to realize that you exist now, in this moment. Not a moment ago, and never mind what's going to happen a moment from now. But you exist in this moment as Pure Intelligence, Unqualified Love, Absolute Reality, Unconditioned Oneness. That's you. You live in that reality. And again, that sets you free.

Principle Number Four

Principle number four is simply this: You have a deep conviction, a deep understanding, a deep feeling, of what Self-realization of Noble Wisdom really is. What is Self-realization of Noble Wisdom to you? You can never know by trying to find out what it is, because it's Absolute Reality. You can only know by finding out what it is not.

So you say, it is not my body, it is not my mind, it is not my organs, it is not my thoughts, it is not my world, it is not my universe, it is not the animals, or the trees, or the moon, or the sun, or the stars, it is not any of those things. When you've gone through everything and there's nothing left, that's what it is. Nothing. Emptiness. Nirvana. Ultimate Oneness.

You say, "I perceive and understand what realization is. I know, something within me understands and feels what Self-realization is," and you keep still. Believe me, the answer will come to you. The only way you can find out is through negation. So you can say to yourself, "It's not the sun because the sun is a projection of my mind. It's not the moon." Same thing. "It's not my husband or my wife, it's not my body or my organs. It's not peace. It's not the war." Everything you name, it's not. When you get tired of naming things, you keep silent, and that's what it is. Everything is Silence. The four principles and the Silence are all the same. Now, what's number four?

It has something to do with "we are nothing."
(laughing) Everything has to do with that. But it's actually to have an understanding, and a deep realization, of what Self-realization of Noble Wisdom is.

And how is noble wisdom defined from regular wisdom?
It's the same thing. Just more wordy. It's a Buddhist expression.

They have all these real long expressions. And then they say what it is.
The eight-fold path. And then they take years explaining it. But when you get into the highest teaching there's nothing. So the fourth one is, the only way to know what Self-realization is, is by knowing what it is not. And whatever is left, that's what it is. So you say it's not the body, it's not the mind, it's not my organs, it's not my thoughts, it's not the world, it's not

the sun, it's not the universe, it's not God, it's not creation, and you go on and on and on. When you get out of breath and out of words, that's it.

Is that what the expression "neti, neti" means?
Yes.

Is it boring? If all that goes away, and there is nothing?
(laughing) No! See, that's what people think. That's why I explained before, the mind will make you say that because it doesn't want to be annihilated. It wants to rule you and control you completely. Because that's its nature. That's the nature of the mind that doesn't exist.

When you're meditating, are you totally separate from this physical world?
When who's meditating? When I'm meditating personally? Well, I don't usually meditate. I sit sometimes with my eyes closed but I just rest my eyelids.

Because there's no one there, right? There's no one to meditate.
There has to be someone to meditate. That doesn't mean you should stop meditating. It means you should look at these four principles and compare them to where you are yourself, and work on yourself so that you can apply these principles to yourself everyday, until the day comes when you don't have to talk about it any longer. You just become a total manifestation of those principles. You just realize; you become aware.

Now, what's the fourth principle?
None of these principles exist.

You're right. I usually don't do this. But I'm giving you these principles to help you. (Robert laughs) Right. They don't exist. But as long as you believe your body exists, they exist also. As long as you feel the world exists, and your body exists, and the mind exists, then the principles also exist. And karma exists, and God exists, and creation exists.

You have to have a strong feeling and realization of what Self-realization means. And what's the only way you can do that? Remember?

Practice the other three principles?

That helps. By realizing what it is not. You can't know what Self-realization is because you are already That. But you can know what it's not. So, by eliminating everything, then what is left is Self-realization. You can't explain it, so you negate it. In other words, you think of what it isn't. Self-realization is not the world, it's not the universe, it's not my body, it's not anything I can think about. It's not my mind. Then what is Self-realization? Whatever answer comes to you is wrong, for it has no answer. There are no words that can describe it. Forget about your intelligence. Human intelligence sucks. It doesn't exist. Why? Because it dies with you. We're talking about something that's eternal, that has always been, and will always be.

You have to become aware of these principles. I give you these things with great compassion, that you have something to do every day besides watching TV or reading comic books. Think, but not intellectually.

You Are Not the World

This is not a formal talk. I can only tell you about my own experiences, not what I read. I can tell you that nothing exists the way it appears. Everything is appearance. The trap is, that we get pulled into the appearance. We react to it. We feel hurt. We feel slandered. We feel something is wrong. We have negative emotions because we are falling for a false premise—that the world is real.

In fact, the world is not real and neither are you. What we have to do is stop reacting to anything. The only way to do that is to discover who you are. When you discover your true nature, everything becomes perfectly clear. You are at peace. If something works out, it works out. If it doesn't, it doesn't. Your feelings have been transmuted. You never even feel what human beings feel. You just have a great love and compassion for all things. You know that the substratum of all existence is harmony, peace, emptiness. You feel wonderful all the time. What can disturb you if you are at peace? If you find true peace, what can possibly disturb you?

The world comes and goes. One day it is like this, the next day, it is like that. But what does it have to do with you? Nothing. You are free, you are not the world. You are not your body, you are not your mind. You are total freedom, total joy, total love. You have to awaken to this fact—it's truth.

We speak many words and take many actions, but to what avail? Does it matter in the end? We build our life, we earn positions, we father children, and what happens at the end? Poof! It's all gone. Everything disappears. (Robert laughs) There is nothing. So what's the purpose?

People say, "I must leave this world better for my children." They are dreaming. The world will never be better or be worse. The world is a dream of existence; like this one day, like that another. But you are not the world. Awaken to that fact.

You are not your thoughts, you are not your karmic expressions, you are not your inclinations from past lives.

Things appear real as long as you believe in them. If I believe in the devil, the devil would appear to me. I would create him myself. If you believe in God, your god would appear to you. Ramakrishna believed in the goddess Kali. Kali became very real to him. He used to dance and sing with Kali. (Robert laughs) He created Kali. That is why no one else saw Kali but him. That is how we create our lives.

Think of the things you fear in your life. You fear becoming sick. You fear poverty. You fear getting divorced, you fear getting married. Whatever you fear is a concept created by your own mind. There is no question of should I get married or shouldn't I get married. It doesn't matter. What matters is how you react to it and what you expect of it. This is true in every aspect of your life. That is what you have been trained to believe since you were a little kid. Your teachers brainwashed you, your parents brainwashed you, the outside world brainwashed you, and here you are.

You are filled with ideas, concepts, emotions, attitudes, and that makes you what you are—miserable. (laughter) As soon as you wake up, all that disappears. Nothing can ever happen to you of a destructive nature. There is absolutely nothing that can destroy you. You cannot be destroyed. Your body may appear to vanish, but that is like a dream. You dream that you are doing something, then you get shot and disappear. Then you wake up.

My question to you is, "What do you believe about yourself and about the world? What is most important to you?" I feel that a true spiritual path should be the first thing of importance in your life. Why? Because it wakes you up. No matter how good a life you live, you may become the richest and most famous person on earth, you'll have to experience the other side of the coin one day and be the poorest, most miserable person on earth. That's the way it works. You may say to me, "My neighbor never has any problems. It's like he fell into a pot of gold. Everything he touches turns into money. He's as happy as a horse. He's got a beautiful wife, a big house, everything he could possibly need, and look at me! You know, that guy's life hasn't changed for forty years."

You're making your own conclusion. He has earned this karmically, and if he doesn't pull away from it, he might spend his whole life in goodness, human goodness. But then he will be drawn back again by the law of karma, which is in his mind and he doesn't know it, and next time he will be a homeless person. Whatever he does, he won't be able to make a dime. He'll try his best, but he'll always be poverty stricken. He won't be able to earn a dime no matter how hard he tries. This is why we should never judge. You have no idea what your neighbor's going through. Never say he or she has a wonderful life and look at mine. Why am I poor, why am I sick, why am I this way or that way. The idea is to wake up, not to look at yourself, not to feel sorry for yourself, not to compare yourself with others, but to awaken.

When you awaken, something happens that is unexplainable. There are no human words to explain it. When you awaken you just understand, you know, you feel—and these words are inadequate—you become Divine harmony. You are no longer fooled by person, place or thing. You no longer react.

As an example, someone tells you that you won the lotto, you won fifty billion dollars. You do not become a slave to that. Someone tells you that you lost fifty billion dollars. Same thing, same reaction. You do not become a slave to that. What happens in the human life does not matter. When you know who you are, you do not say it doesn't matter. You simply exist. You exist as yourself. You're at peace. No one can ever take the peace away from you no matter how hard they try. You are not fooled by things.

What you do is deal with yourself. You can give of yourself because you become your living self. Therefore, you can give yourself away and you're still there, for you've become the Infinite Self, the Divine Mother, Omnipresence, Total Oneness with all things. So you can give of yourself, and yet you're always there.

When Ramana Maharshi was being robbed, his devotees wanted to attack the robbers, and he said, "No, no, no. It's our dharma to be what we are, and it's their dharma to be what they are. We should not interfere with their dharma, therefore give them what they want." That's very profound. We are spiritual people. The world is not. We act in accordance with spiritual principles.

What this really means is that we, as human beings, become last, not first. That's what Jesus meant when he said, "Those who go first will be last, and those who are last will be first." You have to develop great humility. Do not long for anything. Do not want to be rich, or famous or great, and do not say, I want to be poor and have nothing, either. They're both wrong. Just be yourself. When you are yourself, you will be amazed how the universe takes care of you.

It's like the body with vitamins and medicines. Your body is a natural healing factory and able to heal itself. When you start taking too many vitamins, when you start taking medicines too much, the body says, "Well, you've made that into your God, so now you have to depend on it." Then you have to keep taking vitamins for the rest of your life or you get sick. Think about that.

You've got to depend on yourself to take care of everything. Now, your Self is yourself. There's one Self, so we take care of each other. Did you ever think of that? When you think of others you're making a mistake. The feeling will come to you one day that you are all others. There are no others, there is just the Self appearing as others. So, how do you treat others? As you treat yourself. You don't think about it. You don't think that that person's worthy and that person's not, so I'm going to help this person, not that person. You give of yourself automatically. You do not think about it because everything is yourself, and that includes the mineral kingdom, the vegetable kingdom, the animal kingdom, the human kingdom, and everything else you don't understand. They're all part of the One. What you do to the One, you do to everything. How you treat one person is how you treat the whole universe because everything is One.

Now, these four principles I gave you have to do with all these things. You're supposed to ponder these things.

You Are Not Your Problems

Most of us have been searching for reality for many years. We've been to many teachers, many groups. But we still haven't found peace. Why? Because we're searching. That's a direct, succinct answer. Because we're searching for something. No matter how many times I emphasize there's nothing to search for, people still search. Sometimes it would be better if we tore up all the books. Books are only to motivate us, to make us know there's something else. But there comes a time when we have to go within and try to understand what this body really is. The truth, of course, is not a teaching. I do not philosophize. I do not give a teaching, as a rule. I simply give a confession, and to most people it means nothing. But we're not trying to attract most people. Those who feel something in their heart will always come to satsang. And you'll always attract a teacher that is more to your liking.

I do not consider myself a teacher or a guru. I do not consider myself anything at all. But, the Reality that is left over is your reality. It is Omnipresence. There is one Unqualified Reality, and this is it, right here, right now. There are no bodies here. What you see is your own business. When you see others, you're making a mistake. There never were others. We're always looking for something. We want to find the right teacher. The right teacher is where you are. Person, place or thing is not the right teacher. You probably saw the movie *Siddhartha*, where he found the river and the peace of the forest. Even that's a mistake, because he took the river seriously, and made too much of the forest. He was the forest. He was the river. What we're seeking is utter foolishness. There's nothing to seek.

I get so many calls. People tell me their problems all the time. And I really don't know how to respond. To whom shall I tell my problems? There just are not any problems. There are no problems. You may say to yourself, "If he only knew my problems." But, if you live in the moment, is there a problem right now, this second? There's nothing. Nothing is your real nature. A problem begins only when you start thinking. But if you learn not to think, where's the problem? So, we have to empty the mind, and then get rid of the mind. And we cannot empty the mind by thinking. Only by observation. Only when there is no thought is there reality. There's no sense saying to yourself, "I am Parabrahman, Absolute Reality. I am unborn."

Those are just words. And the next moment you have a problem, you have an emotion. You feel something is wrong. But you keep declaring, "I am unborn. I am the Absolute Reality." It is better to say nothing, to believe nothing, to be nothing, and that's just being yourself. It's better just to sit, and think of nothing and try to become nothing, than it is to chant mantras, or to make affirmations, or to keep saying, "I am Brahman." Just by sitting, you will become yourself.

Can you say the Self is real or is 'real' a term that doesn't exist?
If you say the Self is real, you don't really mean it. If you meant it you wouldn't have to say it, but you can say it when you are truly yourself, because it makes you feel better. It helps you live. It's better than saying that my world is real or my problem is real. It's better to say the Self is real than to say that.

What is better than that, to say nothingness is real?
Keep silent. Say nothing. When you ask yourself the question, "Where does my mind come from or where do my problems come from," and you keep still, that's real. The emptiness is real.

Isn't the emptiness the same as the Self?
Yes, but when you speak, you spoil it to an extent.

That's right because the Self doesn't know.
When you say the Self is real, that becomes personal. When there's silence, it becomes omnipresent.
Silence is always the best policy after you say all those things to yourself. It's in the Silence that your problems just

dissolve. Try it. It really works. When you keep still after saying a lot of these things, your problems will dissolve by themselves. Do not think, "I am getting rid of my problems," because that enhances the problems. Do not think about the problems at all, but work on yourself to see your own reality, and in reality there are no problems.

We can also note that to most people, no matter how many times I say this, their problems are very real to them. The problems hold them like a vice. They really feel their problems. To those people I say, "To the extent that you can realize that your mind is creating these problems, in reality you are mindless." To that extent the problems begin to dissolve." Repeat this when you wake up, when you open your eyes in the morning. Do not go through the four principles all at once. Take one at a time, even if you don't get to the second that morning, and spend an hour or two working on the first one, that is good. You can do these things all your life if necessary instead of worrying about your problems. Take them one at a time.

There are two things that you said which I had difficulty with. One of the things you said is, never deal with a problem.
Right.

And I know we should concentrate on the positive things you were speaking about, that's the essential teaching, to stress all the ideas you already talked about today. But still, in this period of life that we have, as we make these statements, as we move towards this goal which I can accept, still there is the life to be lived. There are issues to deal with. So it seems to me that when you say, don't deal with the problem, this leads to enormous problems.

On the contrary. You're separating both. You're putting them into categories. There's only One. As an example, say somebody cheated you, and you sue them in court. When you sue somebody and you're getting involved in something like that, you're sending up an energy. Even if you win the case, you're going to have to sue somebody else and then sue somebody else, and it never stops. You've set up a pattern for yourself. But if you go about it the other way, and if you know the truth about yourself, you also know the truth about the guy who cheated because you both are One.

Robert, let me give you another example. Let's say that we all stay here and we have no money. Tomorrow we're all hungry in the morning, and we say we're not going to deal with this problem, but because our hunger is so great and keeps mounting, we really can't think of anything else. Eventually, we can't think of any of these ideas that you told us about because we're so extremely hungry.

Your first premise is wrong. It doesn't work like that. It would never work like that. If you're hungry, something will happen to appease your hunger. What you're thinking about is that you sit down and you do nothing. It doesn't work like that. When you know the truth, somebody will knock on the door and bring you food.

Something will take care of you. When you came to this earth, everything was predestined. And everything is aware of how to take care of you, and what you're going to go through. But it has nothing to do with you. The secret is not to react. Just do what has to be done. And you will do what has to be done. You can't help it.

I brought up the example a week or two ago about the holocaust, and remember I said how the attitude of the Jewish people and especially the Rabbis was that God is living in Nazis, God has manifested himself through Auschwitz and the others, and so we must go along with this. Would you say that's the attitude the Jewish people should have had?

On the contrary, because that's an attitude. I'm not talking about attitudes. I'm talking about realization. Reading the Bible and making quotations is one thing. Being a living embodiment of the Truth is another thing.

There's a difference in knowing the Truth, and just letting yourself be walked on. This does not mean you become a rug for somebody to step on you. You become a doormat for no one. You are abiding in the Self. When you abide in the Self, everything will be OK. You're not a coward. You're not running from anything. You're abiding in the Self. When you abide in the Self, if you have to pick up a sword and fight, you will. If you have to run, you will. But you will do what you have to do. But it has nothing to do with you. It's different than you think. It's not like you think.

Then, you're saying to deal with the problem.

On the contrary, if you become the truth, the problem will take care of itself.

Yes, but you're speaking of a state to which we are aspiring, and I believe that would happen, but we're not in that state. We are not fully in that state because we cannot fully grasp it and manifest it.

If you take it personally, and you work on yourself as I said, you will do what's right. You will not be passive.

Theoretically, it all makes sense. In actual practice is where I get confused.

If it made sense it wouldn't be the truth. (everyone laughs)

So you didn't exactly say, don't deal with the problem, just realize that the body doesn't really exist. Your body will do the right thing by itself.

As long as you're aware that it has nothing to do with you, you are not your body, you are not your mind, you are not the situation, you are free from it.

Remember what Christ said when he said, 'Put you first the kingdom of Heaven and all the rest will be added unto you'. Isn't that something you're saying?

That's right.

I have no argument with the concept, the idea, the goal, and the abstract reality. I am talking about the interim period that we live in our daily lives during the day. That's why I bring up these problems, and the food as examples of what we have to deal with every moment.

Your body and mind are motivated by karma. The law of karma takes care of them. But you are not your body. If you are aware that you are not your body, the right action will ensue.

You mean you can be aware that you're not your body, yet your body will go out and get food.

Exactly.

But you would know that you are not the doer. If you are aware, those are key words, if you are aware that you are not the body. I would say from my understanding that there are degrees of awareness. If you are completely, absolutely, totally and wholly aware that you are not the body, then I grant you that. But there are these degrees of awareness, and if you are not at that particular state, then you must render to Caesar what is Caesar's.

In reality, there are no degrees. You either are or you're not. If you think you're not, then you have to fetch for yourself. If you think you are, you'll think about these things, and then you'll go and do something. But you won't be doing it. It will do itself. See, when you say it's not me doing it, you believe that you are the one, you are the body. You don't say it's not me doing it. You ask the question, "To whom does it come?" There's a difference. It keeps the me out of it completely.

What kind of answer can one expect when you ask who is it for?

No answer.

So, therefore, the action would be non-personal.

Exactly. If there's an answer, it's the wrong answer. See, all these years we've been dealing with a finite mind, with our own intellectual processes, with our preconceived ideas, with our concepts. But I'm saying we have to transcend those, and use a new part of us that we've never used before. And that's the Self. So when you abide in the Self, everything will be OK. Everything will work out. It has nothing to do with being passive, or being violent or anything else. It's a completely new ball game. You're on God's team, and you're well taken care of, but it's different. There are no words to explain it.

You have to go inside to understand it.

Yes, you have a deep understanding, and a deep knowledge, that all is well and everything is unfolding as it should.

That's what I was going to say. Robert was telling us before about not being the doer, the realization that you are not the doer is what Christ was talking about. That is, you dwell on the Self, on Self-realization, and your body will continue to do whatever is necessary karmically, but your realization that you're not the body and you're not the doer doesn't mean it doesn't get done.

Well, now we're getting down to the nitty gritty. Then what you're suggesting is this. Let's talk about tomorrow morning. My body-mind says go out and try to find some money to get breakfast, but all the time that I'm doing this I can still think that I am not doing this. I am not going to be getting the money. I am not going to be eating it.

No, no, no. When you work on the principles and you are hungry in your body, you will automatically, spontaneously go get food, but you won't dwell on it. Your mind will be somewhere else.

Take my life, for instance. When I get up in the morning, I have no idea what is going to happen that day, but I am acting and interacting. I do certain things, but not purposely; it happens spontaneously. I didn't ask to teach classes like these. It happened. I never asked for anything. It happens because my body does it, spontaneously. My mind is not aware, involved. I don't plan, except maybe to spend a couple of hours in Venice. But I have no long range plans. Everything works out. I know it is hard to perceive this.

My second point is related to that. You quoted Ramana telling his devotees to give to the robbers, but couldn't his karma have been to protect?

It was not his dharma, his way, his truth.

Another teacher could have told his followers to kill the robbers.

That's right. In the Bhagavad Gita, Krishna told Arjuna to fight. It depends on the path you are on. Notice that Krishna did not have to fight. He told Arjuna to fight. When you get to the highest there is peace. There is no need to do anything. In the martial arts, when one becomes proficient to the highest degree, they do nothing. They don't even defend themselves. They go the other way. They accept being killed. Arjuna was not up there.

The highest teaching is that everything is being taken care of. Ramana, as a boy, would have died if it were not for this mysterious power that took care of him. He went into the jungle and into a cave and sat there. He didn't know where his food would come from. He didn't even think about it. It didn't enter his mind. He just sat there for days until a woman came to help and started to feed him. If you have trust and faith, there is a mysterious power that will take care of you and supply all you need.

But while you are paying attention to the Spirit, you must function in the world and deal with problems.

You are speaking from your own point of view. You are speaking of appearances. This is how you see it now. But it is not like that.

I first came because someone said it would be a good thing to do. It just happened. I didn't go to him asking for places to see. Yet, each week I have to consciously arrange to come here. Both energies exist on the same plane simultaneously.

No. This plane you speak of doesn't exist. As long as you believe it does, it does, because you are creating it. You give it its power. You are its power source. When you take the power away, everything just is.

When you realize you are not the doer, your body will do whatever it has come to earth to do. Your body follows karma. But your body is not you. That can only be experienced. To most people this is ridiculous. All that I have said does not mean a thing. Most people want something practical, to accentuate the humanhood in them. The highest truth is that humanhood does not exist. When you come to that conclusion, your life will be bliss.

So what you're also saying then, is in predestination, the soul chooses to be born in a particular time or to a particular life in order to continue with its existence.

That's part of the appearance. And if you believe in your body, and you believe in your mind, then karma is real, and predestination is real. But if you abide in the Self, everything else becomes redundant. But in the meantime on this earthly plane, or this particular plane, one way of describing it is predestination. The answer is there, but if you look at it as a continuum, it's part of the four principles. Nothing appears in the beginning, no end.

And if you become realized, you can get off the karmic wheel.

Yes, exactly. To put it in an easier point of view so you can understand it, if you believe in your body, again, if you believe in your mind, if you believe that you are a body, then everything else exists; karma, God, creation, everything exists. But when the realization comes to you that I am not the body, and I am not the mind, everything disappears. Like the four principles. So that's why the secret is to practice abiding in the Self. Then everything else will happen by itself. You don't try to get rid of your karma, or get rid of the negative situation, because that's like cutting off a tumor on one arm and it grows back on the other arm. You go right to the source, the Self. And then everything is resolved.

What Does Jnana Marga Teach?

Please do not be shocked at some of the things I may say. I am not a teacher, nor am I a lecturer, nor am I a minister. I am merely a looking glass, so that you can see your own reflection. What you think of yourself, you see in me. I may say certain things you're not used to. Bear with me. You should not accept anything I say, nor should you believe anything I say, until you're able to prove it to yourself. I simply give my confession, that I am not the body nor the mind, nor the phenomenal world, that I am Pure Intelligence, Absolute Reality, Sat-Chit-Ananda, Divine Mind, Unborn, Emptiness.

When I use the word "I Am," I am not referring to Robert. I am referring to "I Am That, I Am," Omnipresence, the Infinite.

I get lots of phone calls from people asking me all kinds of questions. One question that most people keep asking again and again is, "What can I do to resolve my problems? Can you give me an affirmation, a mantra, a meditation, a breathing exercise, something I can use?" These things have their place, but they will not awaken you to your true Self. In all of the higher scriptures it is written that the path of Advaita Vedanta, or Jnana Marga, is only for mature souls.

Now what does that mean? It is for those who, in a previous lifetime, have already practiced sadhanas, breathing exercises, yoga techniques, etc., and now they're ready to awaken through this type of teaching. And the Buddhist scripture declares that those who want to do yogas, or breathing exercises, are the simple minded and ignorant. (Robert chuckles) Now, what do they mean? They don't mean to insult you, but they are referring to those who are attached to the world, those who believe the world is real, and who feel the pull of the world. They want to use all kinds of gimmicks to free themselves from their problems, but not to be totally free.

Now, what does Jnana Marga teach? We teach simply this: not to accept anything, unless you can demonstrate it. Not to believe anything, unless you can demonstrate it. Not to believe anything, unless you can use it for yourself, and you can see it's true. To do affirmations, mantras, yoga exercises and so forth, will not awaken you. You start from the beginning. You simply admit to yourself that you exist. This is the truth. You do exist, don't you? So you say to yourself, "I exist. I know that for sure. I exist. I exist. That's all I know. I'm ignorant of everything else, but I do know that I exist, because here I am." And, as you keep saying this to yourself, "I exist," you begin to put more space between the "I" and "exist." "I . . . exist."

If you're doing this correctly, you'll soon find that "I" and "exist" are two separate words. In other words, you'll come to the conclusion that you exist as I. You'll have to ask yourself, ponder, "Who is this I that exists? What is I?" You never answer. It will come to you of its own accord. When you sleep and you awaken, you say, "I slept." When you dream you say, "I had a dream." And when you're awake, of course, you say, "I am awake." But that I is always there. You start to inquire within yourself, "What is this 'I' that exists at all times? It exists when I'm asleep, when I'm awake, when I dream. Who is this 'I'?" And now the inquiry starts. "Where does this 'I' come from? From whence cometh the 'I'?" You ask yourself. The answers are within yourself. And you keep asking yourself, over, and over, and over, and over again, "From whence cometh the 'I'? Where does the 'I' come from?" Or, again, "From whence cometh the 'I'? Where does the 'I' come from?" Or, "Who am I?" And you wait a little while, and you repeat the same question, "Where does the 'I' come from?"

While you're doing that, you follow the "I" deep, deep, within. You keep following the "I." You go deeper and deeper into the "I." Where does this 'I' come from? Who is this 'I'? Whatever answer comes to you is the wrong answer. Do not accept it, but do not deny it. You simply put it aside. And you continue with the Self-inquiry. "Who am I?" And you wait. And you ask again, "Who am I?" It is not a mantra. "Where did the 'I' come from? How did it get there? Who gave it birth? What is the source of the 'I'?" You continue to abide in the "I."

As you continue this process, someday something will happen. To some people it comes like an explosion within where all your thoughts are wiped away. For you see, "I" is the first pronoun, and every thought that you have in the world, is attached to the "I." It is secondary. Think about that. Whatever you have to say about yourself has "I" in it. Everything in the world is about yourself. "I" am going to the movies. "I" am going bowling. "I" feel like crying. "I" feel terrible. "I" feel wonderful. "I" feel sick. "I" feel well. There's always an "I," "I," "I." What is this "I," and what is it all about? Everything is attached to the "I." Subsequently, when the "I" is wiped out, everything else is wiped out, and the troubles are over. All thoughts go with the "I."

Now, there's no answer to "Who am I?" When you get to the answer there will be emptiness, a void. You will be of the unborn. But it is not a void like you think. It is not emptiness like you think. For want of a better word you can call it Godliness, Nirvana, Sat-Chit-Ananda, Bliss Consciousness, Absolute Reality. It doesn't matter what name you give it. You will become That, and there will be no explanation. You will just become That, and you will feel a profound peace that you have never felt before. You will feel a bliss that is unqualified. You will try to explain it to yourself and to your friends, but you cannot. For the finite cannot comprehend the Infinite. There are no words.

That's the method you use. Self-inquiry. You follow the I-thought to its source. How long does it take? It depends on yourself, how sincere you are, what else you're doing with your life. If you're using this like you do everything else—for instance if you say, "Well today I'm going to practice the I-thought, then I'm going to go to a movie, then I'm going to go bowling, then I'm going to watch TV, then tomorrow I'll do the same thing," of course, what's going to happen in a case like that? Very little. But if you put your energy into it, and you practice it every chance you get, and you put this first in your life, you will see amazing results. Amazing results. But you have to put it first in your life.

Think right now. What is first in your life? Don't tell me but just think. What comes first in your life? Can you take it with you when you die? Don't you see by now that you live in a world of constant change? That the only thing permanent in life is change. All facts change. Only truth is real. And truth is personal. For the sincere devotees or students, they will put this first in their life, and then they will start seeing results. You have to find it for yourself. But if you're still worrying, and fearing something, and you think other duties come first, then you've got to work on yourself.

That's why, with great compassion, I give you certain things you can do before you get into Self-realization. Just before you become Self-realized, you begin to feel certain things. And those are the four principles I gave you. That comes to you automatically. But, you have to, upon awakening, become aware of these principles. You cannot think of them at your leisure. But you sort of have to coax the mind. You have to coax your mind to think upon the four principles as soon as you open your eyes in the morning.

So you have two things to do. When you open your eyes you can either ask yourself, "Where did the 'I' come from? Who am I that slept last night? Who am I that has just awakened? Who am I that exists now?" Or you can think about the four principles. Whatever is convenient for you. But, by all means, if you want Self-realization, and you want to become free, and you want to be free from the ocean of samsara, worldliness, and become blissful, then it's up to you. I can share these things with you, but I can't make you do them. It's just like I can bring you to the gold mine, but you've got to do your own digging. What comes first in your life again? Whatever comes first in your life, that's what you become. In the end, you're going to have to leave your body, your thoughts, your possessions, your loved ones. Everything is going to be left in the end. So the wise person searches for truth now, and tries to become free now.

So let's briefly go over the four principles again, for I feel they're very important. Another thing I do is this: Most ministers, teachers, whatever, philosophers, they always search for new knowledge. They research, research, research, and then they share with their congregations or students something profound, something new every Sunday. And, of course, you always forget the previous Sunday, and you go into new words. It's a game of words. You may learn about the astral planes, the causal planes, reincarnation. You may learn about how to become positive in your life, how to attract the right mate, how to attract money, health, and all kinds of stuff. How to channel, how to do this, and it's very exciting to the ego. What we do here is, we try for you to remove your ego so you do not get caught up in the world. That's the only way to become happy, truly happy, and Self-realized. This is why I reiterate, and repeat again and again, the same principle, so it can soak deep into your subconscious mind, and you can become a living embodiment of this truth.

Could you state the four principles again, as clearly as possible?
(1) I understand, I feel, I perceive, that everything, every-thing—and emphasize the second everything—is a mani-festation of my mind.
(2) I feel and understand deeply, that I am unborn, I do not prevail, and I do not disappear.
(3) I feel and understand the egolessness of everything, of all creation.
(4) I have a deep understanding of what Self-realization is by what it is not.
That's it.

What if we don't feel that, should we say that?
Say it when you wake up. It starts something goin,

During the day should we say that?
Make it a little different. Think that everything is a projection of your mind. In the morning it is good to say, I perceive, I understand. When you first open your eyes, you are not awake yet, and you are your real Self. Therefore, you are confessing to yourself your real nature. It goes deep into the subconscious mind as a new idea.

Should we be asking all these questions in satsang?
Real satsang is not intellectual, it is the reality of the person giving it. New students all ask the same questions. That is their perception. No matter what I say, they never will be able to see it until they become it, because they identify with their bodies.

It is the ego that wants to know. When you begin to feel that you know less, that is a good sign, because you know less about the world and more about the Self. The more confounded you become, the more the ego breaks up.

Isn't the purpose of satsang to ask questions?
Yes, but you have to practice the things I tell you and watch what happens. When you leave here you have to work on yourself and not just get caught up in the world until the next meeting. You'll see what happens.

The Three Vehicles of Self-Realization

After you learn the four principles, and they become a living embodiment within yourself, then you learn about the three vehicles, which carry you over the ocean of samsara, into the land of Self-realization of Noble Wisdom. That's why they're called vehicles. But you can only feel these vehicles when you've mastered the previous.

The first one is this: You have a deep feeling . . . now remember, this is before Self-realization, afterwards it doesn't matter what you do . . . you have a deep longing, a deep feeling, to be by yourself. Now, in the West they tell you this is antisocial behavior, but you have a feeling. In other words, you don't mentally say to yourself, "I want to be alone," like Greta Garbo. It's not a mental game you're playing. Because of your inquiry and your feeling and knowing the four principles, you have a feeling to be by yourself, so you are not pulled down by the world, to give you an opportunity to make the four principles and Self-inquiry work for you. So you enjoy being alone. You want to be by yourself. You look for times that you can be by yourself, so you can work on yourself, and that becomes a total joy for you. It's like total heaven to be by yourself, not all the time, but most of the time. It's only when you're by yourself that you can argue with yourself, and you can tell off your mind, and you can scream a little, if you like, and do what ever you have to do to get rid of the ego and the mind. That's the first vehicle.

The second vehicle is: You have a deep feeling, a deep desire, to always be at satsang. Now, satsang is not just a spiritual meeting, as most of you know. It's not a gathering of people when they hear a lecture. Who can explain what satsang is? How about you, Narada? What is satsang to you?

Well, ultimately, I suppose it can't really be put into words, so to realize that. I understand what the essence of satsang is, that it can't be put into words. Satsang is like the embodiment of the teaching. So I think that there's a growth in satsang, that takes place, a growth that does not take place in the words.

OK, that's a good explanation. Anybody else like to say what satsang is?

Abiding in the Self.

Yes, exactly. Being together with people who abide in the Self; the realization that there is one Self, and you are That. So being in satsang is being at the feet of God. That's what it literally means. Sitting at the feet of God. And God is none other than your Self. So you want to be with your Self when you come together with us. And you're still alone. You're still by your Self. Because all the people with you are your Self.

Doesn't it usually involve the presence of a sage?

Yes. But remember, the sage, the guru, and God are your Self. It's all the same. What I mean by that is, I don't want you to look at me as being a sage, or being anything at all. When you see me, as I mentioned in the beginning, I am a mirror. You see yourself. And when you see yourself as divinity, you will also see everyone else here as divinity. We're all one. There's no difference.

Number three: You will have a deep feeling, and a deep desire, to be around people like yourself. In other words your old relatives, your old friends, your old cronies that you used to drink with, and get high with, or whatever you did with them; they don't turn you on any more. You want to be with spiritual people like yourself. You're not putting it on. You're not intellectualizing it. You're not imagining that you want to do that because I told you to. From your practice you become like that. It's an inner feeling, a deep inner feeling. Those are the three vehicles.

Three Methods on the Path

There are three methods we use to help us on the path, so we can realize what we were talking about before. Number one is self-surrender, where we surrender completely to God, or to your Self. But that's hard to do for most people. It sounds easy, but it's not. It means that you have no life of your own. You surrender completely and totally, everything to God. Totally. Every part of your life goes to God. "Not my will, but Thine." That's devotion, bhakti. Again, it sounds easy to some people, but it's not when you get into it, because it means every decision that you have to make is left up to God. You give your mind to God, totally, completely, absolutely. And that leads you to Self-realization.

Number two is mindfulness, which we were talking about. Becoming the witness. Watching yourself continuously. Watching your thoughts, watching your actions. Sitting in meditation and watching what goes on in your mind. Not trying to change anything or correct anything. Just observing. Becoming the witness to your thoughts in meditation, and to your actions in the waking state.

And number three is the one that I advocate, Self-inquiry. Asking yourself, "To whom do these troubles come? To whom does this karma come? To whom does this suffering come? It comes to me. Well, what is 'me'? I am me. Who am I? From where did the I come from?" And following the "I" to its source.

You can use any of those three methods, the one that suits you best. But by all means, do something. Don't waste your life with frivolities. Work on yourself, if you want to become free. It doesn't mean you have to give up going to the movies, or going to work, or anything. You give nothing up. You just become aware of what you're doing. You become a conscious being. You become conscious of your actions. You become loving, compassionate, gentle to all people. You stop watching out for number one. Most of us say, "Number one, I'm number one." Forget it. That's how you suffer. That's ego. It's hard to understand, when you give up your ego, how you can have a better life, but you do. Try it and you'll see. When you stop thinking of yourself, and you start thinking on your Self, but yourself becomes Omnipresence, that means you're thinking of everybody else as yourself. So if any human being suffers, you suffer too.

But, in a way, we differ from Buddhism. Not much, but a little. Because the bodhisattva says he will not be realized until everybody else is realized. But then they have a higher bodhisattva called the Arhat. It's like the Avadhoot in Hinduism, who becomes Self-realized by himself, because he understands that his self is the Self of all. And that's what we accept. In other words, if you want to help your fellow man, if you want to make this world a better world in which to live, find yourself first, and everything else will take care of itself.

Happiness Is
Your Real Nature

Feel the Presence within yourself.
Feel the happiness and the joy that you really are.
Feel it! You can feel it.

No matter how many so-called problems
you may appear to have,
no matter what is going on in your life, good or bad,
forget about that. It doesn't matter.
Feel the Presence. The Presence of Consciousness.
The Presence of Pure Awareness.
Feel this in yourself. Do not think about it—just feel it.
When you begin to think about it, you spoil it.

Allow the mind to rave on.
Do not pay a bit of attention to the mind,
whatever thoughts it brings you, whatever it tells you.
Pay no attention whatsoever to the mind.
Feel the bliss. You ARE the bliss.
There is absolutely nothing that you need
or have to become.

Do not search for enlightenment or liberation.
You'll never find it. There's nowhere to look for it.
When you look with your senses, where is liberation?
Where's freedom?
It doesn't exist.
When you go beyond the senses,
when you pay no attention to the senses
and you go beyond them
by observing them, looking at them,
and not reacting to them,
then you find that you've always been in bliss.

Bliss happiness is your very nature.
You are That.

Happiness Is Unconditioned

How many of us are really happy today? Really, really happy. Really, really, really happy? Now. Not because things are going your way. Not because you like what you see. You're just happy because *you are*. There is no reason for it. Just to serve Consciousness, happiness. That's our real state of consciousness, who we really are.

We're really happy people. We don't know it. We think that things have to go a certain way for us to be happy. This is not true. Not true at all. You can be happy when you have good things, and be very depressed when you don't have them any more. Happiness has nothing to do with person, place or thing. Real happiness has absolutely nothing to do with person, place or thing. Real happiness comes from realization. Realization that you are not the body, you're not the mind, you're not your affairs, you're not the world. When you can drop all these things, you'll be very happy. It'll come by itself. Otherwise you'll have a false sense of happiness.

Most of us walk around with a false sense of happiness. You're happy because it is a beautiful day, the sun is shining, the flowers are blooming, you go to the beach, the movies. We think we're happy, but if you search deep within yourself, you'll realize there's a big sadness, a large unhappiness inside. This is true of all human beings. As long as you believe that you are a human being, it is virtually impossible for you to be happy, really happy. That's what I'm referring to. The happiness I'm referring to is beyond humanity, beyond good and bad, beyond experiences. It is your real state. It's what you are. But again to experience it, you have to let go of everything else. You cannot be attached to anything.

Happiness and Bliss are synonymous. It has absolutely nothing to do with this world in which we live. In this world all kinds of things happen. And we believe we have to live a certain kind of life to be happy. We believe we have to have certain kinds of possessions to be happy. It's all false. It is the happiness that will bring the good to you. It's opposite. It is the reverse. In other words if you want to be happy, happiness is the same as abundance, health, joy, peace, harmony. These things come to you as a result of your happiness. It's the other way around. Most of us believe that if we have certain things we'll be happy. But I'm saying to you, be happy first and the other things will come to you on their own volition. Ponder this.

Everyone wants something. If your mind stops thinking, what happens? Some of you believe you will not have anything, that you will have more problems. But it's in reverse. You solve problems; you want something and you can't get it. But when you do not need anything or want anything, true Bliss comes into the picture. You experience Bliss, Joy and Happiness, when you don't want anything. From what we know, people want something and when they get it they become more miserable than ever before. Leave the world alone. Leave people alone. Leave everything alone.

Know Yourself; Know Happiness

When you really understand who you are, you will experience unalloyed happiness. Happiness that you only dreamed about, happiness in the Silence, when nothing is happening but you're happy. Always happy, always at peace. All of the gods that you have been praying to all your life, all of the

Buddhas you've taken refuge in, the Krishnas, the Kalmias, the Shivas, the Christ, Allah, they're all within you. You are That. There is only the one Self and you are That. Ponder this.

The knowledge of this brings you eternally infinite happiness instantly. When you begin to understand who you are, your Divine nature, that you are not the body, you're not the mind, once you understand your Infinite nature, who you really are and there's nothing else, you immediately become instantly happy. For happiness is your very nature. Happiness, the Self, are synonymous. Consciousness, Absolute Reality, Pure Awareness, are all synonymous. There is only One. It has many names, but the One pervades all of space and time. And it is the only existence and you are That. There is no other existence. Awaken to this truth. You are the only One that does exist. And you are Consciousness.

The reason why somebody really is not happy, is because they don't really know yet who they are. That's the only reason. If you really were aware of who you really are, your real nature, happiness would exude from every pore of your body. It's just wonderful. Happiness *is*. There is really no reason for anyone to be unhappy. People who are unhappy take the world too seriously. They take themselves too seriously. They take life too seriously. They think things are real, and they're going to last. It makes no difference what position you're in right now. It makes no difference what's going on in your life. It makes no difference where you are, who you are. The only thing you have to do is come to terms with yourself. When you understand yourself, how can you possibly be unhappy. Your Self is the Self of the universe. Your Self is Consciousness. Consciousness is just being conscious of your happiness, being totally conscious. When you're totally conscious you have to be happy. Why? Because what we call happiness is the substratum of existence. It's the underlying cause of everything. Do not judge by appearances. Do not look at things and believe that's the way they are.

We all want to be happy. How to become happy? What do we have to do? Sit by yourself, go deep within yourself, and realize the truth about yourself. Which is, you are not the subject or the object. You are not the seer or the thing seen. You are the witness to all these things. The witness, everything you see. The witness is the witness. You watch, you look, you observe. And yet, you're not the observer, you're not the watcher, you're not the looker.

You're like a clay pot. A clay pot has space inside of it and outside of it. The space inside is not any different than the space outside. When the clay pot breaks, the space merges with inside and the outside. It's only one space. So it is with us. Your body is like a clay pot, and it appears you have to go within to find the truth. The outward appears to be within you. The outward is also without you. There's boundless space. When the body is transcended, it's like a broken clay pot. The Self within you becomes the Self outside of you. Always merges with the Self. As it's always been. The Self merges with the Self. Some people call the inner Self the Atman. And yet it is called Brahman. When there is no body in the way, the Atman and the Brahman become One. They become Brahman, One-ness, Absolute Reality, Pure Awareness. They become free and liberated.

We don't have to wait until the body dies for this to happen, it can happen to us now. You can become totally free and liberated now, if you will. All you have to do is let go. You let go of everything that's been keeping you in bondage mentally. Listen to your heart. Observe yourself. Become cognizant of your feelings, your emotions. Is this really you? Are you really your emotions? Are you really your feelings that you observe? Where do these feelings come from? Ask yourself, "Who am I? Where do my feelings come from? Where do my thoughts come from? Where does my life come from? Who is playing the game? Who is being alive? Who is growing up, becoming old and dying? Who is playing this game? Who is the I that is playing this game? Who am I?"

Just by thinking about these things all the time, something begins to happen to you, something wonderful. Do not think about the weather, or about the day's work, or your problems. For all the thinkers, who thinks? Find out who has the problems? Who has problems? Find out who you really are, who am I? It's up to you to awaken from this mortal dream. You can keep on going like you are right now, with the good things and the bad things. Yet you live in a universe of dualities. Which means for every good there is a bad. For every bad there is a good. It's a false world in which you live. You need to awaken to this truth.

Always realize that you're like the ocean. Any thoughts, ideas, body, beliefs, are simply ripples on the ocean. Bubbles come and go. The bubbles appear, stay for a time and disappear. The ocean always remains the same. This is like us. Our true reality never changes, but the body appears and the body disappears. New bodies come, they appear, and disappear. Things come, things go. The ocean will remain the same. Know the truth about yourself. Never forget it. Understand who you really are. Be aware of yourself, always. The world has its own karma. The world goes through its own karma. It has absolutely nothing to do with you. You belong to God. Everything you see is God. This is why you should be non-judgmental. Leave everything alone. By practicing these things, you become radiantly happy.

There never was a time when you were not the Self, Pure Awareness, Consciousness. This is your destiny, to awaken into Consciousness. Yet you can do it now, or you can do it in a thousand lives from now. It all depends on you. It's the way you are reacting as yourself to the world which determines the directions you are going in. There are no mistakes. Nothing is wrong. Everything is right just the way it is. Do not try to understand this or figure it out. Leave it alone. It will happen by itself, by keeping yourself quiet and still. You quiet the mind because of realization. Let it be calm. In all situations be calm. Let it be still and quiet.

The world doesn't need any help from you. Aren't you the world, aren't you the Creator? You created the world the way it is. It came out of you, of your mind. Or else where does it come from? The world that you are in, is a creation of your own mind. The mind becomes still, the world begins to disappear. And you're in divine harmony and joy. Therefore happiness comes to you when you stop thinking, when you stop judging, when you stop being afraid. When you begin to contemplate what is happiness.

All the answers are within you. Everything you're looking for is within you—everything. Nobody can help you but yourself. Know who you are. You are the Power. All the power of the universe is within you. You have all the power you need. All is well, exceedingly well. It has always been well, it will always be well. Act like a god or a goddess. Do not act like a human being any longer. Stop feeling sorry for yourself, saying you're unhappy. Stand up tall. Know the truth about yourself. Become the witness of all phenomena that you see, and be free.

Happiness Is Here and Now

Live in the moment. Can you be unhappy in the moment? The only reason, again, you're unhappy is because you're thinking of some condition or situation you don't like. True. You're thinking about something from the past or you're worried about something that's going to happen in the future. That's the only reason you're sad or unhappy. But if you learn to live in the moment, if you learn to become aware now, how can you possibly be unhappy? Because now is Bliss. Just don't think. Experience now. If you're really not thinking and you're experiencing now, you're in Bliss. Now is Reality. Now is ultimate Oneness. Now is liberation.

But as soon as you allow your mind to tell you, "Oh, this is nothing but a bunch of B.S.," why do you think so? You are thinking of a condition. You are thinking of a situation in your life that you don't like. You're thinking of something that's wrong some place, someone, and you believe that's going to last forever. We do not change conditions. We change ourselves. As you know, you've changed conditions most of your life, and when we get to a new situation everything seems rosy. But then, after a while, you turn right back to your old ways. The novelty has worn off and again, you're unhappy. You therefore have to do things to be happy. You have to watch a lot of TV, or go to the movies, or read newspapers, or read books, or get involved in some kind of situation, so you don't think. The only reason you get involved in all kinds of physical material situations is so you'll not have to think. You'll be too busy to think. But when you're alone, when you're by yourself, when there is no one around, how long can you sit by yourself before you become mad at yourself or angry over something? And you turn on the TV, or drink a bottle of beer, or go bowling, or do something. Even those of you who go and look at nature, climb mountains, enjoy flowers and the trees, are doing so because you really believe that the joy and the love and the experience you see out there is external to you. So even the beauty of the so-called world is erroneous.

You're running away from something. You're looking for beauty outside of yourself. You have to learn that you are the beauty. You are the joy. You are the flowers that you enjoy so much. You are the trees and the ocean and the sky and the mountains. It's all coming from you. If you really realize that you are That, would you run around seeking things? Everything that you want is within you. You are That. Even relationships. You look for a relationship with so and so to make you happy, so you can enjoy their company, so you can love them, so you can be with them. But I can assure you, that within yourself is a greater love, a greater joy, a greater peace than you can ever find anywhere else. It's true. You've got it all. There is nothing, no thing that you need from the outside. And nothing can ever happen to you, because there is no one to make it happen except yourself.

When you begin to think erroneously, you imagine all sorts of things are going to happen to you. You imagine that you lose your job, that you'll be bankrupt, you'll get sick, you'll die from disease, you have all kinds of imaginings. This is the only thing that makes you miserable. If you can only learn to look within. If you can only learn to dive deep within yourself and identify with the Self, merge with the Self. I can't begin to tell you the joy you would feel. There is nowhere you have to go. There is no one you really have to meet. There is no thing you have to do. You simply have to be yourself. You are the joy of the world.

The question arises, is a guru necessary? Is a teacher necessary? Think of that question. The definition of a guru is from darkness into light. Gu is darkness and ru is light. That's why when you hear children saying gu gu (laughter) they're in darkness. They're experiencing the world, so they say gu gu, for they already self consciously realize that the world is darkness. But when you say guru, that's the light. Therefore a guru should always be a sage who takes you from darkness into light. How does the sage take you from darkness into light? By doing certain things in order to make you realize that you are the One. Not by saying, "I'm the guru and you are my disciples." By making you see that you are that One who has never been born, who can never die, who is imperishable, who is absolutely Sat-Chit-Ananda. You are that One. And you are that One just the way you are right now.

If, right now, you are thinking about your body, or you are the doer, or you've got problems, or there's something wrong, that's not you. But if you're living right now, in the Now, the eternal Now, then you are that One, just the way you are right now, right now, in this split second. If you think, you spoil it. For thoughts are always about the past and the future. Even if it's the past minute or a minute into the future, you're spoiling it, because you're not centered in the Now. So you are Brahman just the way you are right now. The guru should be able to tell you that, and make you understand and make you see it and feel it.

Not everyone needs a guru. A guru can be a tree, a mountain, a lake, a flower. You've heard this before, but let me explain it. When a tree becomes your guru, the tree is no longer an ordinary tree. It's you. You are identifying with the essence of the tree, which is Consciousness. You are not seeing the tree as a tree. It's the beauty of the tree or the mountain, or the lake, or whatever, that first attracts you. But if you just see the tree as a tree, you'll be disappointed. For the leaves drop off, bugs attack it, people chop it down, yet if you identify with that tree spontaneously, intelligently, that tree becomes you, and the essence is the beauty, is the essence of your beauty. In that respect, the tree is your guru. Therefore, a guru in the human form is a being whose words in the Silence you feel in your heart. And just like the tree, the essence of the guru is your essence. There is only One. Therefore when you are sincere in your spiritual practice, when you put that first before anything else, when you continue to work on yourself, automatically the guru within yourself, the essence within yourself, like a magnet will attract and pull you to a guru outside of yourself which is really yourself. This can cause you to rise higher and become liberated.

You've got to stop seeing yourself as a human being. You've got to catch yourself whenever you think something is wrong, someone has hurt you, someone has rubbed you the wrong way, when things do not go right at your job or at home. Do not be like the ordinary person and react to it. And do not believe that if you do not react, things will get worse. I cannot tell you enough that every situation that happens to you is necessary for your growth. There are no mistakes. Everything that you've been through, everything that you're going through, is absolutely necessary for your spiritual growth. If it does not look kosher to you, realize it's your mind reacting. It's your ego reacting. And the way to handle it is just to observe. Do not get involved by arguing, fighting, trying to change things. Just observe. If you can observe without getting excited, then you've passed that test and you'll not have to repeat it. But if you get angry, if you get upset, you want to get even, you're always thinking about it, and you've got hate and you've got animosity. Even though you move away from that situation, you will meet that situation again and again and again until you learn not to react to it.

The universe is a university to educate the soul. Before we go any higher and awaken, we have to have these little realizations where we begin to feel that there is nothing wrong. There is absolutely no thing wrong. All the good of the universe is yours. There is absolutely nothing wrong—nothing.

If you can only live in the moment and feel what I'm saying, everything in this world, in this universe, will become you. That's why people like Jesus and others have been able to say, all that I have is yours. Meaning that Consciousness is Bliss, and Bliss is expressing itself as the world, as the universe, as yourself. Live in that Bliss. Refuse to acknowledge anything else. It appears that if you do not acknowledge something, something will go wrong in your life. But you are not made for something to go wrong in your life. There is absolutely nothing wrong anywhere, so how can anything go wrong in your life? God can be good and bad—whatever—in a capricious universe. In a capricious universe, the moon would crash into the sun, wheat would grow one time and roses would grow another time from the same seed, when we live in a capricious universe. There are not two powers here, there is one power and you can call that God, it is All-Pervading and there is no place where it is not, how can there be a problem. For in order for there to be a problem, there has to be God and something else, but all you've got to do is a little meditation, and you will see that there is only God as everything. There is no room for God and anything else.

So you say, "Where does sickness come from? Where does lack and limitation come from? Where does man's inhumanity to man come from?" I have to ask you, who sees it? Who sees this? Most of the world's populace. Most of the world sees lack, limitation, disease, man's inhumanity to man, and this is why these things perpetuate themselves, and appear to be collectively everywhere in the Universe. But then there are the few of us who step out of the parade. And they hear the beat of a different drummer. That's how it begins. They no longer acknowledge evil as a reality. It may be a fact, but whose fact? Those who are living in a dream world. And again, all facts are subject to change. Therefore, anything that's a fact can never be reality. Reality presumes that it is the same forever and ever without change. Harmony is Reality. Love is Reality. Joy is Reality. Bliss is Reality. You are Reality, just the way you are, not what you think. When you begin to think, you can argue with me and say, "How can I be Reality when I'm experiencing this and experiencing that?" You're thinking, that's why you say this. But if you stay just as you are, in the moment, then you're Reality.

As you begin to think about these things, you raise yourself higher and higher. And again, because you're cleansing your personal consciousness from all past karma and samskaras. The inner Self, the Guru within, will lead you to the guru without, and when you sit in satsang you will hear all the truths which are spoken in the Silence and something will happen. You will begin to feel that there is no birth, there is no cause for this universe. It will just come to you. Situations are not what they appear to be. The universe is but a dream. It will come to you all by itself.

For instance, the rishis of old did not have pen and pencils to write notes, or have tape recorders to record tapes, or have newspapers or books to read. Yet if you read the Upanishads, the Vedas, you will find that these rishis, these sages, even though they didn't know each other, all came to the same conclusion about Reality. For they were able to dive deep within themselves. And they were able to see that this world does not exist, the body does not exist, the mind is non-Reality. They were able to merge their body/mind in their own nature, which is Consciousness, Absolute Reality. They then became Absolute Reality, Pure Awareness, and they wanted to spread the word to the world. But they couldn't, because they realized the world doesn't exist. So there is really no one to spread anything to. Yet, when they think of themselves, all others are included. It therefore appears as if there are others. And amongst the others are certain people who are ready to be liberated. And these people sat at the feet of the rishis and they became sages. And that's how the word was spread. Then writing began, and manuscripts were written, and many people were able to come to this truth through reading and through listening to the sage. But now I must tell you the truth. That none of this exists. Everything I told you is for kindergarten students.

Abide in the Now

Why should you have to do anything to awaken, when your Divine nature is already awake? Why should you have to strive or overcome conditions or straighten out your life? In the dream that you are dreaming, you give importance to your humanhood. That's the only problem you really have. Giving importance to your humanhood. And once you do that, every other lie comes into experience. That you've got to straighten conditions out, you've got to do this and you've got to do that, but they're all lies. Consciousness has nothing to do. Absolute Reality is Absolute Reality just the way it is. It doesn't have to practice any sadhanas, chant any mantras, or do anything.

Why not awaken now? What are you waiting for? Make up your mind that you're going to awaken right now, and allow your mind to turn into your Heart, which is Pure Awareness. Do it! Some of you are still asking, how do you do it? Through Silence. Experiencing the Moment, the Now, the Reality. Nothing is happening Now. No one is suffering. Now is the only moment you've got. Abide in the Now. Everything is perfect right now. Feel it. Don't think about it. Feel it. There are no yesterdays, there are no tomorrows. All of your so-called senses have been transcended. No past and no future. You are fully alive now. Right now. Enjoy.

Remember, as your mind starts thinking, grab hold of it by observing it, and go back to the Now. Whenever you fall away in thoughts, keep remembering to catch yourself. There are many of you allowing your minds to run away. Stay in the moment. There is no thing happening in the moment. The moment is eternity. If you're doing this correctly, you should start to feel a joy welling up within you. A joy, a bliss, a peace that you never felt before. Feel it. Nothing else exists except for this Peace, this Love, this Awareness. Call it by any name you like; doesn't matter. You are That.

Satguru

You come to sit with me to realize
that there is no teacher,
there's no truth,
there's no teaching.
There is only the One,
And you are That.
I am not your teacher.
There is no teacher.

I AM.
I AM THE UNIVERSAL I AM THAT I AM.

Guru and Self-Realization

Most of you have come here for one reason. To find freedom from your everyday experiences, to be liberated, to be Self-realized, to attain Nirvana, Satori, to become enlightened. Yet, does the sun have to be enlightened? Your real nature is moksha, liberation. You have always been *That* and nothing else. But some of you do not believe this, do not feel this, have had no experience of this. For this reason it is my responsibility to see that you awaken. That's why I'm here. I'm responsible for you. If you realize this, if you understand what I'm saying, you will let go of everything else. All of your attachments, all of your fears, all of your frustrations, all of the things that you have been holding on to for years will be given up. And when you give up these things, Divine Grace flows by itself. And you will be where you are now, awakened. But you don't know it.

Why do you look at yourself as a simple mortal being with problems? Always thinking about the future. Thinking about your pride and your ego. Drop that. Give it up. So the two things to understand are that Self-realization is not your responsibility, it's mine. For you sought me out. I'm here for you, not for me. But you have to give up the rest. It's up to you to diligently work on yourself to remove all these false concepts that you've had for years, for centuries, for many lives. It means you have to be totally honest with yourself, totally honest, completely honest with yourself to see the way you've been carrying on. To see how your thoughts have been ruling you. Your mind has been telling you, this is like this and this is like that. This is good, this is bad. This is right, this is wrong. Being judgmental all the time. This is what has to be given up totally, completely.

All the tools that you need are within yourself. But you have to make the move to do something. As I said, leave the realization to me. Work on yourself. Get rid of all the stuff that's kept you bound for so many years. You know what it is. The fears, preconceived ideas, all these things that have kept you in bondage all these years. Let go of them. Give them up. Surrender everything. Which means you really have a job on your hands. Yet I tell you all of the time, everything is preordained. Everything is karmic. This is true for the average person who does nothing to find realization for himself. Then your entire life appears to be karmic. Yet when you begin to work on yourself, when you begin to see the truth, when you begin to inquire all day long, "Who am I?" wherever you are, whatever you do, and you go deeper and deeper within, all of karma is transcended. Everything is transcended. You become a totally free being.

You've been in this world for many years, and through practicing spiritual disciplines you've come to the inner conclusion that this world really has nothing to offer you. Even though there appear to be good things in this world, you understand and realize that there is also just a lot of change. Everything in this world must change. Subsequently, there is absolutely nothing that this world can give you. You have to feel this inside. Again, you have to wonder, "Who am I? What am I really? I never asked to be born. I'll live a certain number of years and then I'll die, so to speak. What am I all about? Where did this world come from? Who or what is God? Where did all the animals come from, the bugs and insects, the trees, the mountains, the planets? What is this all about?"

If you've been questioning yourself this way, then satsang is for you. You begin to feel and realize that there is something called Self-realization. When you touch it, it will make you happier than you've ever been in your life. It will bring a profound peace. There will be no doubt in your mind about anything. For you will have surrendered your mind completely and you will be mindless. You have an innate feeling that the real you is boundless space. That you are connected to everything, and everything is connected to you. In other words, you're not just your body. The appearance of your body is a lie. The appearance of the world is a lie. You soon feel this. If you feel this, and this is true if people have only been practicing spiritual discipline and sadhana for many years, many incarnations, then you have to find a sage who has gone all the way and is experiencing realization. Only a sage of this type can bring you forward and cause Self-realization to come to you. Only a sage who has realized himself or herself.

It's up to you to find such a person. When you find such a person, you have to trust that person implicitly, have total faith in that person to lead you on the right path. If you have problems with that, you have to find another sage. All the scriptures, all the books tell you that unless one surrenders totally and completely to the sage, there's no hope for realization. Now it is true that there have been certain people in this world who have realized the Self without any help. These people are few and far between. Very few. The average person needs a sage who has gone all the way. Who has gone beyond eternity. Beyond questions. Beyond the observer and the observed. Beyond all phenomena, and realized all phenomena is a superimposition on the Self. Which means your body, the world in which you live, the animals, everything, the planets, the universe, is only but a superimposition on the Self, like the writings on a chalkboard. Then you can erase it and write something else. You can draw a picture. But the chalkboard always remains the same. Only the images change. And so it is with a Self-realized sage. The realization is that everything is the same phenomena. All phenomena is exactly alike. It comes and goes. But the Self never changes. The Self is silence. No words. There is no logical explanation for the Self. It is beyond everything your mind will think of. You can't find the Self by thinking about it. Only by unthinking! Removing thought.

Love the Sage; Love the Self

When you find such a being who has experienced the Self, you have to learn to love this person, totally, completely, absolutely. You're not really loving the person, you're loving the Self. You may see a person in the sage. But the sage realizes beyond a shadow of a doubt, there's no person present. Therefore, by loving the Self, you're loving the sage. By loving the sage, you're loving your Self. The same thing. The sage is none other than your real Self. The sage is you! But you don't know this, you don't believe this, you've not experienced this. So you think the sage is a person, a place, a thing. Consequently, all you can do is to love the sage. That alone will suffice.

Now a sage, having transcended the body and transcended the world, comes from a completely different space than you do. And he or she may do things totally differently. But you should know this: everything the sage does is only for your realization. This is why the sage or the Jnani exists for you—for your realization, for no other purpose. It's up to you to feel this, to realize this, to understand this.

You really have to learn to love the sage! It is difficult for many of you to love at all. When you think of love, you think of human love. And you think of disappointments, sorrow. But when you love the sage, it's totally different, completely different. When you begin to love the sage you immediately feel bliss inside of yourself. You feel joy and happiness. Why? Because you're loving the Self. The Self is All-Pervading, Infinite Reality, Omnipresence. Knowing the sage is loving your Self. There's only one Self. And you have to really learn to trust the sage in everything you do.

There's a story that reminds me of this. One day Krishna and Arjuna were walking down a path. Towards the evening they became tired and saw a house. In the house was a mean old man. Through some method he acquired lots of money. He was very mean. They knocked on the door. The mean old man came to the door and said, "What do you want?" And Krishna said, "May we have lodging for the night and food to eat?" Usually the mean old man would have shut the door in their face, but he realized it was Krishna and Arjuna, so he reluctantly let them in. He had a scrumptious dinner for himself but he only gave

Arjuna and Krishna bread crumbs to eat. And he had a comfortable bed, but he made Krishna and Arjuna lie down in the corner in the mud to sleep for the night. When morning came, Krishna and Arjuna were about to leave. Krishna put his hand on the old man's head and blessed him and he said, "May you prosper abundantly." And they left.

Evening came again. They came to another house. In this house lived a pious, wonderful, beautiful old man whose only possession was a cow. They knocked on the door and the old man opened the door and when he saw Krishna he prostrated himself and he said, "What a blessing I've got, to have Krishna and Arjuna come to my home! My home is yours." He gave them his dinner. He made them sleep in his bed and he slept on the floor. And he praised them all night. When morning came, Arjuna and Krishna were about to leave, and Krishna put his hand on the old man's head and he said, "May your cow drop dead!" and left.

Arjuna didn't say a word. But he was thinking about this all day. Finally he had the nerve to ask Krishna, "Master, I didn't understand your message. The other night when we came into the house and this old man treated us poorly, was mean to us, you blessed him and told him, may he prosper abundantly. And last evening, when we came to this old man, this pious old man who was wonderful to us, gave us dinner and his bed, you cursed him and said, may his cow die, drop dead. What is the meaning of this?" Krishna explained, "My ways, Arjuna, are not your ways. And your ways are not my ways. You may see me do many things which you don't understand. Never judge me by what you see me do. Only love me. You see, when I cursed the first man, and told him may he prosper abundantly, I realized he would come back many times, many incarnations and have a lot of money, and his relatives would haunt him to get some money. And the IRS would come after him. His relatives would want his money. He will have many lives to work this out. He will suffer many lives because of his greed. Now when I went to the other old man, I realized that he was giving up everything for God. His only possession was the cow. And this was holding him back from Self-realization. So when I removed the cow from him, then he will be Self-realized. This is the game I play with people."

The same is true with us. Never believe the sage thinks like you or does the things that you do. A sage may appear to you to be an ordinary person just like yourself. But that's where the similarity ends. Never try to understand a sage, his methods or what he does. Again, just love him. That's all you have to do. If you can really learn to love the sage, immediately you will see results in your spiritual life.

The first thing you will see, you will feel profound peace in yourself that you never felt before. Then you will feel joy in your heart that you never had before. You will feel love for everything, from the mineral kingdom to the vegetable kingdom, the animal kingdom, the human kingdom. You may be going through some karma, perhaps. Remember, for the sage there is no karma. I know in some of the books it tells you that the reason the sage does certain things is that he or she is going through some prarabdha karma that's left over and it will be all finished when he or she drops the body. This is a lie! These things were just written to appease the people. I'm telling you there's no karma for a sage at all. What you see in the sage is a lie also. As long as you see the sage as a body, your thinking is erroneous. The sage is not a body. Neither are you, because you don't know it. Saying, "I am not the body," is not good enough. You have to experience this truth. What good is this teaching if you can't experience it? Therefore the sage tests you. You may have many personal experiences with the sage. The worst thing you can do is become judgmental. Always remind yourself that the sage is not coming from the place you're coming from. Do not even try to understand the sage. Just love the sage, that is sufficient.

Again, when you really love the sage, you will see very fast changes in your life. This is more important than practicing Self-inquiry, than being the observer or doing other spiritual methods. For if you're loving the sage, Self-inquiry will become easier for you. When you have a hard heart and a head made out of stone, it is difficult for you to love. Therefore you look at yourself as an individual and try to practice spiritual discipline and Self-inquiry, being the observer, pranayama, mantras. Yet, the ego is doing all these things! This is why in Advaita, no spiritual methods are required. No sadhana is required. No discipline is required. Only to love. To love whom? To love the sage as yourself. It's all that is required. Once you are able to do this, everything else will open up for you. It appears difficult in the beginning, especially for a Westerner. For you've been brainwashed to believe that you're the ego and everything that you do in your life comes from the ego point of view. You think you're making progress, then something comes along that makes you angry and upsets you. And you feel you've lost all your progress and you're nowhere. And you become perplexed and wonder about this and you wonder about that. And you say you've been practicing sadhana for three or four or five years. Nothing has happened; twenty years, nothing has happened. You've forgotten one thing: to love the sage as yourself.

True Love Means Surrender

Look back at your own practice and you'll see that this is true, to really love with all of your heart and all of your soul. True love means surrender. What do you surrender? Your *ego*. What else? Give it all to the sage! Become empty, totally free and empty. Then I can assure you, you will feel such bliss and it will never leave you again. You will realize that irrespective of what is happening to your body, *all is well*. You will stop feeling sorry for yourself. You will stop judging yourself. You will begin to leave everything and everybody alone.

Another incidence of this is when I was with Paramahansa Yogananda when I was seventeen years old. He initiated me and he told me, "Robert, do you promise to love me, no matter what you see me do?" So I smiled and I hesitated. I said to myself, "What is this guy going to do?" And yet I felt an overwhelming love and I said, "Certainly, yes, I will." And in the six months that I was with him, I'd see him go into different moods, become angry with certain devotees while loving other devotees. I remember a time during Christmas when many devotees wanted to go home to their families for the holidays. And one went to Yogananda and asked him, "Master, can I go home to my family for Christmas?" And he gave him a warm smile and said, "Yes, of course, go home and enjoy yourself." Someone else would come to him and say, "Master, may I go home for the holidays?" And he said, "What? How dare you ask me a question like this? Of course you can't go home. You have no family. I'm your family. The only family you have is here, your brothers and sisters in satsang." And he would literally scream at him or her and never gave them permission to go home. I observed all this and I watched and I realized at that time also, I'm not here to judge him, to see whether he's right or wrong, good or bad. And there were many incidences that he did in the ashram, which would cause the average person to leave and never come back. But I realized that these were tests to see if people were fit or not. And so it is with us.

What are we really looking for? True spirituality is not easy. It means changing our entire viewpoint, looking at life completely differently. Trying to keep quiet most of the time. Keeping your mind quiet, never allowing it to judge, never allowing your mind to think too much on any one subject. You learn to catch your thoughts. When the mind begins to criticize, catch it before it goes too far. Realize the God within you—your real Self—can never lead you astray.

Ramana Maharshi did many strange things. All sages do. I won't go into them. Suffice it to say, a sage comes with a completely different background than you do. Do not try to train the sage or mold the sage into your image, like you do God! In other words, do not expect the sage to do what you think he should do. Because after all, who is thinking? The ego! Who else?

Realize this. Always remember this. If you learn to surrender to the sage, the sage will always be with you and never leave you. When you're asleep, when you're awake, when you're working, you will never be alone again. Love will always be with you.

But again, this is only for those people who have been through many, many spiritual experiences in their life, that have an inkling of what I'm talking about. You can't pull a person off the street and speak like I'm speaking here tonight. They will laugh in your face and go their merry way. For these people have not yet even begun to learn the lessons of spiritual life.

Only the Self Exists, and You Are That

When I say there's no person, no world, no God, no universe, no life, I speak from experience. Unless you have the same experience, it's better not to think, better not to speak. This makes sense. For when you stop criticizing, you stop speaking, you stop thinking. Only the true Self can emerge from you. Reality comes into your existence. It's always been there. But you've awakened it.

You begin by not believing anything the senses tell you. Don't accept what I'm telling you. You stop worrying about anything and everything. Stop worrying! Remember, all is well. You live in an intelligent universe that knows all about you and it can take care of you and meet all your needs in the right way, in ways that you know not of. *Trust it.* Have faith in that which you do not understand. *Drop all fear.* It's so funny to me that people fear something. There is nothing in this entire universe that has a basis in fear. Fear is a human emotion. If you have no thoughts, there is nobody to fear. It is only when you begin to think and your mind draws pictures for you that you have all sorts of situations that may happen tomorrow or the next day or right now, and then you begin to fear. And you fear for one reason only. You do not understand who you really are! You think you're a human being with all sorts of problems. And you say to yourself, "If I don't think of these things, who will resolve my problems? How will my problems ever become resolved?" That's why I say, do not try to think about them; just love the sage and everything will be taken care of.

But the answer to all this is simple. Do not try to figure it out. For there's not time or space for a problem to begin.

There is not time or space for fear to emerge. Time and space do not exist. Only the Self exists—the Pure Awareness, Absolute Reality, nothing else. And you are That.

I know that some of you listening to these words, you go home and you forget everything I said. And then you become worldly again, start thinking about your income and your sickness, that people don't love you, the job you hate, so forth and so on. But now when you begin to think this way, you have to catch yourself and think of the sage.

How wonderful it is to understand these things! The rest is up to you. Peace.

Who Is the Sage?

Robert, how do you tell a false sage from a real sage?

Your heart will tell you. If you are a sincere devotee, you do not have to worry about anything like that. Something within you will tell you what to do, where to go. But if you're a false devotee, you will go to a false sage. Like attracts like. Therefore, you honestly have to take a good look at yourself, according to what you are, who you are, spiritually in consciousness. That's why I say everybody's in their right place. There are no mistakes. Everybody's where they're supposed to be. *No* mistakes whatsoever. And there are no false sages. Because a false sage has false people. So they're doing what they're supposed to be doing, having a false teaching. Which is right the way it's supposed to be. So if you're sincere, you will attract the right sage.

We don't have to wonder where we will be. It all depends on what we are. What you are speaks so loud I can't hear a word you are saying! So you're always in your right place, where you're supposed to be. Make yourself pure. Dive into your Heart center. Sit in the Silence. Desire Self-realization with all your heart, with all your mind, with all your soul. Cry out for God. And you will be with the right people. Everything will take care of itself.

Robert, is it possible for a Self-realized person to have some negative desires? And thereby use his disciples? I'm thinking of a dozen or so Self-realized beings I've met. There was one I can remember who exuded love but he had one thing on his mind, it seemed; he wanted to know from his disciples how much money they made and tried to exact a check from them every week or month. Now if a person became a servant or slave to such a guru, who was exuding love, I don't know if my calling that negativity is my small-minded interpretation. Would that disciple still receive Grace?

Such a being, a sage like this, is not an enlightened being. He's not realized to begin with.

Are you sure?

Yes. A Self-realized being never needs anything for himself. He never needs anything for himself, never wants anything for himself, but is taken care of by his devotees. A Self-realized being who has a family is taken care of by the devotees. Nothing should be said about this. It should be known by the devotees what to do. But if a sage, so-called, talks about money, and as you say, tries to find out what all the students make, and tells them they have to give him money, such a being is not a Self-realized being. It makes no difference to a liberated sage where they live, what's going on around them, what they own. They do not think of things like this. Yet a sage is no good to the world. He's totally useless to the world. So the devotees have to take care of the sage in their own way.

When you are totally empty, not wanting and not giving—that is for the ego. When you become the Self, you give to the Self. The Self gives to Itself. As long as there's someone left who thinks they don't have to give and there's no need to want, that's still the I-thought that thinks of these things. When there's no I-thought left, there is no doer and the Self acts upon Itself. But as long as you have the thought, "I have to give," or "I don't have to give," they're two sides of the same coin. That's the I-thought playing games with you. When you give, you give without thought. A good example of that is when I had lunch with Henry the other day. A homeless person came over to us and asked us for a couple of dollars and gave us a sob story. I didn't feel that the story was true. But it made no difference. Henry gave the girl five dollars and we forgot about it. There was no judgment. There was no thinking, what is she going to do with it? It was forgotten when the deed was done. And that's how it should be. We have no business judging anything or anyone. Whether we do something or we don't. Then we leave it alone and we go forward.

Robert, you made a statement—if I heard you correctly, I'm not sure—that the sage is no good to the world. By that, did you mean that the sage can't hold down a job that requires thinking in the logical mind, or did you mean something else?

There have been sages who have held down jobs, and who have worked in the world. This is part of the bodily karma. But the truth is, when all bodily karma is destroyed, there is nothing the sage can do in the world. The sage is only good for transmitting Grace, and would not be able to function otherwise.

But true, for a time the two can go together, the prarabdha karma as it's unfolding and wearing itself out can go with the sage. That's known when the Grace is left.
Yes.

What is it the sage cannot do in order to, so-called, work in our world? Is he unable to think with his left brain? (laughter)
There is no brain.

So, there's no thinking?
There's no I-thought, there's no thinking about the world, and about the needs of the world. The world does not exist for the sage. So how can the sage work?

Oh God, I'd better be retired before I become Self-realized.
It will take care of itself.

Robert, it seems like the sages like Jesus, Buddha and Mahatma Gandhi, none of them worked. They didn't have jobs.
So what's the point?

They lived, they survived.
Of course, naturally. When you're speaking about survival, you're speaking about the body. When you're referring to a sage, there's no one left that has to survive, there is no "I" that needs to survive.

Then there's no such thing as fear; that's eliminated.
There is no fear in the sage.
You have to remember what a true Jnani is. The words Jnana and Jnani have been used very loosely in this age. A

person who practices bhakta is a bhakti, devotion, a devotee. So it's easy to say "I am a bhakti," no matter what level of consciousness you're on. But when you come to jnana, it's completely different. You can't say "I am a Jnani" if you're practicing Jnana. A Jnani is a sacred word. It implies that you have transcended the universe. That you are no longer your body or mind phenomena. You are totally liberated. And of course if you were, you would not say that I am a Jnani. For there would be no one left to say that. You would remain silent.

When we speak of such things as spiritual healing, and we try to compare Jnanis to people like Sai Baba, Jesus, and others, we would be better off if we would not compare at all. Every teacher has their place. And every teacher did what they were supposed to do. Those of us who are aspiring Jnanis should not even think of those things. We should not have concepts or preconceived ideas of what somebody is supposed to be or not to be. We should rather practice Self-inquiry or becoming the witness. Spend our time doing that rather than comparing teachers or trying to understand why a Jnani acts the way he or she does. The answer of course is very simple. There is no one home. No one is left to perform miracles. When you perform miracles, it's an emanation of the mind. Miracles are in the mind. There has to be a subject and an object. There has to be a doer and something to be done. Immediately you can see it has nothing to do with Jnana. A Jnani is totally free of those things.

As far as the Jnani is concerned, there are no others. Others are merely himself. So by being in a body, so to speak, a Jnani becomes an asset to all of humanity. The average person should never even think, "Should I or should I not help others?" but should make it a policy to help whomever is in need, if they can, and not think about it. This is your karma in any event. It has been preordained again, every step you're going to take in this body, in this plane of existence. You should take no concern about this. But if the chance arises, when you have an opportunity to help people, by all means do so. But a Jnani has transcended that question. A Jnani is not of this world, even though he or she appears to be in this world. They are Omnipresent, All-Pervading, so their existence is a benefit to all mankind. Just their very existence, because they are Omnipresent, Omnipotent, Omniscient.

If a person advertises himself or herself, makes TV appearances, goes on the radio, writes a lot of books and so forth, you can be assured that person is not a Jnani. That's the first clue to let you know. Why? There has to be a personal I to do these things. In a Jnani there is no personal I. The personal I has been killed. So how can the Jnani act like a personal I? And make public appearances and do all these things? Think about that. There is no ambition left in a Jnani. There are no goals. Jnanis never go out of their way to teach classes. And the last thing they want to do is to build up the classes, to attract hundreds of people. It's not necessary. Those who are so karmically inclined, those who have paid the price in a previous life through meditation, through concentration, through searching in a previous life, will automatically be attracted to the sage. Nothing will be able to stop it.

Everyone in this group who keeps coming back over and over again to satsang, is a person who has perfected himself in a previous life. You have gone through the stage of effortless mindfulness, and now you're ready to go all the way. That doesn't say it's going to take one lifetime, but you're very advanced, and whether you like it or not, this is the truth about you. There's more going on in your consciousness than you can ever imagine. Why do you think you come here? You think you voluntarily come here, but you don't. You are compelled to do so. This is your time.

So you see, a Jnani doesn't go out looking for students. The Jnani doesn't go looking for admiration, or a following, or to build a movement. But the Jnani remains where he or she is. And those students who are ready will be attracted like iron to a magnet. Even if the devotee lives in China or in Japan or in Africa, the vibration of the Jnani is such that he or she will be attracted, and sooner or later will come in contact with the last stage of their life, which is the sage.

You, therefore, have nothing to think about, nothing to plan about, nothing to worry about, nothing to wonder about. You just have to be yourself, and everything will take care of itself. Isn't that wonderful? You don't have to wonder at home, "Shall I go to see Robert this week or shall I go to the movie?" There's something in you that has prearranged everything. You have nothing to say about it. So why try to make decisions? Many of you are learning that when you keep still and sort of get yourself out of your way, things couldn't be better for you. You're finding peace, happiness, freedom. You're beginning to see that all is well and you're no longer concerned about the world situation, about man's inhumanity to man. Those things are important, of course, in this world of illusion, but you begin to look at it from a different angle, a different perspective.

You know it's virtually impossible to change the world no matter how men have tried. The world is unfolding as it should. There will always be man's inhumanity to man. There will always be clashes of personality, conflicts, wars. This is only natural on this illusory plane of existence. For if you understand that this is a plane of duality, how can things be one way? Can you imagine a world that is totally peaceful? Where everyone loves one another? It's idealistic and we wish in our deluded state that it were true. Yet this is not the nature of this planet. This planet is supposed to be as confusing and as confounding as it appears. Everything is supposed to be the way it is. Just to understand this is an advanced state. For you realize you're not saying that you're not going to help others. You're realizing you cannot help others. Even if it appears that you can. It's paradoxical.

Let's say you give a homeless person a good meal. You put him or her up for a couple of days. You give them fifty dollars in their pocket, and they go their way. A few days later, the person is right back where they were before. Yet you have done what you were supposed to do. This is why, when you help someone, you shouldn't think about it. You shouldn't ask what's going on. You shouldn't even wonder if you did the right thing. You are doing what you are supposed to do, and then you drop it and forget it. You do not become part of the karmic game. You have risen above this. And as you become peaceful, anger slowly drops from your consciousness as all anxiety and bitterness and hate are transcended and you begin to feel a wonderful peace, you begin to notice that those people who come into your aura also feel peaceful, feel harmonious. You're not doing anything voluntarily. You have just risen. You have risen to a higher state of consciousness.

A rose need not declare, "I am fragrant." By its very nature, it is fragrant. So you need not declare, "I'm doing a good deed, I am helping others." By your very nature, you can't help helping others, by your very presence. And as you continue to unfold, you notice you are getting less and less involved in the games of this world. You're playing fewer and fewer games. You leave others alone to an extent. If you can't say a good word or help in any way, you say nothing. And by your very silence, you have blessed someone else. When you actually become your real Being, when your real nature of awakening comes, you begin to realize that there is nothing left to do. There is no one to help, for you see that the whole universe is an emanation of yourself. And as you begin to go even further, you are no longer your self with a small 's', but you are the Universal Self, and even as you look at the world, you see the Self. Again, this is paradoxical. A sage looks at the world, he or she sees everything you see, but yet they look right through everything. They see Consciousness, Absolute Reality. It's like a burned rope. A sage realizes that the rope is burned and it is of no use to anyone. Whereas the average person looks at a burned rope and believes the rope is real and can be used. So it is when the average person looks at the world; everything the senses tell them appears to be real. They identify with all these things. They identify with situations, with persons, with places, with things. Whereas the sage sees the same thing, but is only conscious of the Self as the universe. Do not attempt to analyze this. Remember, the finite mind cannot comprehend the Infinite.

What is a Jnani, a sage? To come up with that answer is the question: what is not a sage? A sage is never a yogi or a spiritual teacher, or a meditation teacher. I use the term Jnani and sage interchangeably. A sage has absolutely no teaching to give you. If you want to have a teaching, you'll have to go to a spiritual teacher, a yogi, a meditation master. But a sage never has a teaching to give you whatsoever. The idea is to just be in the presence of the sage; that does the teaching. A sage does not teach tantric yoga, kundalini yoga, hatha yoga, raja yoga, laya yoga, or anything else. For all the teachings are from the mind. Where else would they come from? They are all mental concepts. The sage is beyond the mind, beyond the mental concepts. So how can a sage give a teaching? A sage is Absolute Reality, Pure Awareness. The term sage is loosely termed. Sage is meant All-Pervading. The sage is not confined to a body whatsoever. A sage is the whole Universe, All-Pervading, everywhere present. So to be in contact with the sage, all you have to do is think about the sage.

But there is no teaching to give. The teaching is emptiness. When a person, so-called, becomes enlightened...I don't like to use these terms, they are so meaningless . . . but so you understand what I'm talking about, I use these terms loosely . . . I make it simple for you to understand . . . but a person, a being, so-called, awakens, the awakening has nothing to do with the body whatsoever. This is why throughout history we've had sages who have been kings, queens. Sages have been laborers. They've been married or single. They had boyfriends or girlfriends, whatever the case may be. Some have lived in caves and shunned the world completely. Some traveled from country to country, not interested in one place.

A sage is never looking for anything, for he has nothing left to look for. A sage has attained everything there is to attain. Total freedom is the sage, Absolute Reality, Absolute Freedom. Freedom from desire, freedom from wants. Yet the body of the sage remains the same. Not to the sage, but to the people looking at the sage. The sage realizes he has no body. He has no body. But the body of the sage goes through its karma. In order for a sage to come to this plane, to present himself or herself as a sage, they have to take on a body. Otherwise no one would ever hear of a sage. If Ramana Maharshi didn't have a body, no one would ever have heard of him. So this is true of every sage that ever lived. They have a body in order to teach in their own inimitable way. So everything that the sage does is a teaching, so to speak. The sage is not a teacher, but everything that he does is a teaching.

A sage kills your mind, destroys the mind. When the mind is destroyed there is eternal happiness, total freedom. As long as you have a mind, you're thinking, you never will be happy or peaceful. Impossible. For this is not a world of happiness—or thinking. This world is not a world of peace. Yet the body appears to be doing the same thing everybody else does. It's like the example of the fan. You pull out the plug of the fan, it keeps rotating till it stops. You pull out the plug of the fan, it doesn't stop instantaneously, does it? It keeps going for a while before it stops, slows down and stops. Such is the body of the sage who comes to this plane with the plug out. When the fan stops, so to speak, then the sage disappears. He drops the body and leaves. So while the sage is on this plane, always remember he's like the fan, going without the plug. There is no karma being accrued.

There are many different Jnanis. And we can't judge these things. The worst thing we can ever do is to become judgmental, compare, find fault. As long as we believe we are a body and a mind, we can never really understand what a sage is—never. It's impossible. For the mind is not meant to do that. There are also certain sages in this world called Avadhoots. Avadhoot really means "crazy adept." This sage comes to this world to tear your world apart. He purposely is here to tear your world apart, to see what you believe, your systems. Everything that you stand up for. The sage tears you all to pieces to show you it doesn't matter, not to be wrapped up in anything. In other words, the sage can go into a bar, see a bunch of people drinking, he'll join them drinking, be one of them. He can get twice as drunk as they are. But they will feel the difference by being with the sage. So what happens then, they will become sort of realized inside, and start to pursue a spiritual life. A sage may appear to be a fool, but this comes from your viewpoint. Yet the sage has nothing to do with the body.

Take the example of the screen. You go to see a movie called *The Godfather*. On the screen you see all sorts of violence, murders, mayhem, confusion. All this happens on the screen, blood falling all over the place. But is the screen affected at all? After the movie is over, the screen is just the same as it was before. The screen has not been affected one iota. The images have finished and are gone, and the screen remains the same. That is how it is with the sage. A sage always realizes he is the screen. And all the images are a superimposition on him.

Everything the body of the sage does is simply like the images on the screen. Yet the paradox is the sage knows he is the sage, with other words, with other names. He realizes the body is a body. When you look at the sage, you see something different. You see a human being. You see a person like yourself. And you create a sage in your own image. You want certain expectations with the sage. You expect the sage to behave in a certain way, do certain things that you believe are true and right. You believe it is real.

Whereas the sage is always smiling and happy and observes you and watches you. Leaves you alone. Lets you dig your own grave, so to speak. The sage will never interfere in your life. Remember, the sage is not a problem solver. All problems are of the mind. What does the sage have to do with this? Nothing. *All works out of the mind.* The sage is beyond the mind, beyond thinking, beyond thoughts, beyond doing, beyond appearances. This is why there is nothing more powerful than being with the sage. And having a quiet mind.

Your job is never never to be judgmental whatsoever. Have no opinions for or against anything. Why? Because it's where you are coming from. That's how you see it. But when I speak like this sometimes, it blows the ego. Because the ego's sitting there saying, "You can't say that to me. I've got my own mind. I've got my own opinion." It just keeps you back really, if you're here to try to become enlightened, so to speak, awakened. You hold yourself back because you're judgmental. You've got your own preconceived ideas what a sage is, what you are, what you want, what you need, and it stunts your growth. This is why the best course of action is for you to stop thinking whatsoever. Catch yourself every time you think. And put a stop to it. Stop your mind from thinking totally and completely. For all thoughts are erroneous. I don't care what the thoughts are, how good the thoughts may be, how twisted your thinking may be. As long as you're thinking, you're hindering yourself.

Again, some of you might say, "But what about my work? I've got to think of my future. I've got to think of the present. I've got to think of my bills. I've got to think of my family. I've got to think of this and that." There is a Power which knows the way. If you but surrender to this Power, all your needs will be met from within. All of your needs will be met from within, always. But if you sit there being judgmental, say that you can find peace and happiness by doing certain things, it will never happen. And the body will come back again and again and again on this earth plane. Always searching, always looking for something, but never just being.

A true Jnani is something that you can never understand yourself. It's impossible. You can't understand with your mind. For there are no explanations in the mind. Therefore, you expect the sage to be what you are. And you will say that he is just a person like me. He or she does the same things that I do. Always remember the sage knows he has no body. Even if a body appears to you, the sage knows one hundred percent that he has no body. Never had a body, nor will have a body. And the sage looks at you and sees himself. He looks at the world and sees himself. There's no way else for the world to look to the sage but the Self, because he always sees himself everywhere he looks. By seeing himself, I mean he realizes the whole universe is inside of him. It emanates through his mind, so to speak. It's how it appears to you. You are told not to judge by appearances at all. Every teacher has said this. Do not judge by appearances. Yet most of us do. It's up to each one of us to do the right thing. And learn the truth about your body.

Do not become bored, bored with life. Some of you become bored with satsang. And you look for new teachers, new satsangs, new jobs, new people in our lives. We're looking for happiness, aren't we? Immediately we'll have happiness if we do all these things we just mentioned. Nothing could be further from the truth. It will only be a temporary condition. This is why the wise person hangs on the Jnani in all circumstances. They don't look to be bored or not bored, no matter what's going on. If you're being in the presence of the sage all the time, it'll happen automatically. If you get bored and want to change things, you start all over again. You'll be born again. You go to a new country, you find a so-called teacher, and hear something interesting. Get involved with the teacher. The teacher becomes boring after a couple of years, and you look for somebody else. It never stops. Everything will stop when you stop. When you become still and Consciousness begins to move through you, becomes you, this is the meaning of, "Be still and know that I am God."

Be still. Stop searching. Stop looking. Stop being. Everything, you already have. You are totally free and liberated now. So be it.

Self, Beyond Mind—the Search for Truth

We live in a world of duality. For every up there is a down. For every backward there's a forward. For every amount of pressure that's pressed forward there's an equal amount of pressure that's pressed backward. This is duality.

If you get hooked on the world, you will always be disappointed. Why, therefore, should we quarrel with each other? Why should we be upset with one another? Why should we believe something is wrong somewhere? Because we do not understand. If you try to figure life out in your mind you will get nowhere. Everything will just become more confusing. You cannot understand life the way it appears. No one can. If you try to understand life the way it appears, you will become insane. Take a look at the world. Has there ever been peace? You cannot have peace in a world of duality. For every collective peace in the world there is a collective war, and for every war there is a peace. And so it goes.

If you look at your life in retrospect, you will see you've had all sorts of upside downs and right side ups. Things last for awhile, then they change. Nothing's ever the same. We therefore learn to turn to God. For religions tell us God is the answer. Yet no one understands what God is. What does the word God mean? It is usually something that somebody turns to when their life is in upheaval. When things do not go right in one's life, then they turn to God. But is that the answer? We have had more wars in the name of religion than all the other wars put together. When we begin to have a little wisdom, we begin to recognize that we have to turn within. The only God we will ever discover is "I Am."

We begin to investigate I Am. In the beginning we believe I Am is apart from us. As we pray, as we become peaceful, as we develop humility, as we develop love, we begin to feel something else. We begin to feel that our true nature is expansive. That we are not limited to the body. We begin to understand that this expansiveness is of the mind, and for years we become involved in the mental sciences, realizing that everything comes from the mind and the mind is unlimited. One day we inquire, "Where did the mind come from?" And we come to the conclusion that the mind is the formulation of ideas, imagination, things. In other words we discover the mind is only a bundle of thoughts, thoughts about the past and thoughts about the future.

As we grow, we seek for the way to eliminate the mind, to transcend the mind, to transmute the mind. For we begin to realize it is the mind that keeps us earthbound, that makes us think we're human. And then there's the mind that makes us think we're expansive, that the whole universe is a creation of the mind. All these things are true in our search for truth. There has never been a mistake. There are those people who become involved in different yogas, in particular, raja yoga.

They begin to feel the mind is very powerful and can cause everything and anything to happen. And so it is most people stay at that level for a lifetime, discovering interesting ways to use the mind, trying to become successful through use of the mind, trying to heal through the use of the mind. Unless these people find a proficient teacher who can lift them up out of the mind, they will be involved in mind-stuff for thousands of years. For the mind likes to play games with you. It likes to make you believe that you reincarnate and that you go through astral planes and mental planes and causal planes, that you have lived before thousands of times, that you've had various experiences thousands of times. These things are true for the person that believes in their mind. Just as a dream is true as long as you're dreaming. When you are dreaming you will never believe that your dream is false. When you are working out of your mind, you will never believe that your experience in life is false.

Right now we're all sitting here, and you believe that you're sitting in a group of people and I'm giving a talk and everything is real. But the truth is, none of these things exist. It is most difficult to go beyond the mind. As long as we're working at the level of the mind, we feel safe and secure. We learn that if we don't like a situation, we change our mind. If we want to create a new life we begin to imagine it first in our mind. We use our imagination to picture the situation we would like to be in and then the mind will create it. Now this is true as far as it goes. But it does not bring you freedom, liberation or happiness.

When you play mind games you have to go through all sorts of experiences. Yet if you're truly sincere, as I said, if you've got humility, if you have faith in the unknown, something will happen to you. You may be attracted to a teacher, or it may happen of its own accord, which is very rare. You will come to the conclusion that the mind has to be destroyed, totally annihilated in order to become liberated. And you wonder how to do this. If you don't have the proper teacher, you may go on for incarnation after incarnation, century after century, being stuck in diversions of the mind. But if you have the right attitude within yourself, and I use the word humility again, and you are sincere, either a teacher or a book or something within you which is the Self will tell you the way to destroy the mind is by stopping your thoughts—putting an end to all thinking, causing your mind to be quiescent, having a quiet mind.

Once the mind is free of thoughts, your true nature, realization, comes forth by itself. So you want to free yourself from thinking all thoughts. Remember, I'm not saying you want to change bad thoughts for good thoughts. This is futile. It will only last for a duration. You want to remove all thoughts, arriving at a no-thought state. How to do this? You begin to practice mantras, for it is true, when you are repeating a mantra, you have no time to think. It is the only thought that persists. And if you repeat the mantra correctly and are sincere about it, your mind will slow down. When your concentration becomes one-pointed, you go into a state which is called savikalpa samadhi, when you concentrate on one point, which is your mantra. This takes a long time and is a lot of work. It usually takes many lifetimes before you go to the next state by using mantras.

But a time does come when the mantra begins to do you, and there is silence for a while. The time does come by doing mantras that you experience great periods of deep silence. You merge in Consciousness for awhile and you taste the bliss of eternity. This stage is called nirvikalpa samadhi. But it doesn't last. You may become proficient in nirvikalpa samadhi where you can do feats like being buried alive for a week and then being unburied and you're still living. You may make your heart stop beating and you look as if you're dead, but you have merged with Absolute Reality. But then it always comes back; the world always comes back. And you still relate to your problems. You still relate to the world. You still have a worried mind except for the time you go into nirvikalpa samadhi. But it doesn't last. This is as far as a person can go by themselves. It is only a rare few that go further by themselves.

Guru, Grace, Service, and Liberation

The average meditator has to find a Satguru, an enlightened one who has passed that stage and the enlightened one can give them Grace, so that they may transcend the nirvikalpa samadhi and go into sahaja samadhi, which is becoming normal again but always in a state of bliss, transcending the world, being in a permanent state of liberation and yet back to your normal self. By normal self, I mean you begin to function like everybody else in the world, but deep inside you are not of this world. You have become totally liberated. You have become Absolute Reality, Pure Awareness. You have become all-pervading. You have become totally free.

Many people ask me again and again, "Robert, what is the fastest way to get there?" Many teachings are given to the person. Usually when I'm with someone I am able to see how far they've gone in their spiritual unfoldment and they proceed accordingly. Yet there is one way that is above all ways. There is one way to get there faster than any other way you could possibly have. And I usually share this only with intimate devotees. The reason for this is because others will take it the wrong way. Those that are not prepared to hear this, it's like hitting a nerve. Some people even become upset over it. Yet I feel tonight that everyone here is very sincere about their spiritual life, so I'll share this with you. And it's very simple. It is beyond Self-inquiry, it is beyond becoming the observer, and it is this: being of service to the guru. How does this strike you?

Why? Jay knows why. Why, Jay?

I don't know.

You know. When you are of service to the guru, you are of service to the Self. There is only one Self. Therefore, you are of service to your Self. There are not two entities, the guru and the disciple. You begin to become the Self, for you are serving the Self.

Every great sage has shared this secret with their closest devotee. And it's not for everyone, especially in the West. I feel this evening that I should share this with you.

What do you mean by service?

Treat the teacher as you would treat yourself. In other words, you find no difference. The guru becomes yourself, your lover, your mother, your father. Your Self. When you think of yourself, you want the best for yourself. So when you think of your teacher, you want the best for your teacher. There are no longer two of you. There's only one. This is why many devotees of Ramana Maharshi became Ramana Maharshi. They acted like him, they spoke like him, they had all his mannerisms.

They became liberated. Because there's only one liberator, and that is the Self.

So many of you have asked me the fastest way to get there; I have revealed it. Again, I think this is very important. Therefore if you have any questions, feel free to ask.

Well, if I'm with Ramana, how am I going to give service to him and be as he is, when it's my interpretation of what he is, my perception of what he is?

You have to surrender completely. That's the first thing you do, you surrender all of your thoughts, all of your ambitions, all of your doubts, all of your apprehensions, all of your being to the Self. You become empty of all of your preconceived ideas, all of your concepts. It's like taking a garbage pail and emptying it out, totally and completely, of all of your preconceived ideas, everything you've ever known and learned, giving it all to the Self.

Wouldn't service to any form of life, taken as the Self, be equally effective, not just to a guru?

Not really, due to the fact that when you are of service to a tree and you plant something around the tree and you take care of the tree, you water the tree, you watch the tree grow beautifully. The tree is not activated to give Grace. Only a Self-realized being can give Grace. Therefore when you are giving to humanity, to nature, it is only an aspect of Consciousness. But when you give and surrender to a Satguru or to the Self, then the return comes forth quickly. The Grace comes forth quickly. Again, only when you think of a Self-realized sage, can the Grace come forth so that you become like the sage.

Didn't Ramana talk about the sage Donatrea—that he had twenty-four masters, and I think that included inanimate objects?

Dattatreya. Yes, I know who you are referring to. This is quite true. But as I said before, this is very rare, just like Ramana became Self-realized by himself, and he didn't do anything. But this is very rare. That's why it's dangerous to read books about sages like Dattatreya, especially for Westerners. Because it tells you in the book, like you just said, he surrendered to the trees, to the rivers, to the mountain, to the twenty-four elements, and he became liberated. This is all good and well for him, but how about you? These are very rare beings. Try to remember again, the only reason I'm sharing this with you is because so many of you call me and tell me, "I've been practicing for years, I've been practicing Self-inquiry till it's coming out of my nose, and nothing is happening." Let me tell you again, that practicing Self-inquiry is an excellent practice. If you forget about time and practice, it will take you to the goal eventually. But the fastest way to get there in this life is total service and surrender to the Self. If anyone doesn't feel right about this, tell me. This is why these things are not discussed. I did discuss this with Ramana Maharshi and he agreed with me one hundred percent. But he also added, "This method is only good for ripe devotees."

So, what do you think? I'm not saying this to you for myself. This is why sometimes it is dangerous for me to say things like this. Don't get the wrong idea. I'm really no one important. I'm just revealing the truth to you. You can take it however you like. And I'm only doing this because so many of you have asked me to tell you. And I think this class is ripe for me to share this with you.

Robert, does Self-inquiry lead to the possibility of the person being able to surrender completely to the guru? Because I, at this point, feel that it's so far beyond me; I'm so selfish and so unwilling to give up so many things.

Thank you for being truthful. Most Westerners are like that. They have not been brought up with that kind of understanding. The ego is very big in most Westerners. And I don't even like to talk about things like this. As I mentioned before, it hits a nerve when I talk about things like this. It is only for the few people who are ready to go all the way and become totally liberated in this life.

Robert, if I want to let go of my little mind, I guess you've shown me a doorway of surrendering my mind to the Self-realized person. I've got to be willing to either trust or take a chance, because you know there are always people talking about meeting gurus who turn out to be untrustworthy. So, you've given me a kick in the pants that I think is good. And I may not serve you, because if all these other fifty-five people here start serving you, there won't be any spot for me, so I've got to find somebody else. (laughter)

I'm not particularly saying to you to serve me at all. I am telling you to serve your Self.

I understand, but it tricks me into serving the Self.

There is only one Self. That Self is the tree, the mountain, but it does not give Grace.

Yes, that was a good explanation. Because I wondered about that very thing, and you really explained it well for me. The difference is the Grace.

Most of you were ready for this. That's the reason I shared this with you.

Need for a Living Guru

Does the guru have to be in the body? When having Ramana as a guru . . .

If you really want to make headway fast, follow one direction. Go one way. You may find many contradictions when you read so many books, and you'll become confused and even disgusted. To give you an example. The book by Laksharman Swami, *No Mind. I Am the Self.* Many of you have read this, and you're so excited over that book that I read it, also. I usually don't read books. But I realize the contradictions, and for a person trying to awaken, the contradictions can hurt. It can set you back. For you do not understand. I'll explain one of the contradictions.

Laksharman Swami claims that the only way you can become enlightened is through a living guru. And if the guru passes away, you should find another guru, because that guru is no longer any good for you. It's got to be a living form. To an extent this is true. Yet if you read Ramana's books, Ramana Maharshi tells you, it is better to have a mental guru when your guru passes away. So they asked him, "When you die or give up your body Ramana, shall I find another guru?" And he said "Just think of me. If you think of me, I will always be with you. I will never leave you if you think of me. For after all, the sage is not the body. So what difference does it make if there is a body or not?"

That appears as a contradiction, doesn't it. Yet it's really not. You have to understand where they're coming from.

Laksharman Swami was talking to neophytes when he made that statement—beginners. People who really never practiced. So people who have never practiced or practiced little, are not really devotees. Therefore if the average person found a Satguru, and in a month the Satguru gave up his body and left, they wouldn't really get any benefit from that Satguru because they were not in tune with him for a long time. For them it's better to have a living guru, so that the living guru can teach them. But for the devotees, they need not a living guru. The guru that they've been with will take care of *all* their needs. For their guru can never leave them. After all, the guru and the Self are one, there's no difference. So you can see there appears to be a contradiction, but there's not a contradiction. It depends who he was talking to. So when you read the books, it becomes confusing for you. If you stick to the transcripts, you'll be safe, and you will make headway. Those three things I outlined for you are very important. Sadhana, satsang, and the transcripts. It's easy. Remember those three things. Try to be at satsang all the time, work on your sadhana or Self-inquiry, or whatever you have to do, and keep reading the transcripts.

Robert on Defining the Seeker, Disciple, and Devotee

A "seeker" is a blessed person, who because of experience in different lives, has been fortunate enough to begin searching for truth. A seeker spends many years, perhaps many incarnations, seeking truth. The mistake they make is they go from teacher to teacher, from hatha yoga to karma yoga, bhakti yoga to kundalini yoga. They go from Christianity to Hinduism, from Hinduism to Buddhism. From Buddhism to

Zen, from Zen to Tao; the seeker keeps going from one to the other. The seeker has not yet practiced anything; they just listen at different meetings. They read book after book on all kinds of subjects. They become very intellectual as far as truth teachings are concerned, and are able to discuss anything under the sun; they can talk about everything. They can talk about all kinds of spiritual subjects. Yet, they have never had a spiritual experience!

This can be dangerous if they do not find an efficient teacher who will explain to them what they are doing, for they can go on like that all their lives, and go from one life to the next, one life to the next, one life to the next. They will remain a seeker because the path becomes interesting.

You know what it is like? It is like a king who invited you to the kingdom to share it with him. And he lives on two hundred acres of beautiful land, so you drive in the front gate and you're on the way to the king's house, but you see beautiful flowers and you become fascinated. You forget about the king and get into agriculture and start planting new flowers. Then you remember the king again so you start driving. This time you see beautiful caves and rock formations, and you become fascinated so you stop again and become involved with rock formations and caves!

You forget about the king. Years pass. You remember the king again, so you go forward. And this time you see dancing girls dancing in the flowers and you get fascinated with that. Again years pass. You never get to the king. If you got to the king, he would have shared the kingdom. That is what a seeker does. A seeker becomes fascinated by different teachings and buys every book about that particular teaching and becomes well read, but never has a spiritual experience.

Now we come to the "disciple" or a seeker who has been touched by a teaching. The disciple discovers Zen and just loves it, but instead of staying with one teacher he goes from Zen teacher to Zen teacher. Not like the seeker, who goes from one teacher to the other. At least the disciple is settled down and sits with a teacher awhile, then goes to another Zen teacher and then to another Zen teacher. And they go like this from incarnation to incarnation.

Now a "devotee" is completely different. A devotee has found the path he was looking for and the teacher he wants, so he *becomes* the path. He *becomes* the teaching. He takes care of the particular path he is on. It becomes a reciprocal thing. A devotee realizes the teacher of his path has given up everything to reach the path, so he takes care of the teacher's needs and devotes himself to that path. What happens to that kind of devotee? Pretty soon he merges with the teacher's consciousness. He becomes realized. That's the basic difference between the seeker, disciple and the devotee. Any questions about anything?

So the question is, according to how much I think I am a "me" and I don't believe that things are predetermined.... In other words, I seem to think or feel I have a choice if I want to be a disciple or devotee, or if I'm going to go somewhere or not.

It appears that way, but again you are speaking from an ego viewpoint.

That is the "me" that is blocking understanding?

If you were not a "me" there would be no one to ask the question. The question would not even come up. But as long as you are the "me" then you think whether you have a choice or not. Just the thinking about shows you are "me." You follow? So this is addressed to "me's." (laughter)

I think what is arising within me and what bothered me for a while is that (another teacher) teaches that all you need to do is to believe you are not a "me." Teachings themselves will perform their work even though you still feel like a "me." He will say you should believe you are Krishna and deny that you are Arjuna even while you still feel like you are Arjuna.

He has a point to an extent. It is like a razor's edge. I don't like to say that. It gives new people license to do what they like, to become arrogant and belligerent, to say: "I am total awareness, nothing matters." I have seen many people with those attitudes who were just beginners. So you have to be careful, and this is why Ramana Maharshi was so wise. He taught two ways. One of bhakta. Self-Surrender, and one of Atma Vichara. Maybe both were correct, but to identify with the Self is sometimes not easy. So you have to practice certain disciplines or meditations or surrendering yourself to God. This will make you humble, it will give you humility, and will automatically lead to Atma Vichara, Self-inquiry. Then everything will happen of its own accord. We have to be very careful especially with Westerners, not to believe "I am Consciousness" or "I am God" and "I am Ultimate Oneness." We realize that this is the Ultimate Truth about ourselves. But then watch yourself, your actions, see what you are talking about. Do not use truth to cover up your weakness. For example, if you were a drug user, it is true that if you come to satsang, and you understand Reality, eventually you will stop using drugs. But in the meantime, do the best you can, physically, mentally and otherwise to stop the habit. It is preordained anyway, but do the best you can. As you follow the teachings, everything will take care of itself.

Stump the Guru

It is now time again to play "Stump the Guru."
Did we pass the basket around to get all the
ridiculous questions?

A Dialogue with Robert

Some people wonder if it is good to ask questions at satsang. Some are afraid to appear stupid. If you don't understand the teachings, ask questions. On the other hand, if you come here with the right attitude, all questions will be answered from within yourself. Don't hesitate to ask questions about anything at all.

You say to us, "You don't have to believe me, you don't have to take my word." But I think belief in the words and in the teacher are very important, because there has to be trust to accept the validity of the teachings, the method of the teacher, as well as the general instructions he gives.

I hear you. That's a good point. I'm referring to those seekers who have been around from teacher to teacher and they just accept everything the teacher tells them without investigation. The way it should be done is, if I say something you should investigate it thoroughly within yourself to see if it has any validity. Do not just accept anything I say on blind faith, but intelligently. Look at what I say. Feel it within yourself, and if it's real, something will tell you. And you will feel something. You will feel love for the teacher. That will come as a result of investigation. So I'm really speaking to all the seekers who run from one teacher to the next, and they believe anything. If the teacher tells them flying saucers landed, they just believe that without investigation. So don't just accept that on blind faith. Confirm it within yourself. Your Heart will tell you if it's real or not, and you'll know. Always listen to your Heart.

What does that mean, listen to the Heart?
It means your Heart is your real Self, and it will never lie to you. If you tune in correctly to your Heart center, your real Self will advise you and tell you if your teacher is good for you or not, will advise you and inform you of everything you need to know. Your Heart is the Self, God.

I'm very confused with my mind and my Heart.
Well, you know, the mind is nothing. The mind is only a bunch of thoughts. Thoughts about the past and the future, that's all a mind is. But the Heart is a center of stillness, of quietness, of Absolute Peace. When you rest your mind in your Heart, you feel a joy and a bliss that overwhelms you, and you'll know. Surrender your mind to your Heart and you'll feel it.

If someone believes in the saying, or in the book, that when they feel peace, joy, happiness, and have attained this or that, that's the stuff that shouldn't be believed or accepted because you want to experience the truth.
If you're really going to your Heart, it goes beyond belief. The true Heart is the Self. It cannot fool you. The mind will fool

you. But in a true surrender of the mind into the Heart center, you will actually feel a bliss and a joy that you never felt before.

Well that's what I mean in reference to believing the teacher explaining something.

In this day and age there are many teachers but few disciples. Most people do not want to do anything, but they want to become a teacher. The world is filled with teachers. It is up to you to use your own discernment and find out who the true teacher is.

Isn't it true it's really not an external teacher, that really where the unfoldment happens …

The true teacher is within yourself, and if you're true to yourself, your teacher from within you will lead you to the teacher without, and you'll both be one, and you'll know it.

But even beyond that, whatever I have experienced, I realize very clearly it has nothing to do with the teacher that I've already found and studied. It's always the Self. It has nothing to do, when it comes right down to it, with outside teachers.

The teacher is also a catalyst for you to find yourself.

Actually, effort can only take you so far.

True.

You can't will yourself into Self-realization. You can only go so far, and after a point you become pulled into it. And isn't that the goal of the guru?

You don't even get pulled into him. You simply awaken to yourself. And the guru is a catalyst for that to happen.

You said that it is the happiness that will bring the good to you, that happiness is the same as abundance, health, joy, peace, harmony, that these things come to you as a result of happiness. Many Masters were not very healthy. They had many physical problems.

Who sees those problems? They don't see it. You do. They see happiness and joy. But you see the body wasting away. Find out who they really are. Find out who you really are. You'll see a completely different picture. It's when you see problems, ask who sees all the dastardly things in this universe. We see them. They don't really exist, but we see them. So we have to lift ourselves up to the place where they don't exist. Where harmony exists, bliss, joy, exist. So we have to lift ourselves up.

But they still feel the discomfort.
Who says so?

I don't know.
It's all your pictures. It's all your world. The way you see it. *All is well.*

Robert, I don't know if other people have felt this or feel this. But for myself, I feel a lot of times, I feel trapped between two worlds, so to speak. And I know that's all in my mind thinking. But it feels like I am completely caught between the spiritual part of me, of life, and a more materialistic or a physical sort of existence. I am caught up in my thoughts and my feelings, and I feel really trapped. I feel both of them, sort of warring, two parts of me.

Yes, you have to resolve this when you get up in the morning, when you wake up in the morning, first thing. Look around you. Look at your environment. Look at yourself, and ask the question, "Who am I?" Keep asking yourself, "Who am I?" and everything else will fade away. You will grow spiritually. There will be One, not two. But you'll have to take the bull by the horns, so to speak.

I really understand what you are saying intellectually, but I guess I don't experience it.
When you first get up in the morning, deny the whole world.

That's very difficult to do when I'm going out into that world. I'm really in that world a lot.
The world keeps changing. It's never the same.

That's true.
It's not real. Anything that changes can't be real.

Why?
How can it be real if it disappears? Reality is permanent.

Reality means non-changing?
Yes, that's Reality. Since everything else changes, it can't be Reality. So when you get up in the morning, understand this. First thing when you open your eyes, ask yourself, "Who am I?" Just put this question and see what will happen to you. You'll feel something different. But you'll have to do it every morning. Just try it and see what happens. You'll see Oneness. Keep asking yourself, "Who am I? Who am I?" when you first get up. After that you'll see One Power, One Presence. You are One. Everything will work out for you. Practice.

You must remind yourself as soon as you open your eyes in the morning. You simply remember every day that, "I am not the body/mind phenomena. I am nothing to do with the world. I, is really Consciousness, Emptiness, Nirvana, Sat-Chit-Ananda. I is really Parabrahman. I am That." Just to remember, not to forget to remember, is the important point.

Do not think about world affairs. The world will take care of itself. The world is unfolding as it should. Do not think about your affairs. As far as you know, you are under the law of karma. And the Lord of Karma, Ishvara, will take care of everything. So don't even think about those things. Do not think, in other words, of the world as manifestations, and do not think about the body and its problems, but rather inquire, "To whom does this body come? To whom does the mind come that keeps thinking and thinking and thinking? Who possesses it? I do. But my real I is Absolute Reality. Therefore, the I that appears to have a body and its problems, the I that appears to perceive the world and the universe, must be a false I. Yet where did it originate? What gave it birth?"

Then you can think of the power source, the spiritual Heart on the right side of your chest. If you desire, you may see a picture of your deity that you respect in the center of the ball of light on the right side of your chest. Whether it's the Buddha or Moses or Jesus or whomever. And you watch the I as it comes out of that center and goes up to your brain. And then all of a sudden, you identify with your body and the world comes into being. And the mind appears to sustain it all. That's when you catch yourself. You reverse the process. You watch the I returning from the brain. You abide in the I. You hold onto the I. You follow the I-thread. You trace the I as it returns to the spiritual Heart center and disappears. Then you keep silent. You just keep totally silent. If thoughts do appear, you inquire, "To whom do they come?" and you keep silent again. As you practice this every day, day after day, week after week, month after month, year after year, something will give. Something has to give, and you will become free. Free in the Silence.

Robert, yesterday my wife and I went to a shopping center and had some ice cream, and she asked me if I enjoyed it, and I said, "Yeah." But at the time of enjoying it there was no 'I'. Afterwards came the thought, "I'm enjoying it." When I got home I asked myself, "To whom does this come?" But when I looked at it, while I was experiencing it, there was no 'I' experiencing it, there was just experiencing. Afterward came a thought, "I am experiencing it." At the time of experiencing it, there was no 'I' experiencing it.

Who was eating the ice cream?

There was no 'I' at the time. There was just enjoyment.

Who was the enjoyer?

I don't know. There was just enjoyment. There doesn't seem to be an enjoyer either.

That's good, true. You're right. There is no one there to enjoy anything. There's just enjoyment. When you think you're enjoying it, you're spoiling it all, because if you're enjoying something, the ice cream will be finished and you'll be upset. There's no ice cream left. But if you get yourself out of the way, and there's only enjoyment without a person or a thing being enjoyed, then you can eat ice cream, do anything you like, and you'll always be free and happy.

Robert, is there anything you could say for when a person who has a temporary loss of identification with their body and mind, and during those hours the person has the sense of Being, just Being. Is there anything that can be done during those hours to help prevent the awareness or focus slipping back into body/mind?

What's going to happen will happen of its own accord. When you have periods of nirvikalpa samadhi, that's good. All you've got to do is keep on doing what you're doing, and it will intensify all by itself when you're ready. There's something within you that knows exactly when it's going to happen. Everything is preordained. But your job appears to be to dive deeper into the Self. When you feel yourself coming out if it, pose the question, "Who's coming out of it? Who went in?" The person who went in it doesn't exist any longer. He's been transcended. So who's coming out of it, and in what form? Ask the question to yourself and you will find that you stay in it longer and longer.

But everything is right. There are no mistakes. So when you do come out of it, do not believe there's something wrong, or you've got to stay longer. After all, that's the ego that says that. But simply watch yourself. Observe, look, be, and everything will take care of itself. The worst thing you can do is to analyze. Do not analyze what happened. Just watch, observe. The ego is the great analyzer. It wants to analyze everything. It wants to know. When there is no one left to know, then you will be That all the time. After all, who knows? The Shadow knows. Remember the Shadow?

Yes, Lamont Cranston.
Right.

" 'What evil lurks in the heart of man.' "
That's right.

We're all from the same generation.

I have a question. I have been reading a lot about a few people in Ramana's time. Just by a look or even a hug . . . . There is a story of Annamalai. Ramana ran over to Annamalai, hugged him for two minutes, and he became spontaneously enlightened. And then he spent the next thirty-eight years stabilizing in that, and then certain other cases. . . . So I was wondering if you could speak a little bit about transmission.
Yes. Remember that Annamalai Swami was not an ordinary person. He was extraordinary because he had been in the teachings many years. He had prepared himself and he was very humble, filled with humility.

He was just a boy when it happened.
Yes, he had a joy in his Heart, and looked at Ramana as the Divine Universe. Ramana was the whole Universe to him. So he had something inside of him, so when Ramana hugged him and loved him that way, what was left dropped away, and he became enlightened. Now this is true of us too. We're not different from Annamalai, except that with us, we have such things in our heads that keep us back from being ourselves, we are filled with our own garbage. And when this happens we have a long way to go. So we must first develop humility. We have to develop love, peace. If we stop thinking so much about person, place and things, the sage will give you a hug, or whatever and it will happen to you, too, depending on the person, depending on what's going on, depending on circumstances. There are no mistakes. Everything is in its right place.

So, Robert, that transmission is radiating all the time. It's not that Ramana just all of a sudden turned on the juice, to that one person.

Yes, exactly.

And it's just that the person has to be receptive and open so that the transmission can be received.

Indeed, very true. Grace is always with you. There is never a time when Grace is not. It's up to you to receive it in the right way, by preparing yourself. And the best way you can prepare yourself is to keep the mind still and quiet.

How can a seeker maximize his serious relationship with the sage? What can he do to make the relationship deeper?

Simply by sitting with the Jnani all day long. When you're home, where you're working, think of the sage. When you think of the sage's form, the sage's name, things will begin to happen to you. Find peace. Try it. Then you will be with the sage continuously. Whenever you think of a living sage, the sage becomes part of your Heart, it's the complete Heart. And you feel the love of the sage within you. So if you think of the sage, the sage will think of you. Whatever you think about, that you become ultimately. So you have to be very careful what you think about. Whatever you think about, you become. Think of the sage, you become the sage.

Robert, in talking with some satsang people, some of them say that, "I cannot do much of Self-inquiry," or some of them also say, "I don't care much for Self-inquiry," or, "What I want to do is go and sit with Robert." Would you comment on that?

Well, what can I say? Actually, our being together at satsang is the entire teaching. The words are merely a pointer to be able to sit in the Silence together and find peace. So what you're saying, Jorje, is true. Just being together does the trick.

What's the trick?
The trick is to wake up. I call it a trick, because most people don't realize that all they have to do is keep quiet, and then they'll be awake. So I trick them into making a speech instead of telling them just sit with me, and all will be revealed. Thereby hearing the words, people believe they found something out. But the words are to make you sit quietly and behave yourselves. (laughter)

Robert, you're saying that it's the Grace that flows from the Silence that transforms us?
Oh, yes, true. Grace is already there. You simply have to be quiet enough to pick it up. When your mind is noisy, you pick up the vibration of the world. Just like with a pool of water. When the water is still, it reflects the moon and the stars. But when the water is noisy, it cannot do that at all. It reflects nothing. So when your mind is noisy, it reflects chaos, confusion. When your mind is still and quiet, it reflects your divinity.

Robert, this week you said that the mind has to be destroyed. And in the past you've said there's no mind, the mind doesn't exist. So how can you destroy something that doesn't exist?
To the one who believes he has a mind, he has to destroy the mind. There is nothing to destroy. So it's a question of the person who is seeking, where they're at with their mind. There is no mind. No mind ever existed. But because people have a strong belief they have a mind, just like there is a body. As long as you think there is a strong mind and a strong body,

you have to do things to make it become less and less, destroy the mind and the body. We have to sit around talking like this many times. Depending on who I'm talking to and depending on who's asking the question, certain people will have to do everything they can to obliterate the mind. Other people want to be still for a while and the mind will disappear by itself. Everybody is different. But everybody has a state of mind. Obliterate the mind completely and become liberated. This is everybody's gift. You don't have to stay where you are, you can become liberated. It's a gift to become liberated. But will you do it? I mean you have to want liberation more than anything else in this world. So think of the things you're attached to that come before liberation. That's what I'm talking about. You have to let go of everything. Let go of all your attachments, and liberation will come by itself.

Robert, I've been studying metaphysics most of my life, and I've never been able to get an edge on my suffering. And then after I've been listening to you, there has been a progressive thing happening. At first I was unable to identify with the problems of the world, which was just a tremendous relief to me. And then about a month ago, all of a sudden I was able to not identify any more with the thoughts, the problems with this person. And I found a place where I could be more peaceful and watch this person's thoughts happening. And that's the most freedom I've ever had in my whole life, and the most peace. I'm very grateful to you.

That's wonderful. You're getting rid of the self. You're doing what you're supposed to do. You're making progress. That's wonderful. Keep it up.

I wonder if you could say something about creativity. You said something about the creative life. It is hard to reconcile dropping the mind and using the mind creatively.

Not really. Some of the most famous sculptors, famous artists, did their best work when they did not think. Take Thomas Edison, for example. He used to sit in his rocking chair every day and lose his mind completely. Not think at all. And all the ideas came to him, because it comes out of the Self. The Self of Consciousness is always prevalent. But you give it back, because you're thinking too much. Once the mind stops thinking, Consciousness, the Self, appears by Itself as your creativity, and you become more creative. So do not believe your mind will not be creative. It's not true. You become more creative. Your mind keeps you limited. When your mind is gone, you become more expansive. In any event, what you came to this earth to do in a body, you're going to do, to fulfill. It's all preordained, all predestined. It has absolutely nothing to do with what you think about it, or don't think about it. Your job is to make yourself more peaceful and still, and let nature take its course. Then you'll find that you're totally happy and peaceful, more than you've ever been before.

Are the mind and the ego two separate entities? Or, when you say mind do you mean ego? When you say ego, do you mean mind?

They're both simultaneous. They're both the same.

They are the same?

Yes. In order for us to talk about these things, we have to talk about body and mind, the Self, and ego. There is only One. The One is you. The One is the Self.

Would hypnosis be useful as a means to breaking the hypnosis?

No. Because hypnosis simply contacts the subconscious. It reinforces your ego. You're already hypnotized. So you don't want to double your hypnosis. (laughter) Because then you have to get rid of the hypnotic trance as well as the waking trance.

That's how it appears that it should be.
That's how it appears that it should be? How's that?

That's actually breaking the trance.
Hypnosis can't break the trance. Only you can. By admitting and realizing there never was a trance. That you're already free and liberated now.

Robert, scientists and psychologists and other people, they always try to unlock the limitations of the brain. We use only, say, ten percent of the brain. If we somehow get to the point of using one hundred percent of our brain, would that get us more immersed . . .
More immersed in the ego.

Yes, it is fortunate that we only use ten percent. (laughter)
You're right. (laughter) Because after all, what is the brain? It's an extension of the body. And the more you use the brain, the more lost you become in maya. So you don't want to expand the brain. You want to transcend the brain.

Robert, you said you're not the body, but yet every week I see you and your body looks different to me. Some weeks you look very, very young, and some weeks you look very, very old. Yet I've read in the books that Jnanis have spontaneous transformation, where they would get super rejuvenated. Like they were ready to die, and then all of a sudden they look thirty years younger and have many years to live.

That's what you see.

But when the person is enlightened, and one with this force, this Consciousness, would that have an effect on the appearance of the body?

Only on your appearance. What you see is what you see. The Jnani has no appearance whatsoever. The Jnani is completely empty.

You mean you are the invisible man?

If you see an invisible man, then I am. What you see is what I am.

Sometimes you appear to have no head.

Then I have no head.

It's like the headless horseman.

Whatever you see is what you get. You get what you see.

Robert, when you see someone that you love very much going down a very destructive path, how can you become detached?

You realize that the person does not belong to you. Belongs to God. Therefore, if you have the right wisdom, you'll do something to try to help that person. But then again, karmically, that person has been given to you for you to go through this experience. So the correct answer for this, of course, is to know yourself. If you know yourself, it will take care of the person. For your Self is that person. The greater you know yourself, the greater help the person will receive. For it is only One, and you are That. But when you separate yourself by saying this person is doing this and I'm trying to stop this person, there is duality. And things will get progressively worse. But if you know who you are, then what will happen to this person is what is supposed to happen. I know that's hard. Sometimes you want to grab the person and shake them, and you want to interfere and do something for them. Yet if we could only remember that everything is in its right place and see who we are, that would take care of everything.

We've never done things like this before. We've always taken action. And sometimes the action seems to work. For we've halted a certain situation that appears to be terrible, going in terrible directions, and we've put a stop to it. This is only temporary. Whatever the person has to go through, they will go through, one way or the other. The only relief is to awaken. Consequently, when you awaken, you will see things differently. And this is how you help the person.

Robert, what causes a person to display self-righteous anger to defend another person or a cause? Can you explain?

It's all ego. What else? Only the ego is self-righteous. Only the ego goes for causes. But if you understand what I was talking about today, if you understand slightly how this universe works, you will see that going for causes is not the solution. It appears to be a solution, but it is a temporary solution. Go back in retrospect and see how many justifiable causes there have been in this world since the beginning of time. There have always been causes, righteous causes. Causes for peace and justice. Has the world become any better? Take a look at this world. And yet, the people who are fighting for these causes are necessary. This is their dharma, to do what they're doing, I suppose.

But for the people who come to meetings like this, you have been in this type of teaching for many incarnations. This is why you are able to comprehend something of what I'm talking to you about. The average person on the street has no interest in anything like this. The average activist has nothing to do with things like this. They would have no interest. But you are here. Therefore there is something in your Heart that wants to unfold and become Self-realized and become free.

If I think it enables me to sit in Silence before going to work in the morning, should I actively seek to be transferred closer to home? Or, should I just work on "Who am I?" and trust that right action will take place and my job will be where it's supposed to be, and I should just meekly go where I'm told.

We don't want to be meek, and we don't want to be self-righteous. We want to be the Self, period. Therefore, if you can slow down your mind by allowing it to rest in the Self to an extent, by removing thoughts, feelings, attitudes, and going to a higher plateau by inquiring, "Who am I? To whom do these things come?" then you'll be safe.

But if you see that you cannot do this yet, if you're afraid you'll get fired from your job, you won't have any money, or go to the poorhouse, you'll become a homeless person, then by all means you have to do what you have to do. So you have two choices. Either discover who you are, what your true nature is, by understanding that there is a Power that takes care of you, the Power that knows the way, that will always love you and put you in the right place. Or, you go where you have to go, and do what you have to do. The choice is always yours. There is not one answer or one choice to this question. It depends on the person, where they are, where you're at.

If I took on a person from the street and told her everything will go well with you, don't worry, you don't have to beg, you don't have to steal, that person may starve to death. For that person's karma is to steal and to beg. And we have no right to tell a person how to live. But if that person was able to see the light, so to speak, where the truth is, that they are not the doer, they are not the body, they are not the mind, then they will be lifted up from where they are into a higher state of consciousness and will be taken care of. So you know where you are by the type of thoughts that come into your head. By the type of feelings and emotions that come to you. By how you feel everyday. Take the right action.

There's something within you that knows what to do. There is a Power greater than you, that knows how to take care of you without your help. All you've got to do is to surrender to it. Surrender your thoughts, your mind, your ego, to the Current That Knows The Way. It will take care of you. It will take better care of you than you can ever imagine. Most people are under the mistaken impression that if their thoughts stop, they will vegetate and become a vegetable. On the contrary, you will become spontaneous. You will think just enough to take care of the moment, and everything will be taken care of for you. Try it. We always think we're very important. And we have to think. Only remember the cliché, "I think, therefore I am." It should be, "I am, therefore I don't have to think." (laughter)

When you come in contact with homelessness that you mentioned before, perhaps natural disasters or difficulties that people are going through in different parts of the world or in front of you, what arouses in you, in your state? Does compassion arouse in you? Or, is it arbitrary to you? Meaningless to you? Other people suffering, how do you relate to that, to suffering?

Both are correct. I have a great compassion even though it's meaningless. So I get in there and help. I will give ten dollars to a homeless person. I'll help people in the city. If I'm there I will be part of it. But realize it's meaningless. I'm not the doer. That which appears as a body will do what has to be done. But there is no thought behind it. I do not consider I'm doing something good, I'm doing something bad, I'm helping someone, I'm not helping someone. In reality, no one is doing anything.

What is the so-called blue pearl or the sesame seed?
You mean what Swami Muktananda refers to?

Yes. I heard it referred to by other Swamis or whatever.
The blue pearl is a point of consciousness. Ramana Maharshi uses the right side of the Heart, in the right side of the chest where the Heart, which is Consciousness, resides. So the blue pearl is the same thing. Blue pearl, white pearl, grey pearl, the right Heart, left Heart, it's all the same. It's just a point of reference. It has no real significance. It's a place where you concentrate for the beginner. A beginning student needs to concentrate on a point in the body to become one-pointed, so they stop thinking. So they concentrate on the imaginary blue pearl, or in the Heart in the right side of the chest, or

between the eyebrows, or your navel. And that just makes you one-pointed. When you're one-pointed you can give up all that, and stop thinking all together. Then you become totally free. Catch yourself. What are you thinking about? It's those very thoughts that keep you from awakening. Always catch yourself thinking. And ask yourself, "To whom do these thoughts come?" Even if they're good thoughts. Makes no difference.

Robert, if you see a dream, and a lot of spiritual conditions and religions say that you learn by your dreams, that they guide you. What about this?

There are three states of consciousness, so to speak. The waking, the sleeping, and the dreaming. The deep sleep is when you are Self-realized. There are no thoughts, but you are unconscious of this fact. The dream state is like this. When you are dreaming, you are simply in another state of consciousness that appears very real to you, and is real as long as you are dreaming. And when you awaken from the dream you are in this state of consciousness, which is also a dream. Therefore, what you want to do is to remove all of the dreaming completely and totally, and become absolutely free.

So when you wake up in the morning and you remember your dream ask yourself, "Who dreamt?" And you'll say, "I dreamt." Then you'll realize the dream is part of the "I" again. So inquire, "Who am I?" or, "Where did this I come from?" And follow the I-thread to the source by repeating again and again to yourself, "Who am I? Who am I?" Which really means, "What is the source of the I that has these dreams?" And one day the I will go back into the Heart, into the Heart center which is Consciousness Itself, and you'll be free of all dreams. But your dreams should not be taken too seriously. It is like this life. You're dreaming right now that you are a mortal being. You go through many experiences. You have fears. You have happiness. You have all sorts of emotions. If I tell you you're dreaming this, you won't believe me. You tell me, "Robert, how can I be dreaming? I'm living it." I tell you, "You're dreaming." If you listen to me you will do what you have to do to get out of the dream by inquiring, "Who am I? Where did I come from?" So when you're having a dream at night, it is the same thing. It's merely another dream. But you awaken faster. And then you're in this dream. So stop dreaming completely and awaken and be free.

Is there any difference for visions and dreams?
Oh, no. A dream is like this. The only difference is this is longer. It seems to last longer. But otherwise it's all a mortal dream. When you're dreaming, that's your world for now. You're not conscious through your sleeping or the waking world. But you believe the dream is a waking world. When you wake up, it changes, and this becomes a waking world. But there's no real difference. They're both the same.

And visions are part of the dream?
Visions are all part of the imagination. They're part of the dream. They're a little higher than a dream. But they are in the dream category. Because after all, who is having the vision? The real Self does not need any visions. So a vision is manifested by the mind. Yet as long as you are in your body, you'll have dreams and visions sometimes. But when you are really awake, you will be the witness to your visions, to your dreams, and also to this world.

Robert, when the four principles came to you, was it a dream or a vision, and how do you distinguish between the two?

Well, I don't really know, to tell you the truth. I'm usually aware of what's going on, so all the time I was aware of the vision/dreams taking place.

Including this time.

Yes, I realized I was doing all these things. It was like I was watching everything taking place. But there was never a time when I actually became the dream or the vision.

Or felt totally caught up in it? You were always observing?

Right, I was always observing. But it was like an omnipresent observer.

Could you tell us again—I remember a long time ago, you talked about a vision that you frequently had, in which you would encounter these entities.

Oh, yes. I haven't had that vision in a long time. I had a vision that I was flying through the air and I went to Arunachala, the mountain. I went through the mountain, it was hollow inside. And when I landed in the middle of the mountain, there was Buddha, Krishna, Ramana, Nisargadatta, and many others that I didn't recognize. We all formed a circle. We smiled at each other and we walked toward each other, until we became one blazing light. And the light turned into a lingam. And then I opened my eyes. But I was aware that I was having a vision. And that's it.

And that came to you many times, right?

It used to. It's stopped now.

Did you do Self-inquiry with that?
No. I've never done Self-inquiry. (much laughter)

Why do you recommend it then?
Because it's the way to go.

You're a card.
I'm the whole deck.

Why do you say you've never done it?
Why do I need to do it?

Well, if you studied with these people from the East, my understanding is that that's what they teach.
I didn't go to them for a teaching. I went to confirm my own experiences.

But you said you went to Paramahansa.
Sure, because I was a kid. I had my experiences when I was fourteen years old. And I didn't understand what was going on. So Paramahansa Yogananda explained it to me, and he sent me to India to see Ramana, who explained it further.

Ramana didn't suggest that you do Self-inquiry?
No.

Or "Who am I?"
Never did it.

You didn't need it. You were already . . .
Whatever.

How did Ramana confirm your unitive experience?
With a smile. And most of the things we talked about were mundane.

He just knew that you knew, and smiled?
I have no idea what he knew.

How did you receive his smile?
I smiled back. Then for the rest of the time he inquired about my needs. And he wanted me to tell him about New York.

What did you tell him about New York?
I said, "New York, New York, it's a wonderful town." (laughter)

Robert, is it just insight that you can understand how direct and how powerful Self-inquiry is? Is it just wisdom?
I may make a joke about it, but it works.

So, it's through some kind of inner wisdom that you know?
Definitely.

So once again, Self-inquiry is . . . you could breathe in by saying, "Who am I?" exhale by saying . . .
No, that's not Self-inquiry. Self-inquiry is when you inquire, "Who am I?"

And take it to the Source.
The source of existence. The source of the "I."

Last Thursday you had us go through an exercise which you have us do periodically.

Yes, breathe in saying "I," and exhale saying "Am."

I remember the one she's talking about. You used to also teach us one where we would say, "Who am I?" on the inhale.

Oh yes. When you inhale you say, "Who am I?" before exhaling you say, "I am Consciousness," and when you exhale you say, "I am not the body."

I thought you weren't supposed to answer that question. Just leave it silent and open.

That's the other meditation.

So, the question, "Who am I?" is Self-inquiry?

Yes.

That experience, God knows what it's like, but conceptually it seems like it would be self-authenticated.

It's self-authenticated, but I was a kid. So I felt all these things, and I thought I was going crazy. So I went to find out what was going on.

Even when you're not a kid, you want to understand.

If you're already grown up you can read the books and you can do other things. But in my day there were no teachers except for Joel Goldsmith and Paramahansa Yogananda and people like them . . .

Was the bliss of the Self part of the experience, even though you thought you were going crazy?

Oh yes, of course. By going crazy I mean I no longer conformed to my environment. I didn't care about school, I didn't care about my parents, I was just radiantly happy being by myself. I stopped associating with certain friends.

Why would you need that confirmed? That's self-sufficient.
It's self-sufficient, but I didn't know what it was.

Why do you have to know? Does it require some idea about it?
Because I was still in body consciousness. And the body's got to know. Inquiring minds have to know.

So what you were looking for was a frame of reference, more or less?
Yes, because there was no one close by that I could talk to. And if I did what Ramana did, they would have put me in a psychiatric ward.

Did Yogananda send you directly to Ramana?
He suggested that I go to him.

Had you heard of him before?
Yes, I wanted to become a monk in Self-realization. Yogananda discouraged me.

Why did Yogananda discourage you from becoming a monk?
He told me that's not my path. It's interesting. Whenever I speak of my experiences, people want me to be eaten by snakes, spiders to bite me, they want me to waste away. Then they think I'm a great Soul.

You just haven't suffered enough. Is that true? People really think . . .

Because they read the books of certain saints, and they think certain saints have gone through certain experiences, so everybody has to go through those experiences. That's why I don't talk about myself too much. The truth is, of course, if you really want to know about this body and about the Self in me, know your Self. Find out first who you are. Then you'll know all about me. Otherwise, you'll see me as you see yourself. Do you see what I'm saying?

If you meet a con-man, the con-man's going to look at you and think you're a con-man too. A con-man believes everybody's a con-man. If you meet a person who's filled with love, they will see you as love also. So that's why I say, whatever you are, I am a mirror for you, and you're only seeing yourself.

That's so for everything, though. Not just for you.
For everything, of course.

So what you're saying is, you create your own reality.
Where you are right now, the world that you're seeing is the world that you're creating.

But how does that tie in with everything being predestined?
Everything is predestined.

So you're predestined to create your reality as it is.
That's the way it goes.

That seems paradoxical.
Of course it does. It wouldn't be a truth teaching if it

weren't paradoxical. Everything is preordained if you go to work on yourself to lift yourself up and become free.

There's nothing you can do about it, and yet you have to try to do something about it.
Exactly.

Why is that?
That's the game. And if you try to figure it out, you can't. So don't try.

And that means that when one becomes realized, everything that's preordained doesn't exist anymore, right?
Right. When one becomes realized, the whole game is over. There's nobody to become realized. There's nobody that's not realized. There's no universe, there's no God. There are no others. All is well.

Or, nothing is well, as the case may be.
Touché.

Robert, it seems like it's a gradual realization.
It appears to some people that it's gradual, but when you awaken there never was any graduality. It appears like that sometimes. When you awaken, you know that you've always been awake. There never was a time when you were asleep.

Robert, how did you know enough not to talk about your experience?
In the beginning, I used to ask my teacher about it, and the teacher sent me to the principal. And the principal called my

mother. And my mother did take me to the doctor. And the first doctor said I had hay fever. And then I discussed it with some of my friends and I realized fast I'd better shut up. Even now, my family thinks I'm crazy. I told you before, during Christmas I spoke to my brother who I haven't seen in about sixteen years, and he said, "Are you still good for nothing?" I said, "Yes, are you good for something?" But then I asked him if he was happy and he shut up.

Is it accurate to say that the experiences exemplified by some of these Zen masters is the same as you and Ramana speak of?

There are just different ways of saying it, but Buddhists become enlightened also. Because of karmas and samskaras, we are inclined towards a certain path. It may be Buddhism, it may be mystical Christianity, it may be Advaita Vedanta. We're inclined toward a path from past lives.

Is there a period of assimilation after enlightenment where the understanding deepens and changes one?

There is no deepening involved. You're either awake or you are not. There is an appearance, however, that you become more peaceful, and all the things that used to disturb you seem to dissipate.

So there is a process as realization occurs?

It is not really a process of realization; it's a process to become a better person. Awakening comes by itself and has nothing to do with that. The appearance of improvement happens also, but has nothing to do with realization.

So, you become a better person after Self-realization?
No, not after. After realization there is nobody left to be a better person. The better person comes before. On the other hand, there have been thieves and murderers who suddenly, for some reason or another, have become Self-realized. It depends on the person. Again, you are either awake or asleep. There is no in between. Once you wake up, you realize you have always been awake. There never was a time when you were not. Before that awakening though, you have to go through all kinds of experiences and practices sometimes. It depends on the maturity of the person.

What if the person is immature, and they have a realization of the Self, is the immaturity healed by the realization?
If a person awakens, there is no question of immaturity. There is no one left to be mature or immature. You are just awake. All that we are talking about goes on before awakening.

What about the sinners who have an awakening. What happens to all the karma they generated?
It is completely burnt up. It never existed.

Can you walk over here and wake me up?
As far as I am concerned, you are already awake. You have to be able to see it yourself.

Can someone awaken another by touching them?
It is very rare, but it is possible. It usually happens to a person who has been on a spiritual path for many lives. Then through a touch or a glance, they go all the way and break through maya and become free. If you are asking whether I

can do that, there is no I left to do anything. If I were to do that, there would be a me and a you, but there is no me and there is no you. There is only Ultimate Oneness. There is one Self. There is no one left to do anything to anyone else. The doing is part of the dream. When awakening comes, there is only One. There is no doer. Yogis do things like touching, but not Jnanis. Many awakened people around Ramana Maharshi claimed that when he looked at them or accidentally touched them, it caused an awakening process. He denied everything. It depends on the maturity of the individual. Anything is possible.

Why emphasize freedom so much?
We are not. "Freedom" is just a word to express that you are not what appears to be. You are not bound to anything. There is no bondage. There is no limitation. You are not bound to the earth or to your body.

You nullify everything that is, and what is can be beautiful.
Anything that is beautiful in this world is temporary.

What's wrong with that?
What's wrong is that you are living the mortal dream. Whatever is temporary must come to an end. Then you will experience the other side—unhappiness, sorrow. You experience everything as a mortal being. But who wants to go through life experiencing good and bad, ups and downs? Then you die. Then you repeat everything all over again. You want to get off the wheel and become everlasting joy, Pure Awareness. You want to go beyond what appears to be.

Remember, it is your mortal self who sees the good and bad in the world. Surely you want to go beyond this into Eternity.

If you don't want to, stay where you are. This is why I say, everyone is in their right place. There are no mistakes.

Learn to keep your life simple. Do not become bogged down in this world of effects. The simpler your life is, the better. Practice loving kindness, show peace to all. Do not be swayed by TV or newspapers. Be yourself. Make your life simple, peaceful. Do not listen to rumors. Do not become involved in deep philosophy. Be gentle, humble, and strong. The world may appear hard at times, but don't let it fool you. It has no power over you at all. The reason it appears hard at times is because you allow it to be hard at times. It's just how you see it, how you perceive it. It's all perception. Just look at the world and laugh, and it will go away. Always realize you're Divine protected, Divine guided, to your highest good. You have nothing to fight, nothing to fear. *All is well.*

Silence of the Heart

Everything that you can ever imagine, that you want to be,
you already are.

You are the Imperishable Self that has always been,
that you will always be.
Beyond birth, beyond death, beyond experiences,
beyond doubts, beyond opinions.
Beyond whatever it is your body is going through,
whatever thoughts your mind thinks.

You are beyond that.
You are the Silence,
The Silence of the Heart.

You Are the Silence, the Silence of the Heart

Always ask yourself, "Why am I here?" It is always good to ask yourself this. I don't mean why are you in the universe? Why are you here in this room, in this class, at satsang? What do you want? What are you looking for?

Remember, if you're looking for anything, you're here for the wrong reason. For there is nothing that I can give you really, that you haven't already got. There is absolutely nothing I can do for you. For I am not the doer.

Neither are you. You are already fulfilled. Everything I have is yours. There is absolutely nothing lacking in you. You are Spirit. You are not the body that appears to be a body. You are Spirit. Something absolutely different than what you can ever imagine.

Everything that you can ever imagine, that you want to be, *you already are.* You are the imperishable Self that has always been, that you always will be. Beyond birth, beyond death, beyond experiences, beyond doubts, beyond opinions. Beyond whatever it is your body is going through, whatever thoughts your mind thinks. You are beyond that. You are the Silence, the Silence of the Heart.

Know yourself. Whenever you think of yourself, think of yourself as the Self. Not the I-thought, not the personal self, but as the Supreme Energy, Sat-Chit-Ananda, Nirvana. You are That.

If you really believed you are That, you would be in total peace. There would be no thing in this world that can ever disturb you. You would have no doubts. You would have unalloyed happiness, total joy. It would make no difference what your body is going through, or what thoughts come into your mind. Or what people are doing, or are not doing, who is right, who is wrong, who is enlightened, who is not. You would never think of things like this.

When you think you're human, you have duality to contend with. Right and wrong, healthy or sick, rich or poor, happy or sad, and the rest of it. But when you have transcended this, you see yourself in a completely different light. You see yourself as the light, the light that shineth in the darkness. The eternal glow that can never diminish. Omnipresence, All-Pervading.

You are that One. You have always been that One. You are not what you think you are when you're sad, when you're angry, when you're upset. This is a lie. There is something within you that knows the Truth. That is the Truth. You are That.

Last Thursday I brought to your attention that I wish I could share the things with you that I feel. But they were ineffable. There are no words to describe these things. There is no language that can try to describe the realities, the Pure Awareness. No words.

I received some phone calls from some of you. And they said, "Robert, you can tell me how you feel." (laughter) "You can share it with me." A few people ask me this. I try to explain; if I was able to share it with words, I would. But that's not important.

What's important to you is, how do you feel? Never mind what's going on within me. If you understand who you are, then you understand what is happening within me. Do not spend your time trying to determine what teachers are feeling, or where they are coming from. Rather try to determine where you are coming from, and who is it that thinks? Who is it that has a problem that they can't resolve? Who is it that believes that they want to become enlightened? Find out.

Understand the truth about yourself. Go deeper within yourself. Stop thinking about the world and your problems, or whatever is going on in your life. That will resolve itself when you begin to understand that you are Pure Intelligence.

Your so-called personal life will always resolve itself, will always take care of itself. The power is within you. There is nothing lacking. Never compare yourself to anybody else. Look at yourself with your inner eye.

The Self That I Love Is You

So, some people still ask me, "When you say you feel love, what do you mean?" The love that I feel is totally unconditioned.

This is the reason I can love you no matter what you do. No matter how you act. No matter where you come from. No matter what's going on. I can love you because I love myself. And there is only one Self. So the Self that I love is you. It's not separate.

If I loved you as a separate entity, I'd have a problem. For the separateness would show me different phases of your life. But I can't do that. I can only love. For the Self is love. It is not a personal love. It is All-Pervading. So as I am an embodiment of love, you are in that love also. There is only one love and that love is Consciousness, and you are That.

People ask me, when I see peace, what do I mean? I don't have to see peace where it's peaceful. I feel and see peace in every situation. Whatever there appears to be going on, there is peace. Just as in the center of a hurricane there is a peaceful circle, total stillness at the center of a hurricane. The same is true in the center of a tornado, in the cyclone. There is a center of peace. We are all that center. The true peace is you.

Everything that appears is an image. An image that appears on the Reality of life. There's Reality, Consciousness, and all of the vicissitudes of the world that go on all the time are superimposed on this Consciousness, like a chalkboard.

Images are drawn on the chalkboard. It never affects the chalkboard. They are erased. New images are drawn. The new images never affect the chalkboard. No thing affects the chalkboard. The chalkboard remains the same, whether you decide to draw a fire, a hurricane, a murder, famine, death, or whatever you decide to draw. Wholeness, health, peace, birth, anything. They are all imposters. The chalkboard never changes.

Always think of yourself as the chalkboard. And all the things that go on in this world, try to feel them as images on the chalkboard that change. Change continuously. This will help you. It will help you to understand that you are not the conditioning that goes on in your mind. You are not what your eyes show you in this world. You are not the feelings you feel. You are not the things that you hear. The things that you taste. Those are all the images.

You are totally absolute freedom. Total harmony and joy. This is your true nature. Abide in this truth and become free.

What is love?

Love, happiness, peace, joy, are all your real nature. It is a feeling beyond a feeling. It is a total, ineffable something that you are, and makes you know that you are one with everything. Everyone is your brother and sister, including the flowers, the trees, the animals, the bedbugs, the cockroaches, the mountains, the sky, the sick people, the healthy people, the poor people, the rich people.

When you look at everyone with one eye and not differentiate, then you are in love. But when you pick out somebody special and you think that one you are totally in love with, because he or she has the right features, the right figure, the right assets that you want, this is infatuation. This only lasts for a day until you get what you want. But true love never changes. It doesn't go away because it never came from anywhere. It's just something that *is*. And you are That.

Remember

Well, everything is unfolding as it should.
Be true to yourself and right action
will take place in your life.
Thank you for coming.
I love you.

Remember:
To love yourself.
To worship yourself.
To pray to yourself.
To bow down to yourself.
For God dwells within you as you.

Om, Shanti, Shanti, Shanti, Peace.

A Guide to Sanscrit Terms

Advaita-Vedanta: A subdivision of Vedanta. The non-duality approach.

Ahimsa: [Nonharming]. Abstention from harmful actions, thoughts, and words. An important moral discipline [yama] in Yoga, Buddhism, and Jainism.

Ajnani: One who has not realized the Self.

Ananda: [Bliss]. In Vedanta, the mind-transcending blissfulness of the Ultimate Reality or Self. This is not considered to be a quality but the very essence of Reality.

Arunachala: The holy mountain in India where Shri Ramana spent all his adult life.

Atman: [Self]. The transcendental Self according to the non-dualist [Vedanta] schools of thought, which is identical to Brahman.

Avadhuta: [Cast off]. A radical type of renouncer who abandons all conventions; a crazy adept.

Avatara: [Descent]. An incarnation of the Divine, such as Krishna and Rama.

Avidya: [Ignorance]. Spiritual nescience, which is the root of all human suffering and the cause of one's bondage to egoic states of consciousness.

Bhagavad-Gita: [Lord's Song]. The earliest and most popular scripture of Yoga, containing the teachings of Lord Krishna to Arjuna.

Bhakta: [Devotee]. A follower of Bhakti-Yoga.

Bhakti: [Love, devotion]. The spiritual sentiment of loving participation in the Divine.

Bodhisattva: [Enlightenment being]. In Mahayana Buddhism, the spiritual practitioner who has vowed to commit himself or herself to the liberation of all beings, postponing his or her own ultimate realization.

Brahma: The Creator-God of the famous medieval Hindu triad of gods. The other two are Vishnu [as Preserver] and Shiva [as Destroyer]. Brahma must be carefully distinguished from the Brahman, which is the eternal foundation of existence.

Brahmacarya: [Brahmic Conduct]. The practice of chastity in thought, word, and deed, which is regarded as one of the fundamental disciplines [yama] of Yoga.

Brahman: The impersonal absolute according to Vedanta; the transcendental Ground of the world.

Buddha: [Awakened]. Title of Gautama, founder of Buddhism.

Chit: [Consciousness]. Pure Awareness, or the Transcendental Consciousness beyond all thought; the eternal Witness. See also atman, purusha.

Dharma: The cosmic law or order. Teaching-doctrine.

Dhyana: Meditation.

Diksha: Initiation by the guru.

Gopi: Female shepherd. In Vaishnavism, these terms refer to the devotees of Lord Krishna.

Guna: [Quality]. One of three primary constituents of Nature [prakrity]: Sattva [principle of lucidity], Rajas [principle of activity], and Tamas [principle of inertia]. The interaction between these three types creates the entire manifest and unmanifest cosmos, including all psychomental phenomena.

Guru: [Heavy]. Spiritual Teacher.

Hinayana: [Small Vehicle]. The minority school of Buddhism, which has arhatship or arhantship as its leading ideal.

Ishvara: [Ruler]. Personal God.

Janaka: An Indian king: An account of his Self-realization can be found in The Ashtavakra Gita.

Japa: [Recitation]. Meditative recitation of mantras.

Jiva: [Living Being]. The psyche, or finite conscious human personality, which experiences itself as different from others and does not know the transcendental Self.

Jivan-Mukti: [Living Liberation]. The Self-realized adept who is fully liberated while still embodied.

Jnana: Knowledge of the Self.

Jnani: One who has realized the Self.

Kali-Yuga: [Dark Age]. The modern age of spiritual decline, which requires a new approach to Self-realization. It is thought to have started in 3,012 B.C.

Karma: [Action]. Activity in general of the unenlightened individual, which activates the law of cause and effect.

Krishna: An incarnation [avatara] of Vishnu.

Kundalini: [Serpent Power]. The power that lies dormant in the lowest psychic center of the human body. The ascent of the kundalini to the highest psychic center, at the crown of the head, brings about a temporary state of ecstatic identification with the Self. [In Nirvikalpa Samadhi].

Leela: The play of God.

Linga: [Mark]. The phallus as the symbol of creativity, which is specifically associated with God Shiva.

Mahatma: Great soul, great man or saint.

Mahayana: [Great Vehicle]. The majority branch of Buddhism, which has the bodhisattva as its great ideal.

Mantra: Sound that empowers the mind for concentration and the transcendence of the ordinary states of consciousness. Usually the sacred words are given to a disciple by the guru.

Maya: Illusion

Moksha: [Release]. The highest of possible human pursuits: Liberation. Synonymous with Self-realization.

Mouna: Silence.

Muktas: Liberated ones.

Nadi: [Conduit]. Channels in the body where the prana or energy travels through.

Nirvana: [Extinction]. The transcendence of the ego, a condition that is untouched by space and time.

Nirvikalpa-Samadhi: [Transconceptual Ecstasy]. Samadhi in which no differences are perceived. It is characterised by an absence of body-consciousness. Although one has a temporary awareness of the Self in this state, one is not able to perceive sensory information or function in the world. When body consciousness returns, the ego reappears, so the ego has not been finally eliminated.

Om: The key mantra of Hinduism, symbolizing the Absolute.

Para-Brahman: The Supreme Brahman.

Prana: [Life]. The life-force sustaining the body which has five principals forms.

Pranayama: [Breath Control]. The careful regulation of the breath. This is the most important practice of Hatha-Yoga.

Puja: [Worship]. Ritual veneration of one's teacher as an embodiment of the Divine.

Rama: The main hero of the Ramayana, deified as an incarnation of God Vishnu.

Rishi: A type of Vedic seer, who sees the hymns of Veda.

Sadhana: [Realizing]. The spiritual practice toward Self-realization.

Sadhaka: A spiritual seeker.

Sadhu: A noble person or a spiritual seeker. However, Shri Ramana frequently used this term as a title for someone who has realized the Self.

Sahaja-Samadhi: [Natural Ecstasy]. The effortless ecstasy. This is the state of the Jnani who has finally and irrevocably eliminated his ego. A Jnani in this state is able to function naturally in the world, just as any ordinary person does. Knowing that he is the Self, the Jnani sees no difference between himself and others or the world. For a Jnani, everything is a manifestation of the indivisible Self.

Samsara: [Confluence]. The finite world of change and illusion.

Samskara: [Activator]. Innate tendencies.

Sat-Chit-Ananda: Being-Consciousness-Bliss.

Satsang: [Relationship to the True]. The spiritual practice of being in the presence of someone who has realised the Self. Association with 'being'.

Savikalpa-Samadhi: [Ecstasy with form-ideation]. In this state Self-Awareness is mantained by constant effort. The continuity of the Samadhi is wholly dependent on the effort put it to mantain it. When Self attention wavers, Self-Awareness is obscured by thoughts and imagery.

Shakti: [Power]. The feminine power aspect of the Divine, which is fundamental to the metaphysics and spirituality of Tantrism.

Shanti: [Peace]. Ultimate peace. Quality which coincides with Self-realization.

Siddha: [Accomplished, perfect]. A Self-realized adept. One who has reached perfection.

Siddhi: [Accomplishment]. Paranormal power, that comes as a result of spiritual practice.

Swarupa: Real form or Real Nature.

Tamil: A South Indian language: Shri Ramana's mother tongue.

Tapas: [Glow, heat]. Ascetism, religious austerity, penance, heat.

Tiruvannamalai: A town about a mile from Shri Ramana's Ashram.

Turiya: The Fourth State of Consciousness.

Vajrayana: [Adamantine Vehicle]. The tantric branch of Buddhism, especially of Tibet, which evolved out of the Mahayana.

Vasana: [Trait]. The concatenation of subliminal activators [samskaras], deposited in the depth of consciousness. Mental tendencies.

Vedanta: [Veda's End]. The dominant Hindu tradition, which teaches that Reality is singular and One.

Vedas: Four collections of scriptures dating from 2,000 B.C. to 500 B.C. which are the ultimate source of authority for most Hindus.

Vichara: Self-Enquiry.

Vishnu: One of the three principal deities of Hinduism. Vishnu periodically reincarnates in a human body.

Yoga: [Union]. Spiritual practice in general.

Yoga-Vasishtha: A massive advaitic text attributed to Valmiki in which the Sage Vasishtha answers questions put by Rama, an incarnation of Vishnu. Composed sometime in the tenth century A.D.

Yuga: [Age]. According to Hindu mythology, there are four yugas, each of several thousand years' duration. The present age is kali-yuga.

𝔉riends of The Infinity Institute

"We are on this earth to be of service to humanity."

If you are interested in receiving more information on the publications of The Teaching of Robert Adams or being placed on the mailing list of The Infinity Institute, please contact us at the address below.

We will be happy to send you information regarding the following:

- Books
- *The Infinity-Journal Magazine*
- Monthly Original Transcripts of Live Dialogues and Tapes

The Infinity Institute
2370 W. Highway 89A
Box 11-182
Sedona, Arizona 86336